WHERE RIVERS MEET

THE ARCHAEOLOGY OF CATHOLME AND THE TRENT-TAME CONFLUENCE

Where Rivers Meet

The archaeology of Catholme and the Trent-Tame confluence

Simon Buteux and Henry Chapman

CBA Research Report 161
Council for British Archaeology 2009

Published in 2009 by the Council for British Archaeology
St Mary's House, 66 Bootham, York, YO30 7BZ

British Library cataloguing in Publication Data

A catalogue record for this book is available from the British Library

ISBN 978–1–902771–78–6

Typeset by Carnegie Book Production
Printed and bound by Scotprint

The publisher acknowledges with gratitude a grant from English Heritage towards
the cost of publication

Front cover: The 'sunburst' monument at Catholme (© G Clews)
Back cover: The partial skeleton of the Whitemoor Haye woolly rhinoceros with
its discoverer, Ray Davies; the Alrewas gold torcs (© Birmingham Museum and
Art Gallery)

Contents

List of figures

Acknowledgements

This book describes some of the results of the Where Rivers Meet project. The project was funded by English Heritage through the Aggregates Levy Sustainability Fund. We are grateful to Kath Buxton, Brian Kerr, Caroline Matthews, Sarah Reilly, Ingrid Ward, Buzz Busby, Paul Stamper, Bill Klemperer, Jenny Mariott and Gareth Watkins for their support, advice and patience throughout the project. We also received much advice and assistance from Staffordshire County Council, and thanks are due to Chris Wardle, Ian Wykes and Suzy Blake. We are similarly indebted to Andy Richmond and Gary Coates of Phoenix Consulting Archaeology Ltd. The project developed from proposals first put forward by Vince Gaffney and Gwilym Hughes in the early 1990s, and Vince also helped to get the project off the ground.

A large team from the University of Birmingham collaborated on the project, and we have drawn heavily on their work in this book. Steve Wilkes and Glyn Barratt of the Visual and Spatial Technology Centre (VISTA) undertook the digital landscape modelling and analysis. Neil Davies and Greg Sambrook Smith of the School of Geography, Earth and Environmental Sciences carried out the palaeofluvial analysis, while the hydrogeological modelling was undertaken by Mark Bunch and Mike Riley. Meg Watters undertook the ground-based geophysical survey work, assisted in the field by Kate Bain, Tim Evans, Emma Hancox and Mark Kincey. Mark Hewson compiled the initial gazetteer of sites and excavations, and managed the later stages of the project. GIS-based analysis of the earlier prehistoric landscape was the subject of an MA dissertation by Tim Evans, and has informed much of our discussion of this topic.

We are grateful to Infoterra, which provided the LiDAR data used in the research. Thanks also to Hanson Aggregates, particularly Bob Woodbridge and Roy Bishop, who allowed access to their Barton Quarry, made available their borehole records and provided invaluable advice and assistance during the hydrogeological modelling work.

The excavations at the Catholme Ceremonial Complex were supervised by Kate Bain, Mary Duncan and Emma Hancox, with the assistance of Richard Bacon, Dharminder Chuhan, Keith Hinton, Philip Mann and a team of students and staff from the University of Birmingham. The geoarchaeological work associated with the Catholme excavations was carried out by David Jordan of Terra Nova Ltd, with analysis of the magnetic properties of the deposits undertaken by Mark Hounslow and Vassil Karloukovski of Lancaster University. Especial thanks go to Andy and Keith Mallaber, who farm the land at Catholme, and without whose permission, help and good-natured toleration the fieldwork would not have been possible.

The excavation of the Whitemoor Haye woolly rhinoceros site was part-funded by a grant from English Nature (now Natural England) through their Aggregates Levy Sustainability Fund grant scheme, and we are grateful to Natalie Bennett and David Hodson for their support and advice. We are also grateful to Andy Currant, Danielle Schreve, Andy Howard and their colleagues for permission to provide an outline summary of these investigations prior to full publication. The woolly rhino site investigations would not have been possible without the help and co-operation of Ray Davies (who found the fossil remains) and Ross Halley of Lafarge, operators of the Whitemoor Haye Quarry.

Many thanks are due to those who kindly read and commented on drafts of the book, either in its entirety or on particular chapters. These are Ingrid Ward, Buzz Busby, Bob Meeson, Andy Howard, Danielle Schreve and Ann Woodward, together with two anonymous reviewers, one for English Heritage and one for the Council for British Archaeology. We have benefited much from the comments and advice received, although we have not been able to follow it all. A much better book has resulted, although the undoubted faults that remain are our own.

We are grateful to the following for permission to use illustrations: Figure 1.6, © Graham Clews; Figure 2.1, © NMR; Figure 4.4, by courtesy of Ian Sutton; Figure 4.10, by Graham Norrie, reproduced by courtesy of The Institute of Archaeology and Antiquity; Figure 4.11, by courtesy of Nick Arbor; Figure 5.2, © English Heritage; Figures 5.5 and 5.9, © Graham Clews; Figure 6.2, © David Knight, taken from Losco-Bradley and Kinsley 2002, reproduced by courtesy of the authors and Trent and Peak Archaeology, University of Nottingham; Figure 6.3, after Martin and Allen 2001 © Gifford Ltd; Figure 6.19, © Birmingham Museum and Art Gallery; Figure 6.20, © Birmingham Museum and Art Gallery; Figure 7.3, © English Heritage; Figure 7.4, by courtesy of Henrietta Quinnell; Figure 8.8, © English Heritage.

We must offer particular thanks to Manda Forster, post-excavation manager, and Rebecca Beardmore, both at Birmingham Archaeology, for perseverance and encouragement; to Nigel Dodds and Bryony Ryder for graphical support; and to Caroline Rayner and Jo Adams in the Birmingham Archaeology office for tolerance and understanding.

Finally, we are greatly indebted to Catrina Appleby and Frances Mee at the CBA for their toleration of our repeated shortcomings and delays, and for so expertly steering the book through to publication.

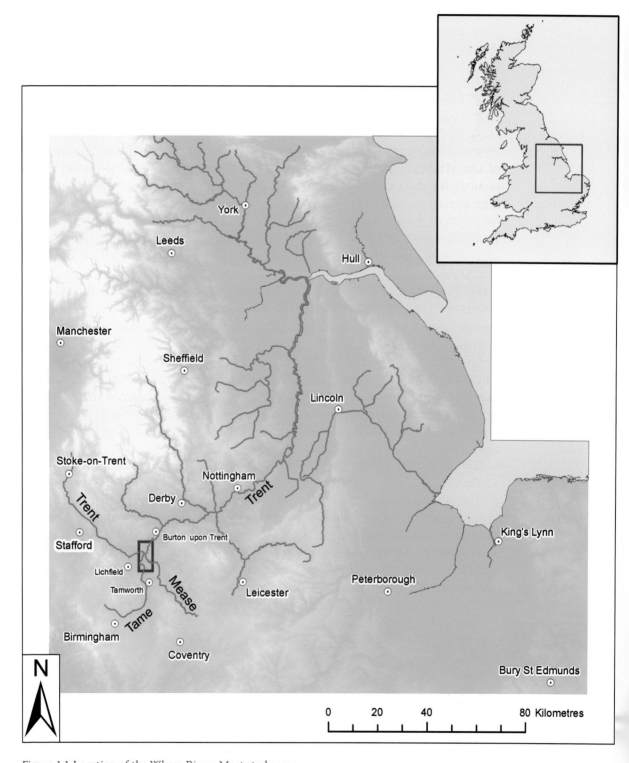

Figure 1.1 Location of the Where Rivers Meet study area

CHAPTER ONE

Introduction

This book sets out to tell the story of a piece of the English landscape in south-eastern Staffordshire, and a small slice of neighbouring Derbyshire, from earliest prehistory down to *c* AD 900 (Fig 1.1). On the surface it seems to be an unremarkable chunk of rural landscape, typical of the lowlands of the Midlands. It is, however, one the most intensively quarried areas of the country for the extraction of sand and gravel. Archaeological research, most of it prompted by quarrying, has revealed that underneath the surface there is – or, for much of the area, was – evidence for a rich and remarkable history of human occupation stretching back to the Ice Age.

The book also sets out to describe how the story of this landscape has been investigated and reconstructed. Conventional archaeological excavation is just one aspect of this and many other techniques have played a part, including some that make use of the latest technology available to archaeologists today.

The Where Rivers Meet project

The book arises out of a project funded by the *Aggregate Levy Sustainability Fund* (ALSF). The ALSF, resourced by a tax on the aggregates industry, was introduced by the government in 2002 to provide funds to help to address the environmental impact of aggregate extraction (in this case quarrying for sands and gravels). One of the impacts of quarrying is on the historic environment, notably on archaeological remains, and one of the distributors of the fund is English Heritage, which funded the Where Rivers Meet project.

The area studied by the project, which we call the 'Where Rivers Meet area' or simply the 'study area', lies at the confluence of the Rivers Trent and the Tame in south-eastern Staffordshire (Fig 1.2). The River Trent flows into the area from the west, having flowed south-eastwards, from Stoke-on-Trent (the stretch of the river known as the Upper Trent). The River Tame, after flowing northwards through Tamworth, joins the Trent near the village of Alrewas. From its confluence with the Tame and the smaller River Mease, the Trent turns north-eastwards, through Burton and on to Newark (the stretch known as the Middle Trent).

The study area is dominated by the two major rivers, their floodplains, and the wide river 'terraces' of sand and gravel that were laid down by the rivers in the past, mainly during the Ice Age. The light, comparatively well-drained soils that developed on these sand and gravel deposits have been exploited for farming for 6000 years. In more recent years, especially since the 1960s, the sands and gravels themselves have been quarried to provide essential materials for the construction industry, the context for most of the archaeological discoveries to be described in this book (Fig 1.3).

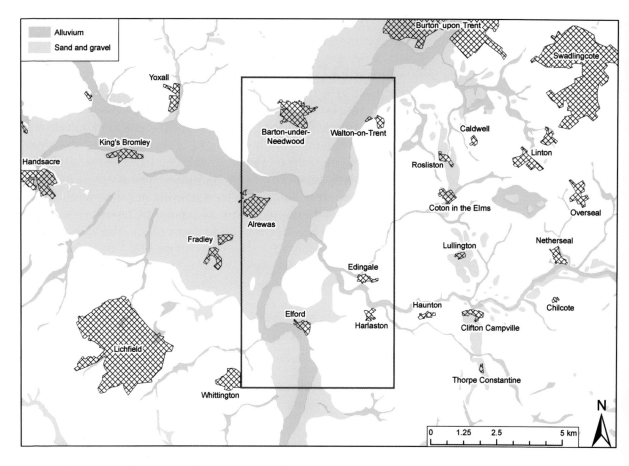

Figure 1.2 Location of the Where Rivers Meet area in its local context, showing extent of sand and gravel deposits, and alluvium

At the time of writing, there are two large active quarries in the Where Rivers Meet area, Lafarge's Whitemoor Haye Quarry to the west of the Tame and, north of the confluence, Hanson's Barton East Quarry to the west of the Trent. However, most other areas along the west banks of both the Tame and the Trent have either been quarried in the past, are still being quarried today, or are designated for quarrying in the future (Fig 1.4). Two important areas of former quarrying are at Fisherwick in the south of the study area, worked mainly in the 1960s and 1970s, and an area immediately to the north of Whitemoor Haye Quarry, where former gravel pits have been restored as the site for the National Memorial Arboretum.

All in all, there are few parts of the Where Rivers Meet area where suitable deposits are present that have not been affected by sand and gravel quarrying. Along the west bank of the Trent north of the Tame confluence these include a small area around Catholme Farm, where some remarkable buried prehistoric monuments revealed through aerial photography have been afforded statutory protection as scheduled ancient monuments. These monuments, which include a 'woodhenge-type' prehistoric temple 4500 years old, have been the subject of the most detailed research carried out by the Where Rivers Meet project.

This intensely quarried landscape provided an important opportunity for a range of archaeological studies related to the impact of sand and gravel extraction on ancient landscapes. Together these interrelated studies comprised the Where Rivers Meet project. A first aim of the project was to produce a synthesis and review of the many archaeological discoveries, excavations and investigations that have taken place in the study area since the 19th century. From the 1960s onwards, much archaeological research has taken place in the area in advance of quarrying. Most of this work has involved the excavation of discrete 'sites' – ancient settlements or burial mounds, for example – which have been published separately in a range of journals and technical monographs over the years. Some, particularly smaller-scale excavations carried out to evaluate the archaeological potential of areas designated for quarrying or other development, have not been fully published and exist only as typescript reports – the 'grey literature' as archaeologists call it. One aim of the project, therefore, was to produce a synthesis of all this diverse evidence so that we could examine not just individual sites in isolation but look at broadly contemporary sites together, these sites forming parts of ancient landscapes. When we look at ancient landscapes it is often the case that the whole is greater than the sum of its parts, and sites that perhaps do not tell us much on their own make much more sense as part of a wider pattern. Much of the book describes the outcome of this archaeological synthesis.

Figure 1.3 Quarrying in progress at Whitemoor Haye Quarry

The area chosen for study was a rectangular block of land, 12km north–south by 6km east–west, covering a total of 72km². It has as its centre the confluence

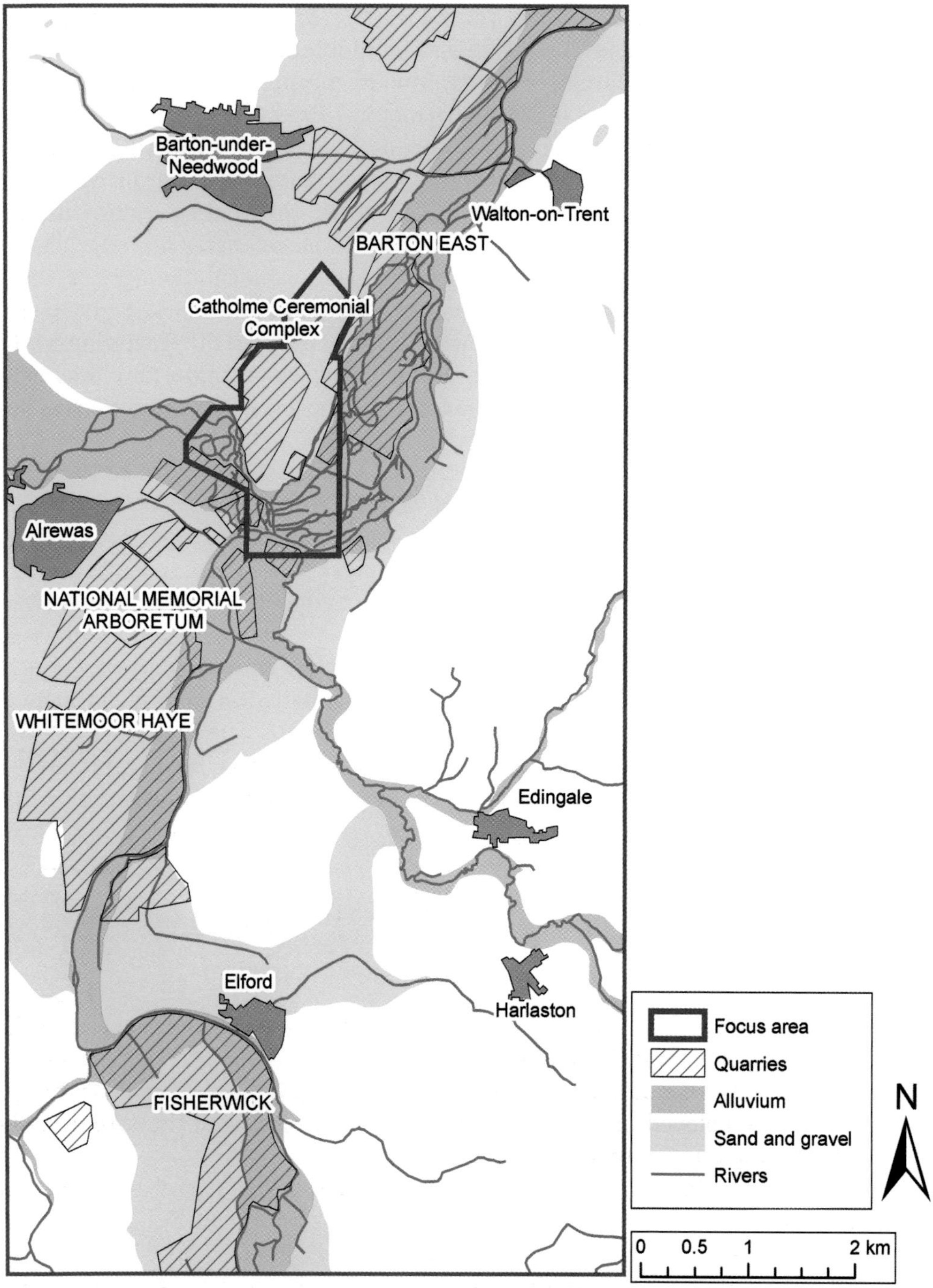

Figure 1.4 The Where Rivers Meet study area, showing areas of quarrying and location of the focus area

of the Trent and the Tame and encompasses most of the areas of quarrying, past and present, around this confluence where significant archaeological remains have been investigated. Other than this, the boundaries of the study area are essentially arbitrary – quite literally, one has to 'draw the line' somewhere.

This means that although only those sites that fall within the study area are described in any detail, we often need to look beyond the study area to set these sites and their landscapes in their wider context. Nevertheless, the study area is sufficiently large that most sites and monuments can be set within their immediate landscape context and can be related to other contemporary sites in the area as part of a broader landscape. For example, for the Iron Age we can look not only at individual farmsteads, and these farmsteads within the fields that often surround them, but we can also look at how the farmsteads and fields relate to each other and to features of the wider cultural and physical landscape – trackways and territorial boundaries, the rivers, land that is likely to have been marsh, meadow, rough pasture or woodland, and so forth. Furthermore, it is clear that the valleys of the Tame and the Trent, which snake their way across the study area from south to north, form in themselves a natural landscape 'unit' connected together by the river corridor itself.

We begin our survey of the Where Rivers Meet area in the Ice Age, when the modern river systems of the Trent and the Tame began to take recognisable form. The upper chronological limit to our study is set at around AD 900. The main reason for this is that we are concerned with a sequence of landscapes that can be reconstructed only (or, from the Roman period onwards, largely) from archaeological evidence. In the decades around AD 900 the landscape as it exists today (or as it existed before the commencement of large-scale quarrying) had already begun to take shape, villages such as Alrewas, Barton-under-Needwood and Walton-on-Trent were developing, and historical sources such as charters and deeds play an increasingly important role in landscape reconstruction.

A second aim of the project was to explore and exploit the potential of some of the tools that are now available to archaeologists seeking to discover, reconstruct and interpret past landscapes. Some of the tools used for archaeological prospection, such as aerial photography and ground-based geophysical survey, have been around for some time. A more recent addition to the armoury is airborne LiDAR (Light Detection and Ranging). GIS (Geographical Information Systems) is not a prospection technique but rather a computer-based tool that enables different types of data – conventional maps, air photographs and satellite imagery, archaeological sites and find-spots, geophysical and LiDAR survey data – to be stored, compared, visualised and analysed (Fig 1.5). All these techniques have been employed on the Where Rivers Meet project, and they are described and explained in Chapter 3.

These techniques, in various combinations, can be used in three main ways, although the goals are not mutually exclusive. The first is for *archaeological prospection* – to try to discover where significant archaeological remains survive and to provide an indication of their character. This information may then be used to target effectively more detailed investigation, for example excavation in advance of quarrying.

A second use of some of these techniques is for the reconstruction of the *physical evolution of the landscape*. River valleys are particularly unstable, changeable landscapes, both as a consequence of natural forces, notably climate change, and

Figure 1.5 Modelling
the landscape
using Geographic
Information Systems
(GIS)

as a result of human action. The latter includes both activity with indirect effects
on the behaviour of rivers, such as woodland clearance and agriculture (which
destabilise soils and can lead to major accumulation of alluvium), and direct
interference with rivers, such as canalisation. As a consequence of these varied
forces the valleys of the Tame and Trent have experienced significant evolution
up to the present day. This needs to be reconstructed both to understand the
patterns of human occupation and resource use in relation to changes in the
configuration of river channels and riverside environments, and to understand
the conditions leading to the preservation or destruction, burial or exposure, of
archaeological remains. With regard to the latter, reconstruction of the physical
evolution of the landscape plays a major role in archaeological prospection and
prediction.

The third way in which the technology now available can be used is to
attempt to *reconstruct, visualise and interpret the ancient cultural landscapes*
themselves – to put the sites, monuments and finds back into the physical
landscapes of which they were a part and to trace their development through
time. Geographical Information Systems (GIS) play a particularly important role
in this process.

To meet the aims of the Where Rivers Meet project a team of specialists with
different skills was needed. Most of the team members were drawn from the staff
of the Institute of Archaeology and Antiquity, the Visual and Spatial Technology
Centre (VISTA), and the School of Geography, Earth and Environmental Sciences
(GEES) at the University of Birmingham.

Steve Wilkes of VISTA coordinated the initial construction of the project GIS,
incorporating Ordnance Survey map data, geological data provided by the British

Geological Survey, vertical aerial photographs, satellite imagery, LiDAR data, and cropmark plots and details of archaeological sites and finds drawn from the Historic Environment Records for Staffordshire and Derbyshire. This work forms the basis for much of the archaeological analysis and reconstruction described in later chapters of this book.

Neil Davies and Greg Sambrook-Smith of GEES undertook the study of the evolution of the river systems in the study area. To achieve this they made use of the GIS constructed for the project, supplemented by fieldwork including the use of ground-penetrating radar and the recording of geological sections exposed in the Whitemoor Haye and Barton East quarries. Furthermore, quarrying does not only affect the configuration of the landscape but also affects the behaviour of adjacent rivers, drainage and the water table. This may have indirect effects on the preservation of archaeological remains even where these are not directly affected by the quarrying itself. For example, some of the most important archaeological remains are those that are preserved in waterlogged conditions; by changing the level of the water table quarrying can act to 'dewater' such remains, leading to their drying out and disintegration. A study of this hydrogeological dimension to the potential impact of quarrying on archaeological remains was carried out by Mark Bunch and Michael Riley of the Hydrogeology Research Group within GEES. As with other aspects of the Where Rivers Meet project, notably the work carried out within the focus area (see below), this research was intended to be of relevance not only to the Where Rivers Meet area but also to investigate phenomena of wider significance and applicability.

Detailed studies in the 'focus area'

Covering a total of 72km², it was not possible to study the whole of the Where Rivers Meet area at a uniform level of detail. Labour-intensive investigative techniques such as new ground-based geophysical survey had to be limited to a small portion of the 'full area'. Furthermore, the fact that much of the full area had been affected by quarrying constrained the parts where such detailed investigations could be carried out. For these reasons a 'focus area', covering some 235 hectares of land within the full area, was defined (Fig 1.4). The area chosen lies just to the north of the confluence of the Trent and the Tame, around Catholme Farm.

As mentioned above, this area contains an important group of prehistoric monuments, predominantly of Neolithic and early Bronze Age date, some of which have been protected as scheduled ancient monuments. These monuments include a 'woodhenge-type' monument consisting of multiple rings of postholes, a 'sunburst' monument consisting of a central ring-ditch with radiating pit-alignments, and a very large ring-ditch. These monuments, together with a number of smaller ring-ditches, a probable cursus and a series of pit-alignments, we have termed collectively the 'Catholme Ceremonial Complex'. (Monument types such as 'cursus' are explained in Chapter 5.)

The monuments of the Catholme Ceremonial Complex lie within what is today arable farmland, and no trace of them can be seen on the surface. The massive timber posts of the 'woodhenge' monument have of course long since rotted away (if they were not deliberately removed or burnt down in antiquity). The earthen banks or mounds that were once associated with the ring-ditches and other structures have been levelled by centuries of ploughing, and the ditches filled in. All these structures were first brought to light as cropmarks visible on aerial photographs (Fig 1.6; see Chapter 2). The appearance and recording of such cropmarks is constrained by a number of factors, including the growing of the 'right type' of crops, the nature of the soil and subsoil, weather conditions and, of course, the presence of an aerial archaeologist at just the right time to record the cropmarks if and when they appear.

An alternative or supplementary approach to 'seeing beneath the soil' is provided by ground-based geophysical survey. Several techniques, such as resistivity, magnetic susceptibility and magnetometry, have been in routine use for archaeological prospection for several decades now. Ground-penetrating radar is a more recent development in archaeology and is not yet used on a routine basis in rural situations. All these techniques operate on different principles, responding to different physical and geochemical properties of buried features, producing different but often complementary results in different circumstances or when used in different ways. While the scientific principles behind these

Figure 1.6 Aerial photograph showing cropmarks at Catholme

techniques are in general well understood, it is less well understood why particular techniques should be successful (ie produce an interpretable 'signature' of buried archaeological remains) in some situations but not in other situations that seem on the face of things to be closely comparable. Subtle factors, at present poorly understood, are evidently involved.

In the Where Rivers Meet area, and more generally in the Trent and Tame valleys, geophysical survey, mainly magnetometry, had been extensively employed prior to the initiation of the Where Rivers Meet project. Much of this survey had been carried out as a method of archaeological prospection in advance of sand and gravel quarrying, for instance in the Whitemoor Haye Quarry. However, the results were largely poor – the surveys failed to produce clear maps of buried archaeological remains even where aerial photography and subsequent excavation showed them to be present. Elsewhere in the country, in what appeared to be comparable circumstances (similar soils, archaeological feature types, depth of burial, etc), good results were produced.

A key aspect of the work undertaken by the Where Rivers Meet project in the focus area was to investigate this problem. A team led by Meg Watters carried out extensive geophysical surveys using the three principal techniques (resistivity, magnetometry and ground-penetrating radar) over the various monuments of the Catholme Ceremonial Complex. This was followed by intensive survey over selected parts of particular monuments, stripping off the topsoil and repeating the exercise, and then limited archaeological excavation.

The main purpose of the excavations was to investigate systematically the precise relationship between what was beneath the ground and the geophysical results, with the aim of better understanding that relationship. Thus the excavations involved detailed field recording and laboratory analysis of the composition of the buried soils and their magnetic properties. The results of this scientific analysis will be published elsewhere and fall outside the scope of this book.

The geophysical work carried out by Meg Watters and her team also involved novel approaches to the integration, display and interpretation of geophysical data, particularly the possibilities for three-dimensional modelling offered by the ground-penetrating radar data. This is further explored in Chapter 3. Although it was not their only purpose, the excavations together with the intensive geophysical survey results also of course shed much light on the monuments of the Catholme Ceremonial Complex themselves. These archaeological results are described in Chapter 5.

The organisation of the book

Following this introductory chapter, Chapter 2 provides some background on the discovery and investigation of ancient landscapes in river valleys. Since the Second World War a combination of aerial photography and excavation, much of it associated with sand and gravel quarrying, has completely transformed our understanding of these landscapes, particularly for prehistoric periods. The discovery and investigation of the ancient landscapes of the Where Rivers Meet area is part of this wider trend, and Chapter 2 aims to set this in its broader context.

More recently, techniques and technologies such as those employed by the Where Rivers Meet project are contributing to a further transformation in our approach to, and understanding of, ancient landscapes. Chapter 3 describes these techniques and technologies in layman's terms, laying particular stress on how they can be used to reconstruct, visualise and hence interpret ancient landscapes in ways that were not previously possible.

Chapters 4 to 8 explore the landscapes of the Ice Age (4), the Neolithic and earlier Bronze Age (5), the later Bronze Age and Iron Age (6), the Roman period (7) and the Anglo-Saxon period (8). Most of the basic archaeological data for the reconstruction of these landscapes derive from archaeological excavations undertaken in advance of quarrying from the late 1960s onwards and is drawn from published sources or archived reports. An exception is Chapter 5, which deals with the Neolithic and earlier Bronze Age. Here much of the account is based on the archaeological results of the detailed investigations undertaken by the Where Rivers Meet project on the monuments of the Catholme Ceremonial Complex within the focus area. A full, technical account of these investigations is beyond the scope of this book and is published elsewhere (Chapman *et al* forthcoming). Chapter 5 provides a summary of the main findings, concentrating on the interpretation of the monuments and setting them in their wider context.

CHAPTER TWO

Ancient landscapes in river valleys: discoveries and challenges

T he discovery of a rich sequence of ancient landscapes in the Where Rivers Meet area is part of a wider phenomenon that has transformed our understanding of the archaeology of river valleys and, especially, our understanding of the prehistoric period in the Midlands. It was not very long ago that the river valleys of the Midlands were considered to have been cloaked in dense woodland and only sparsely inhabited, if inhabited at all, throughout much of prehistory (Piggott 1958, 13). The development of archaeological aerial photography following the Second World War, in tandem with the expansion of sand and gravel quarrying in the post-war years, changed all that.

'Magic writing': the impact of aerial photography

Archaeological aerial photography began in the early decades of the 20th century and advanced greatly during the First and Second World Wars and during the inter-war period. Flyers discovered (even sometimes to the detriment of their

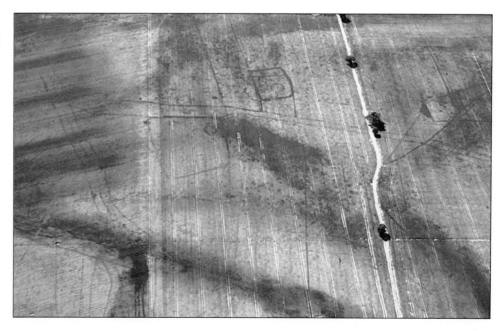

Figure 2.1 Aerial photograph showing a 'palimpsest' of cropmarks (mainly Iron Age and Roman period enclosures and trackways) at Whitemoor Haye

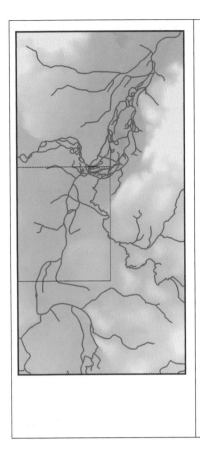 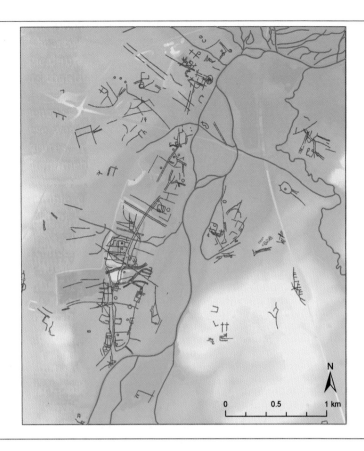

Figure 2.2 A plot of cropmarks at Whitemoor Haye

immediate military duties) that from the air they could see much of archaeological interest that couldn't be seen – or couldn't be made sense of – from the ground. In part it was simply a matter, from their bird's-eye perspective, of being able to see the 'wood' where those on the ground could only see the 'trees'. However, the greatest achievement of aerial photography for archaeology was the recognition of the phenomenon of 'cropmarks' (Fig 2.1).

The basic principles of cropmarks are not complicated. When cut into relatively free-draining subsoil such as gravel, buried archaeological features such as ditches and pits – entirely invisible on the surface and masked by a layer of ploughsoil – will often retain more moisture than the surrounding subsoil. This affects the growth of the crops above. Often they grow higher and more luxuriantly. If the conditions are right, a whole pattern of ancient ditches, pits and postholes appears in the crop for a while, rather like magic writing appearing on a blank sheet of paper, the dark lines of richer crop growth faithfully reflecting the buried ditches and pits below. Buried walls and floors may produce the opposite effect, stunting the growth of the crop above them. The cropmarks are recorded by aerial photography. Aerial shots taken obliquely rather than vertically from the aeroplane generally give the best results. Afterwards, as long as there are sufficient 'control points' on the photograph such as the corners of fields or other landmarks, the aerial photographs can be 'rectified' and the cropmarks plotted on to maps (Fig 2.2). This used to be done laboriously by hand but today there are several computer programs available that do the job much more quickly and accurately.

There is, however, nothing automatic about the appearance of cropmarks – it all depends on the type of crop being grown (and, of course, whether a crop is being grown at all), the type of soil it is grown in, the weather, and a host of other factors. This all means that choosing the right time to fly to photograph cropmarks, and the right places to fly over, is a complicated business, a combination of art with a good measure of luck. There are several other practical limitations too, including the number of aerial archaeologists (which is small), the location of the airfields they fly from, the availability of a plane and restrictions on the use of air space. Finally, the interpretation of aerial photographs is a skilled procedure, requiring much experience.

Despite the limitations, it is impossible to overestimate the impact that aerial photography has had on archaeology. Nowhere has this impact been greater than on the gravel landscapes of England's major river systems – the Thames, the Warwickshire/Worcestershire Avon and the Welland for example, amongst many others, including of course the Trent and the Tame. In the post-war years, quite suddenly it seemed, areas that had appeared to have very few archaeological sites were now awash with them – and not just sites but whole landscapes of monuments and settlements, field systems and routeways.

In the area we are concerned with in this book, the greatest single contribution to archaeological aerial photography was made by Jim Pickering (1915–2004). Pickering learnt to fly with the RAF Volunteer Reserve in 1937 and was a Spitfire pilot throughout the Battle of Britain. After the war he devoted much of his spare time to photographing cropmarked archaeological landscapes in the Midlands, taking tens of thousands of photographs. He continued flying and photographing well into the 1990s, to the age of 80, and was perhaps the most prolific aerial archaeologist in Britain. Technically an amateur, it is possible (there is really no useful way of quantifying such things) that he discovered more archaeological sites than anybody before or since. Pickering, along with a handful of others, was part of a 'Golden Age' of archaeological air photography in the post-war years when each flight might reveal dozens of new sites. Obviously, as the years have gone by, the number of new discoveries compared with repeat photography of previously known sites has tended to decline, although because so many factors are involved in the production of cropmarks there is not a simple 'fall-off' with time.

New perspectives on the past: the 'Ozymandias factor'

All the new discoveries made by aerial photography demanded a radical re-evaluation of what prehistoric and Roman Britain were like, the density of population, and the complexity and sophistication of ancient societies. Before the impact of aerial photography, most rural archaeological sites were known about because something still survived of them to be seen above ground – a Bronze Age barrow (burial mound), for example, the ramparts of an Iron Age hillfort, or the overgrown ruins of a Roman villa. But most of these monuments only survive today because they are located in places that have not been subject to intense occupation and agriculture in subsequent millennia. To put it in modern terms, they did not stand in the way of development.

The monuments that once stood in the much richer agricultural landscapes of the river valleys, however, certainly did stand in the way of development. They were flattened. It is difficult to exaggerate the impact that regular ploughing can have on a monument over the years. Think, for example, of the massive bank that surrounds the stone circles at Avebury, Wiltshire, which once stood to an estimated maximum height of 6.7m (Malone 1994, 11) – that is more than the height of three men. Imagine, furthermore, that this bank had been subject to continual ploughing (as, in fact, it has not). Assume that each year of ploughing removes just 1cm – about the length of a fingernail – from the height of the bank. Then in just 670 years the massive bank at Avebury, more than 4000 years old, could be reduced to nothing. If this had happened, what would have been left? The answer is a buried ditch (which accompanied the bank), still very impressive at up to 10m deep and more than 20m across (*ibid*, 11) but pretty much invisible on the ground. Or invisible unless centuries later a farmer was growing crops over it, the crops and conditions were right, and an expert was up in an aeroplane with a camera.

The destruction by ploughing of a massive earthwork like the Avebury bank is not just hypothetical. Durrington Walls, near Stonehenge, is a monument very similar in size to Avebury, which once consisted of a ditch surrounded on the outside by a massive bank, although in this case the earthworks did not enclose stone circles. Already by the early 19th century, however, when it was first described by the antiquary Sir Richard Colt Hoare, it had been largely flattened by ploughing: 'Having been for many years in tillage, its form is much mutilated; but from what remains it appears to have been of a circular form ...' (Hoare 1812, 169). Over a century later, when Durrington Walls was described again, most of the monument had been almost completely obliterated (Wainwright and Longworth 1971, 7).

The way that natural and human forces, not spectacular in themselves but acting inexorably over long periods of time, can destroy even the mightiest of monuments, may be thought of as the 'Ozymandias factor', after Shelley's famous poem *Ozymandias of Egypt*. The poem describes the shattered ruins of a giant statue of Ozymandias (Rameses II):

> And on the pedestal these words appear:
> 'My name is Ozymandias, king of kings:
> Look on my works, ye Mighty, and despair!'
> Nothing beside remains. Round the decay
> Of that colossal wreck, boundless and bare,
> The lone and level sands stretch far away.

Appreciating the extraordinary destructive power of ploughing prompts the realisation that what survives today as upstanding monuments must be just the tip of the iceberg. If we go on to consider that the areas that are amongst the most favourable for arable farming today, such as the well-drained soils developed on the gravels of river valleys, were also probably the most favourable for agriculture, and therefore settlement, in the ancient past, then perhaps it is just those monuments that were most characteristic and important at the time they were built that have been 'preferentially' flattened. Flattened, but not completely destroyed because the ditches, pits, postholes and other 'negative features' which comprised parts of these monuments have often survived incised into the gravel surface, waiting to be revealed as cropmarks.

Another factor to consider here is the materials from which monuments were built. Stone can survive for thousands of years but, except in exceptional circumstances, wood cannot. Stone circles, for example, even small ones, can be impressive monuments of obvious importance – but were they necessarily as important in their day as perhaps much larger monuments built of timber, employing massive tree trunks? The so-called 'Seahenge', 4000 years old, discovered on the beach at Holme-next-the-Sea on the Norfolk coast in 1998, created a big stir amongst both archaeologists and the wider public. But there is nothing special about it other than its extraordinary preservation caused by waterlogging of the timbers. There are hundreds of examples of broadly similar small, timber-built shrines which survive today only as cropmarks; quality of survival today and importance in the past are two different things.

Very dramatically, then, aerial photography has helped to correct a major bias in the archaeological record – the highly misleading impression that what survives most visibly today is truly representative of the past. The results of aerial photography have offered – indeed forced upon – archaeologists a completely new perspective on the past. They have also presented archaeologists with some major challenges.

Writing on the landscape

One major challenge is how one should go about investigating the ancient landscapes revealed by aerial photography. Although the sites and monuments recognised as cropmarks have inevitably been truncated by ploughing, they nevertheless hold an enormous amount of information about the past. The sheer quantity of cropmark features, however, precludes both the detailed investigation and the preservation of more than a small fraction of them. Yet without further investigation on the ground, as a minimum to establish their date and an indication of probable function, the information they disclose is severely limited.

The cropmarked landscapes revealed by aerial photography are often compared to a 'palimpsest', a piece of parchment or a stone surface, say, that has been written or carved on repeatedly, each new layer of writing superimposed upon and partially erasing the earlier layers. So it is that prehistoric, Roman and medieval settlement have made their marks on the landscape. Some of the marks are deeply incised and clear, others are slight and faint; it is by no means always the case that the most recent marks are the clearest.

In the case of the sands and gravels of river valleys, the analogy of writing carved into a flat stone surface is remarkably precise. Since prehistoric times those who settled the land dug through the topsoil and incised into the surface of the relatively flat gravel the ditches bounding their settlements, fields and roads, the foundations of their houses and monuments, and occasionally even the graves of their dead. Each period of occupation creates a pattern of related marks, stretching for miles up and down the river valley, like a 'text' which the archaeologist seeks to 'read'. And of course each 'text' is just one layer of the palimpsest. Separating out the different layers or 'texts' and attempting to read them demands at least partial excavation.

Sand and gravel quarrying and archaeology: threat and response

At broadly the same time that aerial photography was revealing the extraordinary density of archaeological sites and monuments on the sands and gravels of England's river valleys, so the forces leading to the destruction of these ancient landscapes were on the increase. One of the major threats came from sand and gravel quarrying, which expanded greatly in the post-war years, peaking in 1989. The challenge since the 1960s has been to produce an effective response to this threat and, ultimately, transform it into an opportunity (Cooper 2008). This process is well illustrated by the history of archaeological research in the Where Rivers Meet area.

Before the 1960s only a handful of archaeological discoveries were reported in the Where Rivers Meet area. These were all chance finds, mostly made in the context of quarrying. They include what were evidently Anglo-Saxon cemeteries, uncovered during quarrying at Tucklesholme and Wychnor in 1851 and 1899 respectively, and three Bronze Age cinerary urns found in a gravel pit in 1874. It is noteworthy that these are all very obvious 'finds' – complete pots, metal weapons, jewellery. The more subtle remains of the type of features that produce the majority of cropmarks, with their contents of a few sherds of pottery or a handful of flints, went unnoticed or unremarked upon. Yet it is these latter that make up most of the 'text' that archaeologists wish to 'read'. A few isolated finds do not tell a coherent story.

Archaeological excavation only began in earnest in the area in the 1960s and 1970s, in direct response to the discovery of cropmark sites and the threat to them posed by quarrying. Archaeology in the 1960s was a small undertaking, with only a handful of professional archaeologists working in universities and museums but a rich amateur tradition. The 1970s saw the growth of the 'Rescue' movement. This was essentially an attempt to respond to the realisation of the extent of the destruction of archaeological remains occurring as a consequence of urban and rural development and to organise such limited resources as were available to excavate ('rescue') at least some archaeological sites before they

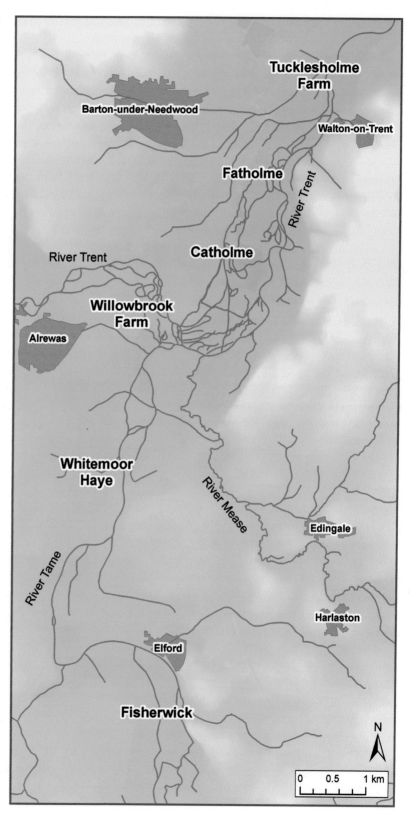

Figure 2.3 The Where Rivers Meet area showing location of principal archaeological excavations

were destroyed. This was an 'heroic age' in the history of British archaeology. Committees were established to coordinate the effort in Britain's historic towns and in the regions. In the area that we are concerned with it was the Trent Valley Archaeological Research Committee that undertook much of the work over this period. Indeed the impetus for the founding of the committee was the mass of cropmarks which had come to light in the valley of the Trent and their likely destruction by quarrying and other development (Salisbury 2002, xi). Much of the (very limited) funding for this sort of work came from the Ancient Monuments Division of the Department of the Environment and, after 1983, from English Heritage (Fig 2.3).

The first excavations carried out under the aegis of the committee in the Where Rivers Meet area took place at Fisherwick in the south of the area, on land being quarried by the Midland Gravel Company and Blue Circle Aggregates. Excavations by Henrietta Miles in 1968 (Miles 1969) targeted a cropmark complex photographed by Jim Pickering. The excavations revealed the remains of a Romano-British farmstead and associated enclosures, and a droveway, as well as ephemeral traces of Neolithic occupation. A further, more extensive programme of excavations coordinated by Christopher Smith followed in the early 1970s, targeting various other cropmark complexes at Fisherwick. These included a middle Bronze Age settlement (Smith 1976) and a well-preserved Iron Age farmstead enclosure with associated field system (Smith 1979). Waterlogged plant remains from the farmstead enclosure ditch provided a rare opportunity for environmental reconstruction (see Chapter 6). Smith's excavations were undertaken in the context of a ground-breaking landscape research project that deployed the cropmark evidence together with extensive fieldwalking, map and documentary research to reconstruct the landscape at various periods from the Neolithic onwards, all along the west bank of the Tame from Fisherwick to the confluence with the Trent (Smith 1980).

However, the most significant excavation carried out in the Where Rivers Meet area under the aegis of the Trent Valley committee during the 1970s was probably that of the Anglo-Saxon settlement at Catholme (Losco-Bradley and Kinsley 2002; see Chapter 8). Again the stimulus was cropmarks, in this case suggestive of Anglo-Saxon *Grubenhäuser* (sunken-floored buildings), threatened by sand and gravel quarrying. Following trial trenching in 1973, which confirmed the Anglo-Saxon date of the site, the excavations directed by Stuart Losco-Bradley were carried out over intermittent seasons from 1973 through to 1980.

During the 1980s there was something of a lull in archaeological excavation in the Where Rivers Meet area, but from the early 1990s the pace of archaeological research increased greatly. The principal stimulus for this was the introduction by the government in November 1990 of *Planning Policy Guidance 16: Archaeology and Planning* (commonly referred to as 'PPG 16'). Prior to the introduction of PPG 16, developers, including quarry companies, were under no obligation to take account of archaeological remains, except in the case of those sites afforded protection as scheduled ancient monuments. Although most quarry companies permitted archaeological excavation of sites that were to be destroyed by quarrying, they were not required to fund these excavations. Given the scale of quarrying and other development, this placed huge pressure on the limited funds available from the government and a few other sources for rescue excavations, and the deployment of these funds had to be extremely selective. The excavations at Fisherwick and Catholme mentioned above were largely carried out with funding from the Department of the Environment.

What PPG 16 has done is to provide planning authorities, including the county-based minerals planning authorities, with guidance that archaeological remains are a 'material consideration' in the planning process, and advice on how they should be dealt with. PPG 16 is guidance, not legislation, but it enables and encourages planning authorities, advised by archaeologists employed within local government, to impose conditions on planning permissions for new development, including quarrying, that protect significant archaeological remains or mitigate the impact of development upon them.

In the context of a proposed new development, the PPG 16 process is usually triggered by a record or records in a local authority 'Historic Environment Record' (HER) of archaeological sites that may be affected by the proposed development. HERs, formerly called 'Sites and Monuments Records' (SMRs), are maintained by almost all local authorities. They essentially comprise a list (nowadays a computer database) of all known sites, monuments and find-spots, accompanied by maps showing their locations and other relevant documentation (including aerial photographs). Each site or find-spot listed in the HER is given a unique reference number, called the 'HER number' (or 'SMR number'). In the kind of landscape we are concerned with here, the majority of sites on the HER will be cropmarks plotted onto maps. The landscape at the confluence of the Trent and the Tame falls mainly within the area covered by the Staffordshire HER, although part of it, along the eastern side, falls within the area of the Derbyshire HER.

While the HER provides the starting point for deciding whether a proposed development may have an impact on archaeological remains, through the provisions of PPG 16 the planning authority is encouraged to put the onus on the prospective developer to provide a suitably rigorous and detailed assessment of the potential archaeological impact of the proposed development. To do this the developer normally employs an independent archaeological consultant or contractor. Generally the process has two distinct stages. First the consultant or contractor will carry out a *desk-based assessment*. This involves using existing information, both that in the HER and anything else relevant that is available, to compile a detailed report on the potential archaeological impact of the proposed development. Where cropmark sites are involved, the original aerial photographs will be re-examined by a specialist and new interpretative plots will be produced, usually to a higher level of accuracy than is available within the HER.

Where more detailed information is required from the planning authority, as it often is, the next stage of assessment will be a *field evaluation*. A variety of techniques is generally used to obtain a better picture of the character, extent, significance, date and preservation of the archaeological remains threatened by the proposed development. These may include fieldwalking (the systematic collection of artefacts, usually pottery and flints, from the surface of ploughed fields, which can provide an indication of the date and character of underlying archaeological remains), geophysical survey, and small-scale trial excavations. The field evaluation will be carried out according to a specification agreed with the planning authority. Based on the assessment reports produced by the archaeological consultant or contractor on behalf of the developer, the planning authority will decide what conditions, if any, should be imposed on the development to mitigate its effects on the archaeological remains.

In the guidance provided in PPG 16, the favoured solution for the protection of archaeological remains is 'preservation *in situ*', that is preservation of the remains in the ground undisturbed or only minimally disturbed to an acceptable degree. Where this is not possible or justifiable, as is often the case where quarrying is involved, an alternative solution is what is called in the jargon 'preservation by record'. Essentially this means *archaeological excavation*, although other methods of investigation may be employed. The idea is that although the archaeological remains are physically destroyed (with the exception of the 'small finds' such as sherds of pottery, flints, bones etc, which are recovered), a record is preserved of them in the form of notes, drawings, photographs and so on; this record is then described and interpreted in an archaeological report. As with the assessment and evaluation stages, the excavation will be carried out in accordance with a written specification agreed with the planning authority.

The great majority of archaeological work carried out in the Where Rivers Meet area since 1990 has been carried out in the context of PPG 16. It has involved dozens of assessments, evaluations and excavations (Fig 2.2). A principal focus of this work, beginning in 1992, has been the Lafarge Aggregates Whitemoor Haye Quarry, occupying the stretch of the west bank of the Tame northwards of Fisherwick towards its confluence with the Trent. Here, elements of landscapes of the Neolithic, Bronze Age, Iron Age and Roman periods have been extensively excavated by the Birmingham University Field Archaeology Unit (now Birmingham Archaeology) in advance of quarrying, mainly since 1997 (Coates 2002; Hewson 2007). A second focus of work, although not on the same scale, has been in the north of the study area, particularly in the parish of Barton-under-Needwood, and has involved numerous assessments, evaluations and smaller-scale excavations, notably of prehistoric ritual and funerary monuments. These investigations have been carried out in response both to quarrying, for example the Barton and Newbold Quarries, and other types of development, for example the Barton Business Park. At the time of writing much of this work has not yet been formally published.

As described in the previous chapter, the intensity of aggregates extraction in the Where Rivers Meet area, combined with the large but necessarily piecemeal amount of archaeological work that has been carried out in response to it, was the stimulus for the Where Rivers Meet project. In the next chapter we describe some of the new techniques and approaches that have been applied to this rich but very complex ancient landscape.

CHAPTER THREE

Studying ancient landscapes in the 21st century

Introduction: the challenge of change

One of the greatest challenges to archaeologists studying past landscapes is change. It is difficult to understand ancient monuments and the relationships between them when they are set amongst the 'clutter' of modern buildings, roads and field boundaries. In some landscapes, changes since the Industrial Revolution – urbanisation, the building of roads, canals and railways, quarrying and other development – have dramatically altered how the landscape looks. Interest in the impact of these types of changes has increased since the 1990s when approaches to understanding archaeological sites and monuments became more concerned with their 'embodiment' in the landscape. Drawing upon themes in the social sciences, archaeologists explore the visual and other relationships between sites, attempting to perceive how they might have worked together and how they relate to their local setting.

In addition to the impact of development on the landscape, natural forces and farming practices can render past landscapes unrecognisable. Changes in sea level have altered our coastlines and affected the nature of rivers far inland, creating areas of wetland. Flooding rivers have deposited silts (alluvium) over the land, often deeply burying archaeological sites. Intensification of arable farming has similarly led to the deposition of hill-wash (colluvium) over areas that may have been occupied in the past. More recently, rivers have been canalised and embanked, narrowing active floodplains; coastal areas have been 'reclaimed' and lowlands have been drained, with the ultimate loss of the diversity of environments.

The landscape surrounding the confluence of the Rivers Trent, Tame and Mease has undergone massive change since it was first occupied by humans. The very fact that the area is dominated by three dynamic rivers implies that much could have altered, and this is confirmed by a cursory glance at the geology maps of the region which show vast areas of alluvium across the floodplains (Figs 1.2 and 1.4). This reflects significant changes to both the nature and courses of the rivers over time. More recently the impact of aggregate quarrying has fundamentally altered the form of the landscape, creating huge hollows and lakes along the courses of the rivers. The development of settlements such as Barton-under-Needwood, Alrewas and Elford, railways and roads, warehouses and other commercial development, and modern farming practices have all dramatically changed the face of the landscape and its ecology.

For the landscape archaeologist such changes present a number of challenges.

The first is simply the discovery of archaeological remains. We saw in the previous chapter how the discovery of archaeological sites was transformed by the development of aerial photography. Even once sites have been identified, however, the interpretation of their landscape context will require some level of 'reconstruction'. This may be attempted to a certain extent using the mind's eye, but normally this is insufficient. Fortunately, there are now numerous tools and techniques, derived from a range of different disciplines, which together can assist in the reconstruction of past landscapes (Gaffney, Fitch and Smith 2009). As we saw in Chapter 1, without breaking the ground, buried archaeology and geology can be modelled using a variety of geophysical techniques, including electrical resistance, magnetics and radar (Fig 3.1). Similarly, the shape of the landscape can be modelled using sophisticated computer software. Geomorphologists (who study land forms) can interpret how features such as rivers may have appeared at different periods. Palaeoecologists (who study past environments) can use the fossil remains of insects and plants, including ancient pollen, and the characteristics of buried soils to reconstruct the patterns of vegetation. A range of scientific dating techniques, including radiocarbon, can be applied to provide a chronology of change. Combining these approaches may allow the reconstruction of the landscape context of a site, in terms of both natural and cultural features. With this framework in place, interpretation of the activities of people within the ancient landscape becomes possible.

Landscape archaeology thus involves a wide range of disciplinary approaches, many of which are intrinsically specialist. Consequently, the best way to approach an archaeological landscape is to establish a team of specialists who will work

Figure 3.1 Some of the geophysical survey techniques used during the project: left, magnetometry; top right, resistance survey; bottom right, ground penetrating radar survey

together on the different aspects of landscape reconstruction and interpretation. However, the quantities of information that are generated from such a multi-faceted approach are often very large and cumbersome. It is here that computer-based modelling approaches become extremely useful. For combining multiple datasets together and obtaining meaningful information from them, the use of Geographical Information System (GIS) software has become extremely popular. This is a type of cartographic programme which also lies at the heart of technologies such as in-car satellite navigation, having the ability to simulate the real world (or, in the case of archaeology, past landscapes) and generate models combining multiple data types. GIS also holds the potential for interrogating the data, examining layers of information together, and even for modelling sites within their three-dimensional landscape, for example elements such as the steepness of slopes or how visible one site may be from another.

For the Where Rivers Meet landscape, a comprehensive suite of state-of-the-art techniques was combined to examine the archaeological features, in addition to their topographic and palaeoecological contexts (Wilkes and Barratt 2004). This chapter outlines the principal methods that were used in the study.

Topography: the bare bones of landscape

The starting point for the study of landscape is the basic shape, or topography, of the landscape surface. Topography is three-dimensional (3D). It is therefore best represented in a computer in a format that enables the generation of three-dimensional simulations. First we start with the topography as it is today and then, using additional sources of information, we can progress to modelling how it might have been in the past.

The Ordnance Survey provides data that can be used for modelling the three-dimensional shape of the present-day landscape surface on a computer. The computer simulates the land surface as a grid of 'cells', each cell representing a square area of fixed size on the ground. For example at 1:10,000, a scale often used for fairly detailed maps, each cell represents a square measuring 10m by 10m on the ground. Each cell has a value representing its height above mean sea level, or elevation. These values are presented in the form of a three-dimensional bar chart, where the position of each cell is determined by its horizontal location, and the height of each bar represents its elevation. Over large areas these individual cells become visually merged, resulting in the appearance of a continuous three-dimensional surface – actually it is a simplified model of that surface. The principle is the same as that used in a digital photograph: the picture looks smooth and continuous until you go up close and see that it is made up of a very large number of discrete pixels.

The main advantage of this type of model is that it is quantifiable. In other words, it is possible to perform calculations on it. By looking at the differences in elevation between adjacent cells, for example, it is possible to calculate slope angles. Similarly, it is possible to examine whether a person standing within a particular cell (perhaps where an archaeological monument is) could see another

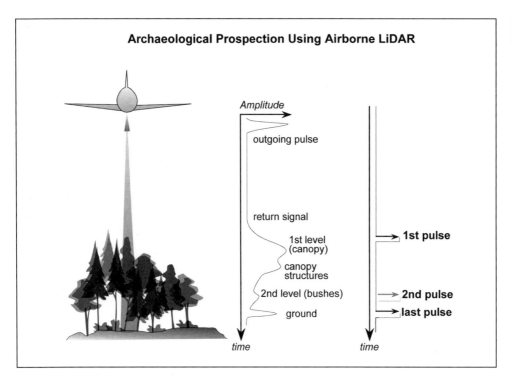

Figure 3.2 How LiDAR works

cell (or another monument). Cell-based data like these are normally referred to as 'raster' data, and it is the same format as that in which aerial photographs, geophysics plots, scanned maps and other images are also stored – each cell (or pixel) contains information.

The Ordnance Survey data provide an excellent overview of the landscape and

Figure 3.3 The results of the LiDAR survey revealed many features within the study area including river courses and quarries visible here, as well as more subtle topographic features including the routes of infilled channels, and the earthwork remains of early agriculture

a good basis for performing analyses, but they are of insufficient resolution for exploring some of the key features of an archaeological landscape. Subtle features such as old river channels can rarely be seen within these types of data. Higher-resolution data were consequently sought from a company called Infoterra (Wilkes and Barratt 2004). These data are generated by having an aircraft with a special type of scanner fly over the landscape. Essentially, the landscape below the aircraft is 'laser scanned' (Fig 3.2). The scanner emits a laser beam which is reflected off the ground surface and then received again by the instrument. The time between the emission of the laser beam and its return is measured and this enables the distance between the scanner and the ground surface to be calculated with great precision. The position of the aircraft is accurately located using Global Positioning System (GPS) equipment, providing a fix for the scanned landscape. The area is flown in transects to ensure that it is all covered.

The results from this type of scanning, which is known as LiDAR (Light Detection and Ranging), provide three-dimensional coordinates at around every metre across the landscape. The reflectance of the laser records both the tops of trees and buildings (first pulse) as well as the ground surface (last pulse), enabling the modelling of tree canopies, as well as the bare landscape, at a very high resolution, and it can even be possible to map the shapes of earthworks hidden within woodland.

The LiDAR survey of the Where Rivers Meet area provided a range of extremely useful information. The modelling of the data by Stephen Wilkes (Wilkes and Barratt 2004) showed that it had captured the shape of the modern landscape, including the alterations to the landscape such as the quarries (Fig 3.3). It also highlighted ancient features of the landscape, such as the trackways and house platforms of deserted medieval settlements, and the subtle depressions of old, infilled river channels (or palaeochannels) (Fig 3.4).

Figure 3.4
Earthworks identified within the results of the LiDAR survey, revealing patterns of medieval agriculture (ridge and furrow) and the channels reflecting medieval water management

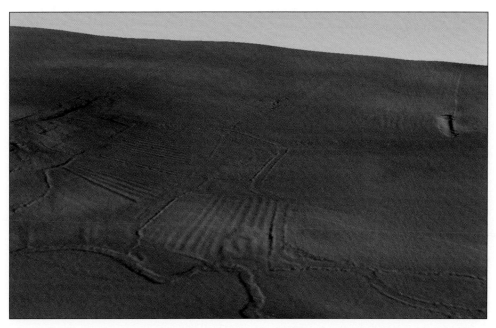

Adding flesh to the bones

By remodelling the LiDAR data in conjunction with the Ordnance Survey data a bare-earth surface was created that would act as the foundation for all further analyses. This formed the basis of the spatial database within the GIS, to which was added a variety of other mapping data and archaeological data from record offices. The Ordnance Survey digital raster mapping was supplemented by digital mapping representing features (roads, buildings etc) as a series of lines, points and polygons, known as 'vectors' in contrast to the raster (cell-based) data format.

Historical mapping was also obtained in a digital raster format. This covered the whole landscape and dated to both sides of 1900 (Ordnance Survey 1st and 2nd edition County Series mapping). These maps provided snapshots of the landscape over a period of more than 100 years. They were supplemented by georeferenced (accurately located in space) vertical aerial photography from 1963, 1971, 1981, and 1992. The earlier photographs were the most useful since they predated the extensive quarrying of the landscape.

Geological mapping was obtained from the British Geological Survey in vector format. Two types of geological mapping were used, that showing the 'solid' geology (the underlying rocks) and that showing the 'drift' (surface) geology. Drift geology includes such things as material washed along and deposited by rivers, which is known as alluvium. This comprises both the sands and gravels deposited by the rivers during the Ice Age (the material the quarrymen are after) and finer silts deposited in more recent times; both can be many metres thick.

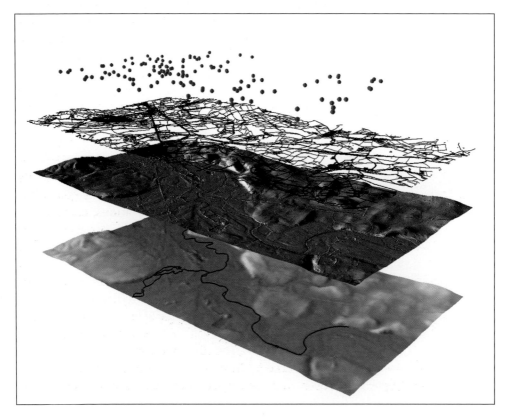

Figure 3.5 The GIS software enables various layers of data to be analysed together. Here the basic topography of the landscape (bottom) is shown in relation to a light-shaded surface, 'vector' mapping lines, and dots showing the positions of archaeological sites in the study area (top)

Databases of archaeological information, including cropmark plots, were obtained from the Historic Environment Records of Staffordshire County Council and Derbyshire County Council, and integrated into the GIS. To supplement these databases, additional archaeological features identified on the aerial photography were digitised and added to the overall database (Fig 3.5). The end result was a very complex database with many 'layers' of data – topography, geology, archaeology, etc, bringing together in the computer as much as possible of all the relevant information that could be obtained. The next stage was to try to make sense of it.

A sense of environment

The examination of the wider environment, and how this had evolved, was clearly of fundamental importance to the interpretation of the landscape. In particular, given their centrality within the landscape, the evolution of the rivers was crucial. A study of the rivers was undertaken by Neil Davies and Gregory Sambrook Smith from the University of Birmingham (Davies and Sambrook Smith 2004; 2006). The study of the rivers and their evolution was approached using a number of different sources of evidence. Mapping the position of previous courses of the rivers was undertaken using a combination of sources providing the locations of channels at different dates back as far as the 17th century. The recent courses of the rivers were obtained from the current 1:10,000 and 1:25,000 OS mapping, in addition to the LiDAR data (2003) and aerial photography (1964). Earlier river courses were mapped from the 1st edition County Series OS mapping (1884) and the 17th-century mapping contained in Robert Plot's *The Natural History of Staffordshire* (Plot 1686). A combination of the modelled LiDAR data, the 1960s (pre-quarrying) aerial photography and geological mapping, along with field observations, enabled the construction of an initial map of the ancient river channels (palaeochannels) and associated features (Fig 3.6).

To provide a higher-resolution interpretation of the palaeochannels and river dynamics, detailed field observations were made of geological exposures in the Barton East and Whitemoor Haye quarries. In addition, a ground-penetrating radar survey was undertaken. Ground-penetrating radar (GPR) used over drift geological deposits such as sands and

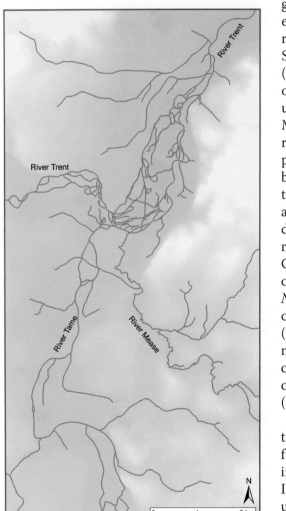

Figure 3.6 The Rivers Trent, Tame and Mease within the study area in relation to the underlying topography of the study area, including the positions of earlier stream courses of these rivers

gravels can reveal differences in sedimentation indicative of formations such as ancient river channels. The GPR survey was focused on areas where the old river channels had not been exposed by quarrying, and was undertaken in transects positioned perpendicular to the direction of flow of the rivers. From this it was possible to interpolate the position of the river channels between the survey transects.

The results of all the different techniques used to map ancient river channels were combined to provide an interpretation of how the river system had changed from the Ice Age onwards. This story is told in the next chapter.

Detailed studies in the 'focus area'

The first phase of work on the Where Rivers Meet project involved collecting and integrating largely pre-existing data relating to the whole 72km^2 of the study area. Detailed field studies were confined to a smaller area (235 hectares), with the aim of better understanding these data, exploring their reliability, investigating the potential of alternative techniques and obtaining new data. This was termed the 'focus area', a relatively small area unaffected by quarrying and centred on the monuments of the so-called Catholme Ceremonial Complex.

The first phase of archaeological fieldwork involved extensive landscape-scale geophysical survey within the focus area, combining resistivity, magnetometry and ground-penetrating radar (see Gaffney and Gater 2003 for a detailed explanation of the methods and their applicability to different archaeological situations). This phase of work was undertaken by Meg Watters, Tim Evans, Mark Kinsey and Kate Bain, from the University of Birmingham (Watters 2003). The initial output from these surveys consisted of a series of images in raster format that could be georeferenced within the project GIS (Fig 3.7). These images comprised maps of differences in electrical resistance, in the case of resistivity; alterations in the local magnetic field caused by various soil properties, in the case of magnetometry; or depth slice reflections from the radar. The 'anomalies' visible on these plots can be interpreted as either natural or archaeological features, and they could be directly compared with the mapping of cropmarks and other features from the aerial photography within the GIS. The anomalies were interpreted and digitised by Meg Watters to generate vector layers.

A major aim of the work in the focus area was to 'ground truth' the geophysical results systematically. 'Ground truthing' is another rather awkward technical term, but useful nevertheless, and some explanation is in order here. 'Remote sensing' is a catch-all term that refers to any technique that uses an instrument to detect indirectly and map an object of interest, whether buried oil deposits or buried archaeological remains. When the remote sensing reveals something that might be of interest against the general background, this is called an 'anomaly', a deliberately neutral term. Anomalies need to be interpreted, and the confidence of our interpretations can vary all the way from 'I'm almost certain I know what this is' to 'I haven't the faintest idea what is causing that anomaly'. Ground truthing is the process of directly investigating precisely what it is that is

Figure 3.7 Phase 1 of
the survey: the results
from the magnetic
(a) and resistance (b)
surveys within the
focus area

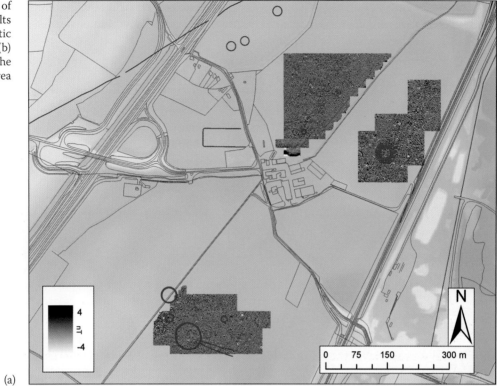

(a)

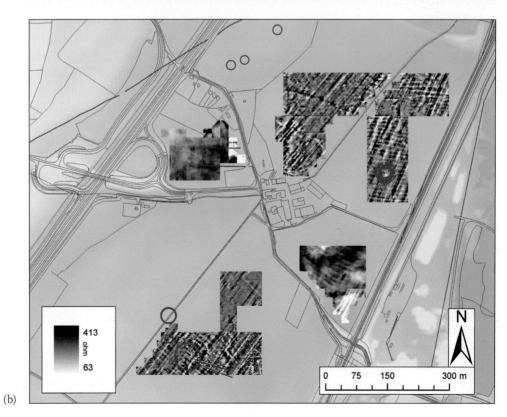

(b)

causing a particular anomaly or type of anomaly. For geophysical survey, 'below-ground truthing' might better capture the idea, because excavation is needed to determine precisely what it is that is causing the anomalies.

Ground truthing is not just about trying to find out what caused a particular geophysical anomaly in a particular case. It is about trying to understand precisely *why* a buried feature produced the type of anomaly that it did. It is also about trying to understand why buried features do not always produce the anomalies that might be expected. Systematic ground truthing is an essential part of the process by which the interpretation of geophysical data can be refined and also by which the geophysical techniques themselves can be improved. Furthermore, when excavations are carried out for ground truthing purposes the information that is sought from the excavations, for example the geophysical and geochemical properties of buried soils, is different from that which is sought during conventional archaeological investigations.

Small areas of the landscape-scale geophysical survey, located mostly over the principal monuments of the Catholme Ceremonial Complex, were selected for the ground truthing work (Fig 3.8). By removing the ploughsoil (c 30cm deep) many of the factors that cause interference to the geophysical equipment sensors are diminished. To provide a comparison of data, and thereby test methods, the areas that were to be excavated were intensively surveyed using the full range of geophysical equipment both before and after the removal of the ploughsoil. The results of this exercise revealed the greatly enhanced results that are possible through the removal of the upper layers of soil, before any archaeological features are reached.

The different geophysical methods used in this exercise produced different types of data. The magnetometry provided two-dimensional (2D) images showing the changes in the magnetic field attributed mainly to disturbances of the ground in the past, and these could be integrated within the GIS using high-accuracy positioning from GPS survey. In contrast, the high-resolution GPR survey generated a dense series of 'profiles' through the subsoil which could be joined together to provide images of anomalies at different depths down the profile. Furthermore, using specialist imaging software, it was possible for Meg to model three-dimensionally specific buried features that were interpreted as being archaeological (Fig 3.9). The type of software used was initially developed for imaging the results of medical CAT scans but it also proves to be very valuable for processing and imaging large quantities of GPR data. This enabled 'volumetric' modelling of features, and provided an extremely useful dataset that could later be compared with the results from the archaeological excavations.

The final stage of the fieldwork was limited archaeological excavation, targeted on areas that had produced different types of geophysical anomaly and also on a control area with no apparent anomalies. Detailed analysis of the physical and chemical properties of the buried soils and deposits, both those comprising the fills of archaeological features (ditches and pits, for example) and those forming the surrounding 'background', was carried out by David Jordan of Terranova (Jordan 2005). The magnetic properties of these deposits were investigated by

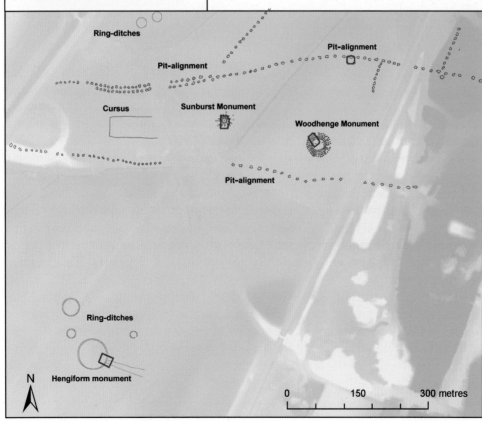

Figure 3.8 Areas within the Catholme Ceremonial Complex chosen for higher-resolution geophysical survey and subsequent 'ground-truthing' through excavation

Ring-ditches

Pit-alignment

Pit-alignment

Cursus

Sunburst Monument

Woodhenge Monument

Pit-alignment

Ring-ditches

N

Hengiform monument

0   150   300 metres

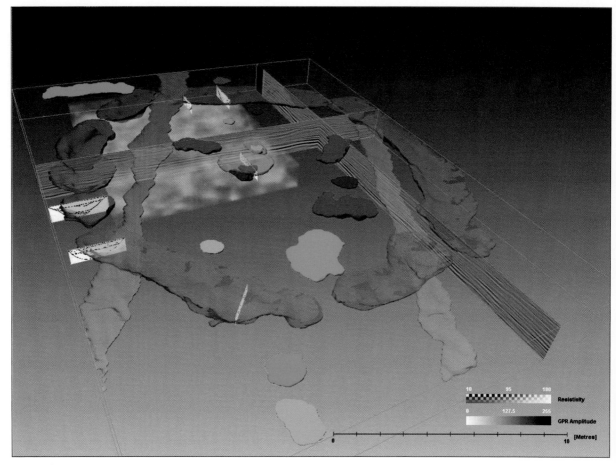

Mark Hounslow and Vassil Karloukovski of Lancaster University. The results of these detailed analyses are outside the scope of this book.

A principal aim of the archaeological excavations, therefore, was better understanding of the applicability of various geophysical techniques, leading to improved interpretation and the development of better methodologies for the future. The excavations did, of course, provide direct information on the monuments of the Catholme Ceremonial Complex themselves, and on their state of preservation. They also provided the opportunity to obtain samples that could be submitted to the laboratory for radiocarbon dating, and for analysis of organic remains, notably wood.

As with all the other information gathered during the Where Rivers Meet project, the results of the investigations in the focus area – the plans and section drawings from the excavations, the geophysical data and the interpretative plots – were incorporated into the project GIS. The results of these excavations, and of earlier excavations within the landscape, are described in the following chapters.

Figure 3.9 3D modelling of the results from the GPR survey in relation to a part of the resistance survey and some of the drawn 'sections' from the excavation of the sunburst monument. The modelling reveals a segmented ring-ditch (mauve), and other features including two later plough scars (beige), a central pit (dark green) and a variety of other pits and features

Bringing it all together

The use of a Geographical Information System as a spatial database where all the different datasets could be combined was established at the outset of the Where Rivers Meet project. Each strand of data from the different types of investigation tells a separate but incomplete story about the landscape archaeology of the study area. Together, the multiple strands of data from all the approaches begin to form a more complete narrative.

A number of issues have to be considered when analysing multiple datasets together. The different forms of data not only tell different stories, but also relate to different scales in terms of both time and space. Often the palaeoecological story, concerning the character of past environments, will present a broad-brush picture of change over large areas and through long time periods. The LiDAR survey provides information about the modern landscape at a 1m surface resolution, whereas the mapping of cropmarks may contain surface errors of several metres in some cases. The GPR data in contrast was collected over smaller areas at 0.25m resolution. The excavation of features was undertaken at an even higher resolution over small sample areas. Dealing with the variety of spatial resolutions, and picking apart the chronological phasing of different elements of the landscape is quite a challenge, both in terms of the practicalities of GIS software and with regards to archaeological understanding.

Some basic correlations can be extremely useful. For example, comparing the distribution of mapped cropmarks with the geology maps can be extremely telling (Fig 3.10). As aerial archaeologists have known for many years, the geology of an area will influence the likelihood of cropmark formation. The critical factor is the drainage potential of different types of geology. Poorly drained geologies are less likely to reveal features because the formation of cropmarks is dependent on differential moisture retention by the soil, which causes differences in the growth of the crop. A comparison between geology and known cropmarks can therefore address important questions: are the gaps in the cropmark record merely the result of geology, or do they represent real differences in land use in the past? Other correlations, such as between cropmark features and geophysical survey results, are equally important. Because the different techniques are reflecting different properties of the burial environment, it is not always the case that they will reveal the same features. By bringing the results from different approaches together it is possible to increase knowledge of the buried archaeological landscape even before breaking the surface of the ground.

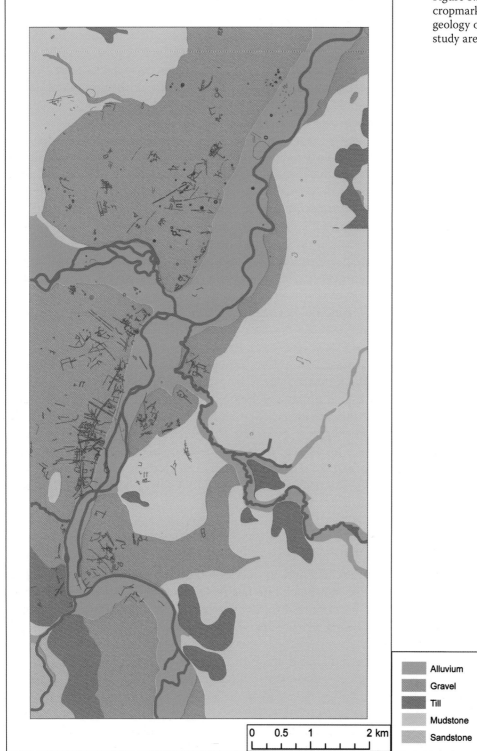

Figure 3.10 The occurrence of cropmarks in relation to the geology of the Where Rivers Meet study area

	Alluvium
	Gravel
	Till
	Mudstone
	Sandstone

0   0.5   1   2 km

Reconstructing the landscape

As mentioned at the beginning of this chapter, the interpretation of an archaeological landscape starts with reconstruction of the physical landscape. Sites may only make sense in relation to natural features such as hills, slopes, lowlands or wetlands. Some of these, for example wetland areas, will change through time, reflecting both their development and drainage. Other factors such as the contemporary vegetation pattern will also have a dramatic impact on the way in which a site or sites may be interpreted.

There have been numerous different approaches to reconstructing past environments, and it must be acknowledged that some elements, such as vegetation, are more difficult to model than others, such as topography. Many of the current approaches to modelling patterns of vegetation, for example, have combined pollen analysis with consideration of the physical configuration of the landscape, such as slope, aspect and elevation. These have been conducted at grand landscape scales (eg Spikins 1999) and at more local scales (eg Gearey and Chapman 2006; Winterbottom and Long 2006), with the results sometimes being used to address other themes such as the visual impact of monuments. Whilst the precise location of every tree and shrub at a certain period will never be known, the modelling of different possibilities provides a stimulating 'way in' to the exploration of past worlds and for engagement with them.

Within the Where Rivers Meet area, the modelling of the landscape at different periods has been based on a wide range of different environmental and archaeological datasets. The combination of these datasets provides a relatively clear understanding of the major changes to the landscape, and in some areas a higher-resolution understanding. There remain many gaps and uncertainties, however, as the later chapters of this book will show. Modelling within a GIS essentially creates a 'best-fit' picture of a landscape on the basis of current knowledge. In this way, the models should be considered as hypothetical, or perhaps even heuristic – a platform from which to generate interpretations of cultural activity throughout time.

Landscape archaeology in the 21st century

Although 'landscape archaeology' as a concept in archaeology goes back a long way, in recent decades this sub-discipline has really taken off, with landscapes being investigated from a number of different perspectives. Critically, the development of 'experiential' approaches to interpreting landscapes – what was it like actually to be in these landscapes and to move about in them? – has highlighted the need to understand how a landscape may have appeared in the past.

In recent years this has been achieved by developments in digital technologies, both in terms of capturing data and modelling it. The use of approaches such as GIS has fundamentally changed the way in which we approach archaeological landscapes (Chapman 2006). We are now able to visualise how a landscape may have looked in a rigorous, repeatable way. Furthermore, models can be altered as new data become available. This has had a dramatic impact on all aspects of landscape archaeology, not only on the interpretation of landscapes but also on how they should be managed. The use of these technologies has become common within planning departments, where decisions regarding new developments are made. The potential impacts of development on archaeology can be understood in increasingly precise ways. Furthermore, the same technology can be used to assess indirect threats to archaeological sites and landscapes, for example the impact of drainage of wetlands (eg Chapman and Cheetham 2002). Part of the research of the Where Rivers Meet project, carried out by Mark Bunch and Mike Riley of the University of Birmingham, investigated the potential affect of 'dewatering', caused by quarrying, on archaeological remains (Bunch and Riley 2004). These new approaches are permeating all areas of the archaeological process.

For the Where Rivers Meet project, the use of state-of-the-art technology has formed the backbone of research. The project has helped to advance the ways in which we use these technologies in the field and how we process the resulting data, including assessing the appropriateness of the different methods for different purposes. We have entered a 'brave new world' of research that will progressively alter the way we view and engage with past landscapes.

CHAPTER FOUR

The Ice Age and after

The Ice Age (or Pleistocene epoch in geological terms) covers approximately the last two million years of history. During this time, the massive natural forces unleashed by the repeated advance and retreat of ice sheets, as the climate swung from cold to warm and back again, shaped and reshaped the landscape. For much of this time, low sea levels meant that Britain was not an island but a peninsula of continental Europe, the western limit of a great plain – sometimes called 'Doggerland' – which stretched across the southern North Sea basin to Scandinavia (Gaffney, Fitch and Smith 2009). The drainage of the land was constantly changing, with new river systems coming into existence and then being obliterated or substantially altered. Plants and animals came and went with the changing climate, including species of early humans, archaeological traces of which are found in the Midlands dating from over 500,000 years ago.

The River Trent in the Ice Age

In our study area, the picture of the landscape only begins to come into focus during the last major cold stage of the Ice Age, which is known in Britain as the Devensian. This last cold stage lasted from a little before 100,000 years ago until around 11,500 years ago, when the climate entered the current warm interglacial period we enjoy today, known as the Holocene. Although temperatures were lower than today's, the Devensian was not one long period of uniform cold but a period of fluctuating climate (Fig 4.1). Nevertheless, the underlying trend was of deteriorating temperatures culminating in the last major ice advance of the Ice Age, the Last Glacial Maximum, centring around 21,000 years ago. At this time the Devensian ice sheet expanded sufficiently far southwards and eastwards from the highland zone to encroach on the study area, with the ice limit around Alrewas. From the trough of the Last Glacial Maximum, temperatures rose relatively rapidly, although not without serious fluctuations, to usher in the Holocene interglacial.

During the Devensian the Where Rivers Meet area was dominated by a river system with a principal direction of flow from the south-west to the north-east. We may call this the River Trent, although its size and course were very variable and the separation of the Trent and Tame rivers as we know them today had not yet taken place. Aspects of this early river system were studied by Neil Davies and Greg Sambrook Smith, of the School of Geography, Earth and Environmental Sciences at the University of Birmingham, as part of the Where Rivers Meet project (Davies and Sambrook Smith 2004; 2006). As we saw in the previous chapter, they were able to make use of three principal sources of evidence: geological exposures in the quarries at Whitemoor Haye and Barton

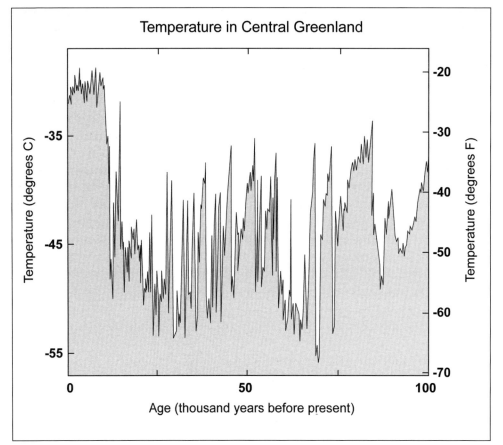

Figure 4.1 Chart showing fluctuations in temperatures over the last 100,000 years, based on data from Greenland ice cores (the average temperatures are those for central Greenland; the relatively stable, warm temperatures of the last 10,000 years are shown on the left)

East; aerial photographs and LiDAR survey data showing the course of early river channels (or 'palaeochannels') (Fig 4.2); and GPR survey data which they collected themselves in order to assess the 3D geometry of the river deposits where no exposures were available. From these various sources of evidence they were able to produce a composite map showing the pattern of former river channels in the study area (Fig 4.3).

The Trent around Catholme during the Devensian may be visualised as a multi-channel ('braided') river system (Fig 4.4) fed mainly by glacial meltwater. The system is likely to have been highly seasonal, with prolonged intense floods during the summer months, but becoming a shallow river wetland in the winter months, with fewer active channels. The river channels were much wider than those of later periods, up to 100m across. Due to the lack of extensive vegetation the banks of the channels would have been unstable and the channels would have changed their course easily and frequently, migrating across the river plain. The whole river system scoured a valley into the underlying Mercia Mudstone bedrock, which had been laid down more than 200 million years earlier during the Triassic period. This river valley is about 5km wide, with the mudstone edges of the valley along its eastern side forming, in places, a pronounced bluff.

Over a period of thousands of years this river system deposited sediments of gravel, sand, mud and clay up to a depth of about 13m, with an average thickness of around 6m. Most of the deposit is gravel, mainly comprising locally derived quartzite and quartz from the Triassic 'Bunter Pebble Beds'. Study of the exposures at the Whitemoor Haye (Fig 4.5) and Barton East quarries suggests that the Ice Age gravels were laid down in 'pulsed' flood events, in sheets or broad channels, reflecting the 'pulsed' seasonal variation in meltwater discharge. Occasional 'cryogenic' features (features caused by the effect of ice) in the gravel deposits, such as ice-wedge casts, indicate permafrost conditions during part of the period of deposition. The channels with a sand fill are narrower and may represent 'overspill' channels transporting fine-grain sediment across bars within the river system. It is of course these valuable sand and gravel deposits that have been, and are being, exploited by the numerous quarries in the Where Rivers Meet area, past and present. Occasionally they reveal a surprise.

Figure 4.2 LiDAR image revealing the complex of wide Pleistocene palaeochannels and narrower Holocene palaeochannels around Catholme Farm (compare Fig 4.4)

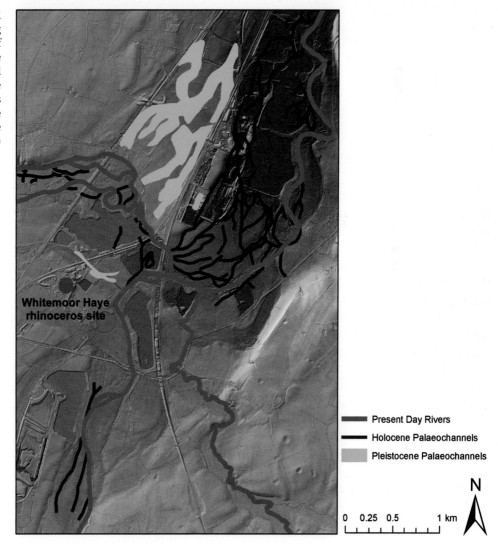

Whitemoor Haye rhinoceros site

Present Day Rivers

Holocene Palaeochannels

Pleistocene Palaeochannels

N

0   0.25   0.5   1 km

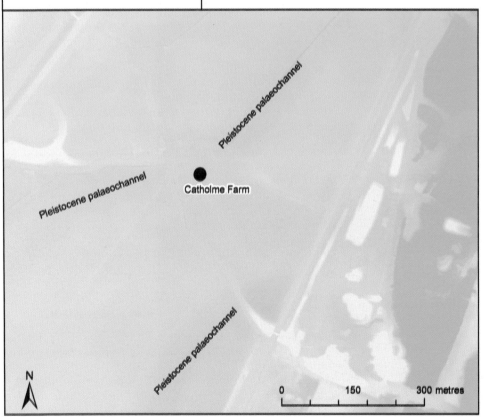

Figure 4.3 Above:
map, compiled
from a variety of
sources of evidence,
showing former
river channels in the
study area; below:
detail of Pleistocene
palaeochannels
around Catholme
Farm as revealed
by the LiDAR data
(after Davies and
Sambrook Smith
2006)

Figure 4.4 A large braided river outwash plain: the River Trent will have looked like this during the cold stages of the Pleistocene

Fig 4.5 Pleistocene deposits exposed in the Whitemoor Haye Quarry – the ranging rods indicate the position of a deposit of organic material filling a former stream channel within the gravels

The discovery of the Whitemoor Haye woolly rhinoceros

On 3 September 2002, Ray Davies, a digger driver at the Lafarge Whitemoor Haye quarry, was working as usual, excavating the gravel and loading it onto large dumper trucks for transport to the processing plant. From deep down in the gravel he pulled up in his machine bucket the skull, lower jaw and most of the other bones representing the front end of a woolly rhinoceros, *Coelodonta antiquitatis* (Fig 4.6). The bones were in a very good state of preservation and had evidently been at least partially articulated (ie still forming a skeleton) prior to their disturbance by the machine bucket.

This was an exceptional find. While it is not uncommon for the occasional tooth or bone of Ice Age 'megafauna' (animals weighing more than a ton) to turn up during quarrying, it is very rare to find such a near-complete specimen. When we consider the number of unlikely circumstances that must occur for a skeleton to survive almost intact we can easily see why this is so. First, the carcass has to survive the usual depredations of scavengers such as the spotted hyena. Then, somehow, it has to become embedded in a soft deposit within the river bed that will keep it intact and will, somehow, survive the violence of Ice Age rivers in flood for thousands of years. Normally, if bones do manage to make it into the river, they are scattered and smashed so that all that remains, if anything remains at all, are a few isolated scraps, particularly teeth, which are the toughest part of the skeleton. The odds against a skeleton surviving even partially intact are enormous.

The unexpected discovery of the woolly rhinoceros skeleton was followed up by detailed investigations at the find spot and in its environs. These were led by Andy Currant of the Natural History Museum, London, and Danielle Schreve of Royal Holloway, University of London, both specialists in the study of Ice

Figure 4.6 The partial skeleton of the Whitemoor Haye woolly rhinoceros with its discoverer, machine operator Ray Davies

Figure 4.7
Reconstruction
painting of a woolly
rhinoceros

Age mammals. The work was in part funded by English Nature (now Natural England) through their Aggregates Levy grant scheme, with much practical assistance being provided by the quarry operator, Lafarge.

One aspect of the investigations involved a careful search of the quarry floor for further remains, both of the woolly rhinoceros itself and for the remains of other Ice Age animals that might have survived. At the location of the original find an area measuring *c* 50m by 30m was carefully and expertly stripped down to the bedrock by the machine drivers working at the quarry. By the conclusion of the investigations, a considerable group of bones of large Ice Age mammals had been collected. These included further bones of the original woolly rhinoceros (although not its pelvis and the other major bones of its rear end, which had evidently been destroyed), together with bones of other woolly rhinoceri, wolves, mammoths, horse, reindeer and bison (Currant and Schreve 2003).

The parts of the woolly rhinoceros skeleton that were collected include the cranium and lower jaw, some of the vertebrae and ribs, a single shoulder blade and the major parts of the front limbs. The excellent preservation of the bones that did survive, along with details such as the preservation of plant remains in the upper teeth, points to the very rapid burial of the carcass, probably in a frozen state. It seems likely that the rear part of the carcass was re-exposed some time after deposition and was dispersed by the river. Figure 4.7 provides an artist's reconstruction of a woolly rhinoceros in a tundra landscape, not unlike that which would have existed at Whitemoor Haye around 30,000 years ago.

Another aspect of the investigations was the collection of data that would place the rhinoceros find in its environmental context and provide evidence for its date. Not only did the bones of large mammals survive in the Ice Age deposits, but also the macroscopic (stems and leaves) and microscopic (pollen and spores) remains of plants, together with beetles and other insects. Study of these, in tandem with geological analysis of the deposits in which the remains are found, enables the climate and environment at the time of deposition to be reconstructed.

Dating evidence is provided by radiocarbon dating of the mammal bones, together with a technique called Optically Stimulated Luminescence (OSL) (see Box 1). OSL dating is a technique that enables scientists to estimate the date at which grains of sand (quartz) were laid down by water or wind and then buried in the accumulating deposits. Fossil remains contained within these deposits may be dated by association with the dated layer.

Box 1: Optically Stimulated Luminescence (OSL) dating

The OSL dating technique is based on the fact that all sediments are very slightly radioactive. Quartz or feldspar grains in the sediment absorb this radiation, which builds up slowly in the grains over time. Exposure to sunlight, which occurs when the deposits are laid down by wind or water, sets the radioactive signal in the grains to zero. After the grains are buried the radiation levels build up again, and by measuring the amount of radiation that has built up in a grain an estimate can be made of the time that has passed since the grains were buried. This is done in the laboratory by making the grains emit their stored radiation in the form of light (luminescence), hence the description 'optically stimulated luminescence'.

On the 'Mammoth Steppe' in Staffordshire

At the time of writing, the scientific study of the fossil remains (mammalian, insect and plant) from Whitemoor Haye has not been completed. Nor are the full results of the programme of OSL and radiocarbon dating available; these will be published in a scientific report (Schreve *et al* forthcoming). What we can provide here is just a preliminary outline account of some of the main findings and a sketch of what the landscape of the Where Rivers Meet area may have been like at the time that the Whitemoor Haye woolly rhinoceros died (Buteux *et al* 2003).

The preliminary results of the OSL (Toms 2003) and radiocarbon dating suggest that the Whitemoor Haye fossils are *c* 30,000 years old. This places them in the latter part of a worldwide climatic stage known as Marine Oxygen Isotope Stage 3 or MIS 3, which lasted overall from *c* 60,000 years ago to 25,000 years ago (see Box 2).

Box 2: Marine Oxygen Isotope Stages

The most complete, continuous record of worldwide climate change during the Ice Age has come from long cores drilled into the soft seabed at various locations around the world's oceans. The seabed sediments at these locations contain the microscopic skeletons, made from calcium carbonate, of millions of dead sea creatures. When these animals die their remains rain down on the seabed and build up deposits many metres thick. The chemical composition of these skeletons contains information about the chemical composition of the sea water at the time the animals died. Extracting a core from the seabed and determining the chemical composition of the skeletons of the microscopic animals at different levels through the seabed deposits provides a method for determining how the chemical composition of the sea water has changed through time.

The aspect of the chemical composition of the sea water that tells us about changing climate is the relative proportion of two different versions (isotopes) of the oxygen atom. The isotope ^{16}O is lighter than the isotope ^{18}O and more of it evaporates from the sea water. In cold climatic periods more of the lighter isotope (^{16}O) is 'locked up' in ice sheets and glaciers and thus the sea water is relatively enriched in the heaver isotope (^{18}O). In warm periods, when more of the lighter ^{16}O is returned to the oceans in the form of precipitation, the proportion of the two isotopes shifts. Thus the proportions of the two isotopes in the sea water at any time, determined indirectly from their proportions in the skeletons of the tiny sea creatures at different levels in the sea-bed deposits, reflects (amongst other things) the size of ice sheets and glaciers and also sea levels: when water is 'locked up' in glaciers global sea levels are lower. These factors in turn provide us with a broad picture of changing climate.

The record of changing climate determined from the deep-sea cores, known for reasons that will now be apparent as the marine oxygen isotope record, has been divided into a number of alternating cold and warm stages, known as Marine Oxygen Isotope Stages. The stages are numbered backwards in time, starting with the present warm interglacial stage, which has now lasted for more than 10,000 years, Marine Oxygen Isotope Stage 1 (MIS 1). MIS 2 is the last glacial period, which peaked around 21,000 years ago. The way that the numbering system works means that warm stages will always be denoted by an odd number and cold stages by an even number.

The 'warm' period to which the Whitemoor Haye woolly rhinoceros belongs is MIS 3, which lasted from around 60,000 years ago to around 25,000 years ago. 'Warm' is in inverted commas because the climate during this long stage was in fact extremely variable, generally deteriorating from its beginning to its end, with several very cold episodes (including that in which the rhinoceros lived and died). A more fine-grained climatic record for the period is provided by cores drilled into ice sheets, as is described in the main text.

At this time the landscape of southern Britain formed part of what has been called the 'Mammoth Steppe'. The Mammoth Steppe was an extraordinary phenomenon, with no real parallel today. It stretched uninterrupted half way around the top of the world, from England in the west across 'Doggerland' (ie the area that is now covered by the southern North Sea), the North European Plain and Siberia all the way to Alaska in the 'east'. The low sea levels meant that many areas now under the sea were dry land. These included the southern part of the North Sea and also part of the Bering Sea between the north-east corner of Siberia and Alaska, a lost area known as 'Beringia' (Fig 4.8) (Gaffney, Fitch and Smith 2009, chapter 5). The grasslands of the Mammoth Steppe supported a wide range of large herbivores, such as bison, horse, musk ox and reindeer as well as woolly mammoth, together with the carnivores that preyed on them or smaller animals, including cave bear, hyena and wolf. Some of these animals, such as the mammoth, were found across the whole range; others, such as the woolly rhinoceros, were confined to Eurasia.

Cores almost two miles long drilled into the Greenland ice sheet provide a detailed record of climate change during MIS 3, much more fine-grained than the record from the deep-sea cores (Figure 4.1 shows the fluctuation in temperatures based on data from a Greenland ice core). From these ice cores it is clear that the period from *c* 60,000 to 25,000 years ago was one of very unstable climate, characterised by rapid, often millennial-scale, climate oscillations. The warm peaks were 6–7°C warmer than the intervening cold episodes, which towards the end of MIS 3 equalled those of the Last Glacial Maximum. Such rapid climate change must have had a profound effect on the landscape, vegetation and fauna of the Mammoth Steppe, which may be characterised as a highly diverse 'mosaic' environment. The details of this environment and regional variation are poorly understood, however, which is what makes sites like Whitemoor

Figure 4.8 The global extent of the Mammoth Steppe

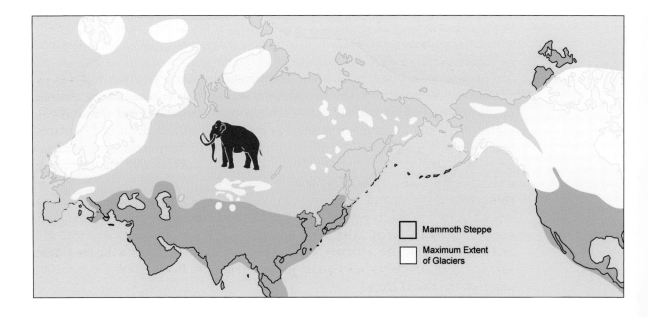

Mammoth Steppe

Maximum Extent of Glaciers

Figure 4.9 *Dryas octopetala*, the mountain avens, typical of arctic and alpine environments

Haye so important for scientists trying to understand past environments and environmental change.

What was the local environment like at the time that the Whitemoor Haye woolly rhinoceros died? From the geological evidence we have already been able to form a good picture of the river, with its broad, unstable multiple channels criss-crossing the broad plain, sometimes in violent flood but at other times more quiescent. During these quieter periods, or beyond the edges of the main channel belt, conditions were sufficiently gentle for organic deposits to accumulate, containing both macroscopic plant remains (leaves, stems and fruits) and microscopic pollen grains. The preservation of some of the plant remains was so good that it was hard to believe that they were around 30,000 years old.

A sample of organic deposit was taken from the spot where the first woolly rhinoceros remains were discovered, and preliminary analysis of its content of macroscopic plant remains was carried out by Dr Mike Field (Field 2003). Only a fairly narrow range of plants was present. Grassland, disturbed in places and perhaps with patches of bare soil, was suggested by grasses, types of flax, cinquefoil, dandelion and other plants. It is quite possible that the disturbed areas may have been caused by the movement of large animals, including woolly rhinoceros and mammoth, to and from the river. A tundra-type environment was suggested by dwarf arctic-alpine plants, most commonly dwarf willow, with occasional dwarf birch. Also represented was one of the most characteristic arctic-alpine plants, *Dryas octopetala* – a pretty little white flower, the mountain avens – that flourishes on barren ground (Fig 4.9). It was probably growing amongst the dwarf trees.

Figure 4.10
Preserved remains
of a *Chrysomela
cerealis* L. beetle
from a fragment of
organic sediment
associated with
one of the shallow
channels on the
Whitemoor Haye
woolly rhinoceros
site. It is estimated
to be *c* 50,000 years
old

Perhaps surprisingly to the uninitiated, the study of insect remains is one
of the key techniques used in the reconstruction of climate and temperature
during the Ice Age. Three types of insects from Whitemoor Haye were studied
but here we will just mention the preliminary results of the study of the beetles,
which was carried out by Professor Russell Coope and Dr David Smith (Coope
and Smith 2003). The use of beetles to reconstruct past climates is a particularly
well-developed technique. Beetles have not evolved since the Ice Age so that
the modern temperature and precipitation ranges of different species can be
reliably used to infer past temperature and precipitation. Different species have
different tolerances, so that by comparing the 'range overlap' of the various
species represented in a fossil assemblage a more precise 'fix' on the past climatic
conditions can be obtained.

Around one third of the beetle species present were species that are no
longer found in Britain (Fig 4.10). All the exotic species found in the samples
from Whitemoor Haye were species that are associated today with high Arctic
tundra or Alpine conditions. Examples of these include *Helophorus obscurellus*,
now found only to the east of the Kanin Peninsula in arctic Russia, and
Heloboraephilus nordenskioeli, limited to the tundra landscapes of northern
Scandinavia and Siberia. The preliminary work on the beetles suggested a July
mean temperature of 10°C and January mean temperatures as low as –15°C.

In terms of landscape reconstruction the range of beetle species suggested a
tundra scrub with sand and gravelly ground. The species of water beetles identified

were all of types associated with slow-flowing and usually vegetated waters, providing a further clue to conditions under which the woolly rhinoceros carcass became buried. The wide range of *Aphodius* dung beetles that was encountered provides indirect evidence of the rich fauna of large grazing mammals that must have inhabited the landscape around Whitemoor Haye (Fig 4.11).

Overall, by combining evidence from sources as diverse as deep-sea cores and ice cores, old maps and LiDAR, ground-penetrating radar and the geological recording in quarries, macroscopic and microscopic remains of plants and animals, and dating by means of OSL and radiocarbon, we can build up a rich and detailed picture of the Where Rivers Meet area during the Ice Age, tens of thousands of years ago.

Figure 4.11 Cold climate fauna of the Late Pleistocene, showing many of the species uncovered at Whitemoor Haye

On the trail of the Ice Age hunters

We have seen how the discoveries at Whitemoor Haye, which all started when Ray Davies pulled up some large bones in his machine bucket, enable the Ice Age environment of some 30,000 year ago to be reconstructed in considerable detail, with the promise of more detailed and accurate reconstructions when the scientific research has been completed (Schreve *et al* forthcoming).

But were humans also on the scene? Although no direct evidence in the form of stone tools has yet been found anywhere in the study area, it is easy in the mind's eye to populate the landscape not only with the range of grazing animals discovered but also with the early humans that may have hunted them. The Mammoth Steppe provided an excellent hunting ground.

The period around 30,000 years ago is a very interesting one because it was around this time that the Neanderthals were replaced by modern humans (*Homo sapiens*), with a possible overlap of several thousand years when both species may have co-existed in western Europe. There is no doubt that both Neanderthals and the earliest modern humans in Britain penetrated into the Midlands and that the River Trent would have been familiar to them. Stone tools characteristic of both species have been found in caves at Creswell Crags, a dramatic limestone gorge immediately north of the Trent valley on the Derbyshire/Nottinghamshire border. Although such stone tools have not yet been found in the Trent valley itself, this would surely have been part of the range of mobile hunting bands. However, the discovery of these tools requires that somebody is looking for them and that they know where to look. This is where modelling past environments comes in: it provides clues as to where the promising deposits may be found.

As we have seen, this was a time of fluctuating climate, and the presence of humans, either Neanderthals or *Homo sapiens*, ebbed and flowed with the changing climate and environment. It seems probable that no humans were present during the episode in which the Whitemoor Haye woolly rhinoceros died, as this was likely to have been just too cold for human occupation this far north. But, as the evidence from Creswell Crags shows, they were clearly present at other times.

From around 25,000 years ago the climate deteriorated even further, entering into the Last Glacial Maximum (MIS 2). During this long period of intense cold, with the ice sheets spreading across much of Britain, the whole country was abandoned by humans. The hunters did not return until around 15,000 years ago, following the rich herds of game which also migrated northwards, tracking the now warming climate. The human presence (now only *Homo sapiens*, the Neanderthals having become extinct long since) appears to have been more numerous than before the glacial maximum. Once again their presence in the Midlands is demonstrated by the discovery of their stone tools and other artefacts (including cave art only recently discovered) in the caves at Creswell Crags. Indeed the dominant stone tool tradition of this period in Britain takes its name, the 'Creswellian', from Creswell Crags. Furthermore, although there is still no direct evidence of occupation in the Where Rivers Meet area, scattered flint artefacts of the period have been found elsewhere along the Trent valley, for example downstream at Potlock, Derbyshire (Howard and Knight 2004, 23), and there is little doubt that hunters were operating in our area, on the tracks of such prey as reindeer, horse and bison.

The end of the Ice Age

Soon after 13,000 years ago, the Earth plunged into the last convulsion of the Ice Age, a period of severe cold known as the Younger Dryas. It is named after *Dryas octopetala*, a plant often found in environmental samples from this period. We saw above that this wildflower, the mountain avens, which was also associated with the Whitemoor Haye woolly rhinoceros skeleton, is typical of tundra or Alpine conditions. The ice sheets advanced again, although it is unclear whether Britain was once again wholly abandoned by humans.

Around 11,500 years ago the Younger Dryas came to an abrupt end, ushering in the present warm and climatically relatively stable interglacial period known as the Holocene. At first, however, the Where Rivers Meet area was once again dominated by a powerful, unstable multi-channel ('braided') river system, fed by meltwaters. The discharge was still great enough for the formation of a gravel-bed stream, with very broad, shallow channels prone to constant shifting of their course. While the river still flowed towards the north-east, the active floodplain now moved to the south-east, closer to its present position (Davies and Sambrook Smith 2004).

As the climate ameliorated, the discharge of the river diminished, the width of the active river system narrowed and less sediment was transported and deposited. As a consequence, a river terrace was cut into the Ice Age gravels during the early Holocene. It is on this terrace, now submerged only during extreme flooding events, that almost all subsequent archaeological evidence of human occupation has been found in the Where Rivers Meet area. It was around this time that the north-east-flowing river system separated into two rivers, the Trent and the Tame, each with their own drainage areas. The Trent flowed into the area from the west before turning north-east past Alrewas; the Tame flowed in from the south (*ibid*).

Climatic amelioration brought with it warmth-loving plants and animals, migrating from their southern refuges. Birch and pine woodland came first but was replaced over time by hazel and elm, followed by oak, lime, alder and ash, so that gradually much of the Midlands became a densely forested landscape. The changed landscape was inhabited by a range of animals adapted to it, including red and roe deer, aurochs (wild cattle), boar and elk.

Reduced flow and the development of a densely vegetated landscape had a major effect on the river system. As some of the channels became the dominant water discharge routes, those that were abandoned were quickly colonised by vegetation and stabilised by roots, making channel shifting more difficult and helping to stabilise the river system as a whole. Gradually both the Trent and the Tame settled down into a relatively stable multi-channel form, in contrast to the highly unstable multi-channel rivers they had been previously. Between the river channels numerous small vegetation-stabilised 'islands' were formed, where peat and wet soils developed. It was now only during the more extreme flood events that these 'islands' were submerged and became covered by a layer of gravel. Following such flood events, the channel system would redevelop, the river finding new courses for its multiple channels (*ibid*).

This was the basic pattern of the Trent and Tame down until recent centuries and it is critically important both for the effect it had on the pattern of land use, settlement and river exploitation down to modern times, and for the effect it has had on the pattern and interpretation of archaeological discoveries. Many of the places within the Where Rivers Meet area have names ending in 'holme' (eg Catholme, Fatholme, Borough Holme, Cherry Holme). The –*holme* suffix in Norse or Old English denotes an island of stable land within a river or marsh (Gelling 1984).

While extreme flood events are by definition rare, they are not uncommon when viewed in historical perspective, with no fewer than 46 floods known to have affected the Middle Trent recorded between 1255 and 1960 (Brown *et al* 2001). Floods can cause river 'avulsions', when the bank of a river channel is breached and a new river channel is formed. Major avulsions of the Trent, Tame and Mease are known to have taken place within the Where Rivers Meet area in the last 300 years.

We know from the maps in Robert Plot's *The Natural History of Staffordshire* (1686) that at the end of the 17th century the Trent was still predominantly multi-channelled, and north of the confluence with the Tame the main channel followed a course some 500m to the west of the current course of the river. This former channel can be clearly identified from the LiDAR survey (see Chapter 3) and from aerial photographs (Fig 4.3). In fact, the general trend through Holocene times has been for the river to migrate eastwards across the broad valley created by the Pleistocene (Ice Age) river. Thus the prehistoric monuments and settlements at Catholme and Fatholme, to be described in later chapters, were once much closer to the river. Indeed the Anglo-Saxon settlement at Catholme and the Bronze Age settlement underlying it (see Chapters 6 and 8) were right on the terrace edge, overlooking the river.

By 1884, the date of the first Ordnance Survey maps, the main channel of the Trent north of its confluence with the Tame had moved eastwards to adopt its current course, leaving the old course as a subsidiary channel. Furthermore, up until the 18th century the Mease had been a tributary of the Tame, joining it at Whitemoor Haye. By 1884 the Mease had shifted its course dramatically eastwards to its current confluence with the Trent (Fig 4.3). It is likely that these major 'avulsion events' of the Trent and the Mease were triggered by one or more of the major floods that took place during the 18th century, in 1754, 1770 and 1795, the last of these being the largest river flood ever recorded in Britain (Acreman 1989).

The hunters return again

In following changes to the river system during the Holocene we have moved well beyond the chronological scope of this chapter. However, doing so has enabled us to sketch the character of the river system as it emerged from the climatic upheavals of the Ice Age. As the climate ameliorated, and woodland and then forest began to develop, with woodland animals following from their refuges in the south, so hunters returned again in their train.

This archaeological period is known as the Mesolithic (Middle Stone Age), distinguishing it from the Palaeolithic (Old Stone Age) of the Ice Age and the Neolithic (New Stone Age) associated with the advent of agriculture. In Britain the period may be taken as lasting from the end of the Younger Dryas, *c* 11,500 years ago, until the advent of farming and the Neolithic *c* 6500 years ago, so it is no mere interlude.

Archaeologically, the period is most readily characterised by the use of small chipped stone artefacts known as 'microliths'; these were probably the components of a variety of tools, including hunting equipment. It was during the Mesolithic that Britain became, for the last time, an island. During the early part of the Mesolithic Britain still formed just the western part of a vast plain, Doggerland, joining what is now the British Isles to Scandinavia. However, as the ice sheets continued to melt and retreat so the sea level rose, with the Straits of Dover and the Irish Sea starting to open up around 9500 years ago. Also during the Mesolithic period the landscape developed from being relatively open, with birch and pine the principal trees, to being dominated by dense deciduous forest.

Like their predecessors, the Mesolithic hunters were highly mobile, and settlement remains such as the traces of huts or pits are only rarely found. Most usually, Mesolithic remains consist of scatters of flints, generally found during fieldwalking, which from the character and size of the stone tool assemblages may represent anything from 'home bases' to temporary hunting encampments or kill sites. Until recently there was comparatively little evidence of Mesolithic activity in the Trent valley but over the last couple of decades a number of systematic fieldwalking projects, mainly carried out in advance of development or quarrying, have demonstrated a significantly higher density of Mesolithic activity in the Trent valley than had previously been recognised (Knight and Howard 2004, 35).

A handful of probable Mesolithic flints (a flake, a blade and a blade core) have been found in the Where Rivers Meet area. They were found during fieldwalking on the Mercia Mudstone higher ground flanking the east side of the Trent valley near Walton-on-Trent, in the small part of the study area that lies in Derbyshire. An elevated location such as this would have been ideal for surveying the movement of game along the river valley. Although this provides just a trace of Mesolithic activity in the area, it needs to be seen in the context of the spread of finds along the Trent valley as a whole, which would have provided rich hunting grounds for the skilled Mesolithic hunter. These hunters probably operated over very large territories, moving between the southern Pennines (with cave sites such as those at Creswell Crags) and the Trent valley, in an annual round in pursuit of food and raw materials.

CHAPTER FIVE

A ceremonial landscape
(*c* 4500–1500 BC)

D
uring the Neolithic and earlier Bronze Age there existed at the confluence
of the Rivers Trent and Tame a 'ceremonial landscape' comparable, albeit
that the monuments are on a smaller scale, to those of Stonehenge or
Avebury. The investigation of this landscape undertaken by the Where Rivers
Meet project, through a combination of digital survey, geophysical survey,
palaeoenvironmental analysis and excavation (see Chapter 3), has revealed how
the construction and use of monuments was the prevailing theme throughout
this long period. Ultimately, the principal focus for monument construction
became a small area just to the north of the confluence, close to the present-day
Catholme Farm, which we have termed the 'Catholme Ceremonial Complex'.
Before describing and attempting to interpret these monuments, we provide
some background to place these developments in their broader context.

First, a brief note on dating terminology is needed. Up until now, when
discussing the Palaeolithic and Mesolithic periods, we have provided dates in
terms of events happening, approximately, 'X thousand years ago'. Sometimes
these dates are expressed as being 'X years Before Present', or simply 'BP'. This
is how geologists and other earth scientists measure time. Historians, however,
at least those working in the European tradition, express their dates relative to
the conventional date for the birth of Christ, as either BC (Before Christ) or AD
(Anno Domini). Thus a date of 10,000 BP is (as near as makes no difference) the
same as a date of 8000 BC. Archaeologists are caught in the middle. Generally
archaeologists working on the Palaeolithic period use BP dates and those working
on the Neolithic and more recent periods use BC/AD dates. For the Mesolithic
there is no firm convention (we chose BP), which can easily cause confusion, but
from this chapter onwards we switch over to BC/AD. Most of the dates given in
the next couple of chapters are based on calibrated (ie corrected) radiocarbon
determinations. Where specific radiocarbon determinations are mentioned, the
convention 'cal BC' is used.

A new way of life

The date of 4500 BC marks the approximate beginning of the Neolithic period
in Britain. 'Neolithic' is Greek for 'New Stone Age', and this term was coined
by archaeologists in the 19th century to describe a number of changes visible
in the archaeological record. One of these was the appearance of new kinds of
stone tools, notably polished stone axes. Another important change recognised
by archaeologists as characteristic of the Neolithic was the first appearance of

vessels made of fired clay – pottery. It soon became clear that the new types of stone tools and the earliest use of pottery were associated with a third novel phenomenon, the construction of monuments in earth, timber and stone. These monuments appeared to serve ceremonial and religious functions, and often involved human burials or at least rites involving human remains.

Underlying these various changes, a more fundamental transition was recognised: an economic transition from a way of life based on hunting and foraging to one based on farming. In a European context, the essential features of farming are the husbandry of domesticated animals (notably cattle, sheep, goats and pigs) and the cultivation of domesticated plants (notably cereals such as wheat and barley). As a result of breeding, domesticated animals and plants have been genetically modified from their wild progenitors for certain useful qualities such as docility and meatiness in animals or grain size in cereals (which are a type of grass).

In the 1930s the famous prehistorian Gordon Childe highlighted the global significance of the economic transition from a hunting and gathering mode of subsistence to a farming mode of subsistence by describing it as the 'Neolithic Revolution' (Childe 1936). The transition in mode of subsistence entailed a 'package' of other changes in economic and social organisation, in ideology and religion that together were even more revolutionary in their importance for human history than the Industrial Revolution of the 18th century. Fundamental amongst these was the change from the mobile way of life of the hunter-gatherer, who must be on the move with the seasons to where the wild animals and plants are to be found, to the sedentary way of life of the farmer, who must be based largely in one place to cultivate, protect and harvest the crops (the pastoralist may of course lead a more mobile way of life). Another fundamental trait of a farming economy is that it is generally much more efficient, in terms of the number of mouths that can be fed per unit of land, than a foraging economy. Thus a farming way of life allows, and perhaps even encourages, population growth to a level which, given the right circumstances, exceeds that of the hunter-gatherer by several orders of magnitude.

From these two fundamental traits – a sedentary way of life and population growth – many of the other traits of the so-called Neolithic Revolution more-or-less naturally follow. The use of pottery vessels, for example, is only really practical for sedentary communities. They are too heavy and fragile to be carried from place to place by mobile communities, who make use instead of basketry, bark or other lightweight containers (which will only very rarely survive in the archaeological record). The practical purpose of polished stone axes is to fell trees to make clearings for agriculture, although some evidently became symbolic items also. This is shown by examples made of exotic stone, sometimes transported hundreds of miles from their source, and too beautiful and fragile to be of practical purpose. It is also shown by their deliberate deposition at monuments and other places in what appear to be ritual acts.

More importantly, the farming way of life allows the accumulation of resources (herds of animals and stores of grain) beyond what is needed for day-to-day subsistence. In short, it enables some individuals and communities to become rich. Agricultural surpluses may be used to support specialist craftsmen, or to enable communities to release labour for the building of monuments such as temples and tombs. Surpluses may also create 'haves' and 'have-nots', circumstances encouraging the appearance of social stratification and the emergence of chiefs and leaders of various sorts, who may use their wealth to secure power and the allegiance of others. Surpluses also create circumstances which may encourage the development of trade and exchange. Furthermore, while one way to become rich in livestock and in good farming land is by the sweat of your own brow or that of your social inferiors, another is to take what you want by force or the threat of force. The accumulation of resources, including land, creates something worth fighting for and the circumstances for the development of endemic warfare.

Tied up with the economic and social changes consequent upon the transition from hunting and gathering to farming are changes in ideology and religious belief. While the cave paintings, figurines and burials of the Upper Palaeolithic cannot provide us with any kind of direct access to the ideology and religious beliefs underlying them, there are recurrent themes such as the apparent (and unsurprising) importance of wild animals that suggest what might be broadly defined as a 'shamanic' world view. This is supported by the prevalence of shamanic practices amongst hunter-gatherer communities of the present day and recent past. Typically the shaman is an individual who, through working himself into a trance state, enters into the dangerous world of the spirit animals and there undertakes healing, divination and other tasks. While shamans may have continued to play an important role in the beliefs of Neolithic communities, the appearance of monuments such as causewayed enclosures, cursus monuments, henges and elaborate burial mounds, described later in this chapter, points to new ideas more relevant to the farming way of life. These monuments appear to relate to the landscape, to the celestial bodies, and to the ancestors, and thus to aspects of existence of particular importance to the farmer. The importance of land and the landscape to the farmer needs no explanation. The movements of the sun, moon and stars govern the seasonal rhythms of agricultural life in all their precariousness, such as the hoped-for growth, ripening and harvest of the crop. The ancestors, perhaps a very real and powerful presence amongst the living, legitimise your possession of the land and may be called upon for help, although they are also a dangerous force, easily angered, and requiring respect and placation.

Throughout human history, one role of religious beliefs has been to legitimise the existing social order. Origin myths, for example, may be seen as making existing social arrangements appear natural and necessary, and of legitimising the asymmetries of power and wealth within communities. Ritual acts performed in special places not only help to ensure the continued success of the harvest and the fecundity of the herds, but also serve repeatedly to reconstruct and reconfirm social relations. However, new religious beliefs may also challenge the existing social order, by suggesting alternative realities. We can see this uneasy tension between legitimising and challenging the social order in the history of

Christianity. Although we can only glimpse the possible beliefs underlying the monuments of the Neolithic and early Bronze Age, we can perhaps recognise such tensions (and themes such as 'exclusion' and 'inclusion') as the history of the construction, modification and replacement of these monuments unfolds over the millennia.

The origins of the British Neolithic

Before turning to the extraordinary range of Neolithic monuments that has been uncovered in the Where Rivers Meet area, we need briefly to consider the concept of the Neolithic Revolution, sketched in the preceding section, with respect to Neolithic Britain. Although the concept is powerful and coherent, and appears to explain a great deal, in recent years its relevance to the Neolithic period in Britain has been called into question by archaeologists. A major reason for this is that in many parts of Britain, including the Where Rivers Meet area, some of the expectations of the concept are not met. In particular, what is lacking is evidence for the sort of settled farming communities, living in substantial villages or farmsteads, surrounded by organised field systems, that the concept would lead us to expect. In fact, in our area and many other parts of lowland Britain, such evidence is largely lacking for some 3000 years and does not appear until the later Bronze Age, to be described in the next chapter. This suggests that the Neolithic and earlier Bronze Age in Britain had a distinctive character. To explore some of the possible reasons why this might be so, we need to turn briefly to the origins of farming in Britain and Europe more generally.

It is beyond question that farming came to Europe from south-west Asia, the immediate source being Anatolia (modern Turkey). This is so not only because the domesticated plant and animal species involved have been dated earlier in south-west Asia than in Europe, but also because in many cases the natural distributions of the wild ancestors of these domesticates (notably sheep and goat, wheat and barley) were restricted to south-west Asia. The question that has much occupied archaeologists is the *process* by which farming was brought to Europe. Was it the farmers themselves that moved, colonising Europe and bringing their new way of life with them, or was it only the domesticated plants and animals that moved, farming being adopted by the indigenous peoples of Europe (the Mesolithic hunter-gatherers briefly described in the previous chapter)?

This debate is by no means settled (and is complicated because in recent years linguistic and genetic as well as archaeological evidence has been brought into the argument) but the likely answer is that both processes were involved. It is probable that the first farmers to appear in Europe, in Greece and the Balkans from *c* 7000 BC, were colonists from adjacent Anatolia. These colonists lived in villages built of mud-brick, which often occupied the same spot for many years, developing into artificial mounds or 'tells'. From the middle of the 6th millennium BC what appears to be a second colonisation movement spread from western Hungary across central Europe, following the fertile soils of major river valleys such as that of the Danube, arriving in the Rhineland and Paris

Basin by *c* 5200 BC. This whole colonisation movement may have only taken about 300 or 400 years, and is marked by a very distinctive cultural 'package'. Particularly characteristic are hamlets or villages of timber-built longhouses of fairly standardised construction. Archaeologists have suggested that this longhouse tradition may have provided an indirect inspiration for monuments such as long mortuary enclosures ('houses for the dead') found many centuries later in Britain.

A second possible route by which western Europe was colonised by Neolithic farmers is along the seaways of the Mediterranean, around the coasts of Italy, southern France and Spain, and ultimately up the Atlantic coast of Portugal. Beyond these two probable colonising movements, through central Europe and along the Mediterranean coast, many archaeologists see the appearance of agriculture in the rest of Europe as better explained as the gradual adoption of farming by indigenous communities. The regions where such indigenous adoption of farming is likely to have taken place include much of France and Iberia, northern Europe (south Scandinavia) and the whole of the British Isles, already by this time fully an island. We are dealing here, of course, with a huge variety of different environments, some more and some less suitable for farming, and each requiring the adoption and adaptation of different parts of the Neolithic 'package', and the rejection of others.

With this background, it is not surprising that the different indigenous peoples in different parts of Europe developed contrasting Neolithic traditions. There is not a 'European Neolithic' or even a 'British Neolithic' but a series of different local 'Neolithics', of which that of the Where Rivers Meet area and the wider Midlands landscape in which it sits provides one example. In stressing the individuality of the Neolithic in each area, we should not ignore the contacts between areas that drew them together and provide common themes (in monument types, for example) with local variations. Indeed, the earliest of the monument types that we will encounter, the causewayed enclosure, is often interpreted as a meeting place where people from different communities gathered, perhaps to feast, exchange goods and marriage partners, and engage in ceremonial and ritual – all acts which help to forge and cement the kinds of social relationships upon which human life is dependent. Before turning to a description of the range of Neolithic monuments uncovered in the Where Rivers Meet area, a brief account of the environmental background completes our introduction.

Reclaiming the wilderness: the environmental background

Between approximately 6000 BC and 2500 BC average temperatures in Britain were 1–2° warmer than they are today, and it was also drier, although with regional variations. At the outset, the vegetation across much of the country was dominated by dense, mixed, 'wild' woodland, with variations based upon such factors as geology, soil, elevation, slope and hydrology, and a general increase in wetland vegetation, such as alder, in the river floodplains from the Mesolithic onwards.

At the beginning of the Neolithic, *c* 4500–4000 BC, much of the lower reaches of the River Trent comprised multiple-channelled, well-vegetated wetlands. The palaeoenvironmental evidence for the region indicates that mixed, closed-canopy woodland – the 'wildwood' – including oak, elm, beech, lime, ash, hazel and alder, cloaked much of the landscape. It is likely that the area around Catholme was also dominated by such woodland, with the broad floodplain associated with the river confluence being populated by wetland trees and shrubs. Evidence from carbonised remains recovered from early Neolithic features at Whitemoor Haye, within the southern half of the study area, indicates the presence of oak/pine woodland during this period (Coates 2002).

As we saw in the previous chapter, this wildwood landscape was, at the beginning of the Neolithic period, occupied by apparently sparsely distributed and probably highly mobile hunter-gatherer communities. In the simple model we outlined at the beginning of this chapter, the adoption of agriculture by communities such as these should have led to fairly rapid woodland clearance and the establishment of settled farming communities. In our region, however, and indeed in many other regions, this does not seem to be what happened. Although the environmental evidence for the west Midlands is not as comprehensive as we would like (Greig 2007), the dominant theme throughout the earlier Neolithic, up to at least 2500 BC, is of the persistence of woodland. Evidence for the creation of clearings in this wildwood is modest and that for the cultivation of cereals slight. It is against this background that we must set the appearance of the earliest Neolithic monuments in the Where Rivers Meet area. Today the buried remains of these monuments appear in an open landscape, with a pattern of fields stretching off in all directions as far as the eye can see. This was not, however, the situation when the monuments were built. Then, the monuments lay within woodland clearings, and the wildwood would have dominated the landscape, broken by the courses of the major rivers, providing the major routes of communication. Reclaiming this wilderness was, as we shall see, a long, slow process spread over thousands of years.

Causewayed enclosures: the earlier Neolithic landscape (c 4000–3400 BC)

Monument construction in the Where Rivers Meet area began in the earlier Neolithic period. Within this landscape, the earlier Neolithic is characterised by a number of causewayed enclosures (also known as interrupted ditch enclosures), monuments that have been dated to the earlier 4th millennium BC, perhaps continuing up to 3400 BC. These monuments typically consist of multiple circuits of interrupted ditches surrounding an area of land that is normally quite large compared with funerary sites, perhaps 200m across. The function of causewayed enclosures is difficult to determine and there have been numerous interpretations. Settlement has been suggested for a number of sites, although it has been noted from the causewayed enclosure on Windmill Hill in Wiltshire, for example, that the excavated domestic material actually predates the construction of the enclosure and therefore appears to relate to an earlier phase of activity. A second suggested function has been defence, and evidence of palisades inside the causewayed rings at sites such as Hambledon Hill in Dorset is seen as support for this theory, although it may be that they were intended to keep out wild animals rather than people. Furthermore, the fact that the ditches are interrupted by frequent causeways generally contradicts a defensive purpose. Other suggested functions have included cattle compounds, trading centres, communal meeting places, ritual centres, burial sites, and places of excarnation (where corpses are left exposed to natural decay). Whilst we cannot be certain that all causewayed enclosures shared the same function or functions, it seems most likely that they were generally focused on what may be termed 'non-domestic' activities, acting as meeting places or ceremonial locales. In this respect they may be compared with medieval churches, which were the focus of both secular and ceremonial activities.

Figure 5.1 The location of the Alrewas and Mavesyn Ridware causewayed enclosures just outside the study area

Within the region of the Trent/Tame confluence, the two best examples of causewayed enclosures are located just beyond the western boundary of the study area (Fig 5.1). The nearest lies just west of Alrewas. The Alrewas

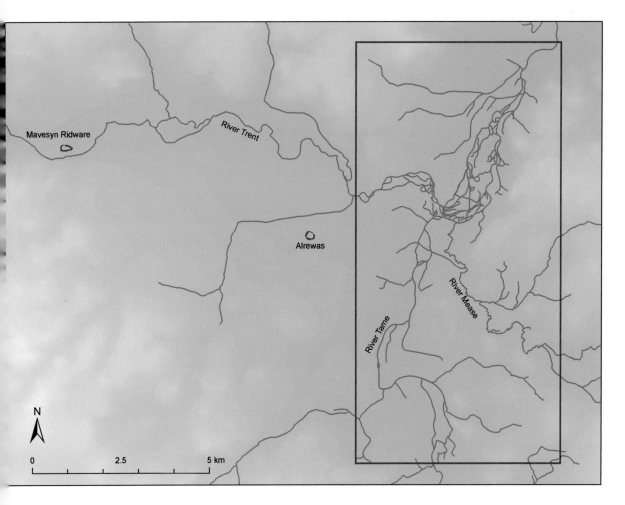

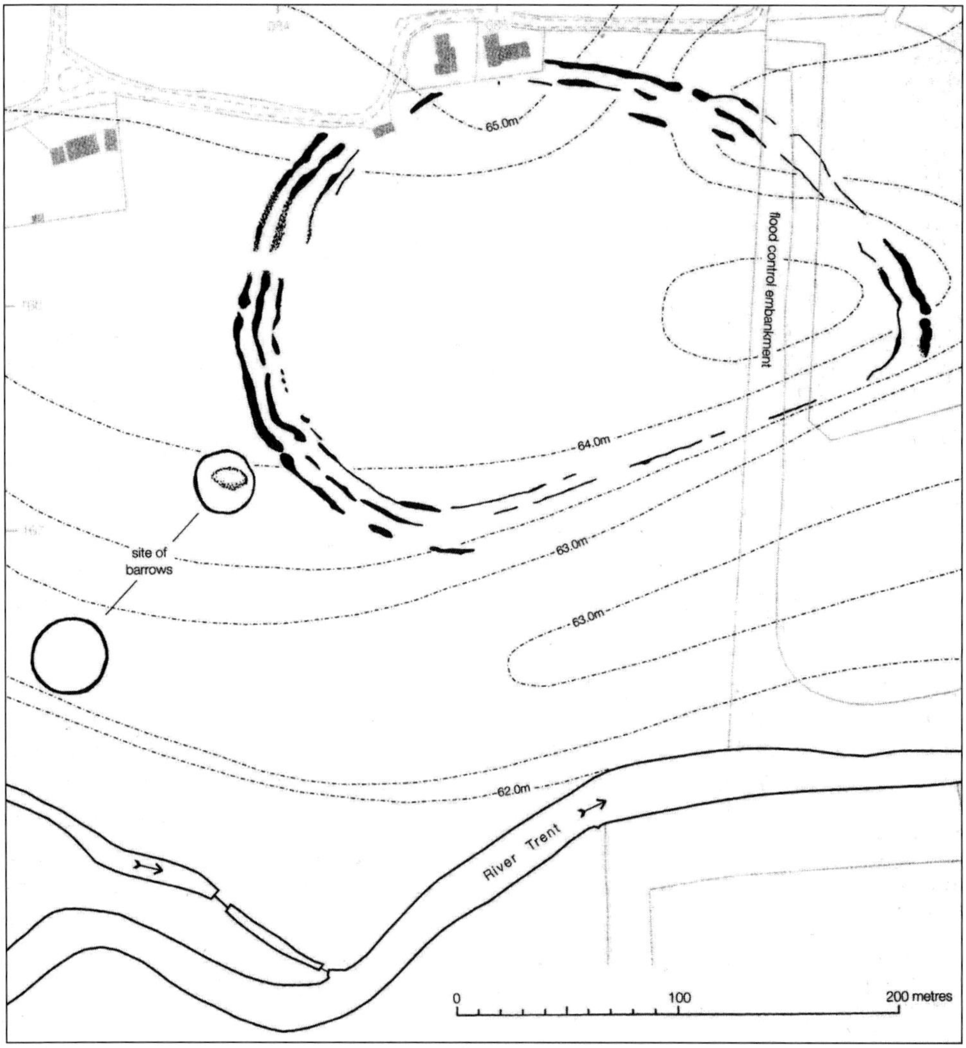

Figure 5.2 The Mavesyn Ridware causewayed enclosure (from Oswald *et al* 2001)

enclosure (Palmer 1976; Hodder 1982) consists of three close-set circuits of causewayed ditch, covering a total area of 250m by 210m. The second enclosure lies approximately 6km further to the west at Mavesyn Ridware (Oswald *et al* 2001; Fig 5.2), again represented by three concentric rings of interrupted ditch enclosing an area similar in size to the example at Alrewas. Neither of these sites has been excavated so their dating to the earlier Neolithic is based upon morphological similarities with sites elsewhere.

The causewayed enclosures at Alrewas and Mavesyn Ridware, with their close morphological similarities to better-known, excavated examples in southern Britain beyond the west Midlands, are perhaps best seen as meeting places and ceremonial centres to which people came from afar, and where large gatherings involving such activities as exchange and communal feasting took place. Already by the early Neolithic, they are marking out the special importance of this natural meeting place, at the hub of the natural routeways provided by the major river valleys. This point is emphasised by the fact that nowhere else in the west Midlands have comparable large causewayed enclosures been definitely located. Indeed, until a few years ago, they were considered to be the most northerly expression of the tradition, although recently sites have been found as far north as Scotland (Oswald *et al* 2001).

New linear monument types (c 3500–2900 BC)

From the middle part of the Neolithic, from around 3500 BC, new classes of monument were being constructed in Britain. The emphasis shifted from the circular monuments of the earlier Neolithic, which perhaps reflected natural clearances in the woodland, towards linear structures, called cursus monuments, which necessitated making considerable changes to the local environment.

The cursus tradition appears to have evolved from earlier types of linear monuments, such as long mortuary enclosures and bank barrows. In turn, as we mentioned earlier in this chapter, the ultimate inspiration for these monuments may have been a ritual transformation, from houses for the living to houses for the dead, of the longhouse architectural tradition of the first farmers to have colonised north-western Europe.

Cursus monuments are normally long enclosures defined by ditches (and sometimes pits), with either squared or rounded terminals. A recent definition of these structures is 'parallel-sided sites closed by at least one terminal and defined by ditches or pits/posts' (Loveday 2006, 25). These sites can be constructed on a wide variety of scales, from perhaps 100m in length up to 10km, as in the case of the massive Dorset Cursus. In terms of width, whilst there are possible examples as narrow as 25m, the majority of sites are in excess of 40m wide. Recent dating evidence has indicated that these structures were constructed during the second half of the 4th millennium BC, between perhaps 3640–3380 BC and 3260–2920 BC, suggesting that they were constructed over a period of *c* 200 to 650 years (Barclay and Bayliss 1999). This places them within the middle period of the Neolithic, or at the transition between the earlier and later Neolithic, and there remains some debate over whether they overlap chronologically with the earlier causewayed enclosures. Cursus monuments are commonly laid out in relation to rivers, either running parallel to them, or crossing them, or both, as in the case of Rudston, East Yorkshire (Chapman 2005).

In the 18th century, the pioneering antiquary William Stukeley interpreted cursus monuments as ancient race tracks, hence the name. Today they are generally interpreted as serving a ceremonial function, particularly types of activity that involved procession along these long structures. The cursus enclosures are normally considered as marking out a sacred area or *temenos*, often defining alignments within the landscape.

Within the Where Rivers Meet area there are three or four possible cursus monuments, each defined from aerial photography and each preserved in only a fragmentary way (Palmer 1976; Hodder 1982; Jones 1992; Fig 5.3). In addition to these monuments, the ditches of a possible 'bank barrow' have been very tentatively identified to the south of Catholme (Evans 2006). This structure consists of two ditches extending for at least 80m, positioned about 5m apart at the western end of the structure but widening to about 14m apart at its eastern end. Geophysical survey (Watters 2003) and excavation (Bain *et al* 2004) of the western end of this feature revealed how it had been truncated by a large ring-ditch following considerable silting, indicating that it was earlier in date than the ring-ditch, which we interpret as possibly defining a 'hengiform' monument (see below). Tentative morphological parallels for this putative bank barrow include West Cotton in the Nene valley (Windell 1989) and Milfield in Northumberland (Harding 1981), where similar features are located within clusters of other, later monuments, as at Catholme (Evans 2006).

The first of the possible cursus monuments in the study area (Cursus 1; Fig 5.3) is recorded in the Staffordshire Sites and Monuments Record (SMR 208, SAM ST222) and lies on a small raised area on the western side of the River Trent, to the north-west of Walton Bridge. This fragment survives as a cropmark less than 30m long forming the southern terminus of a monument that is only approximately 12m wide. An aerial photographic assessment in 1995 failed to identify this possible cursus, and it was concluded that the remains may in fact be no more than relict field boundaries (Deegan and Cox 1995).

The second possible cursus monument (Cursus 2; SMR 204, SAM ST216) is located in the vicinity of Catholme Bridge, on the

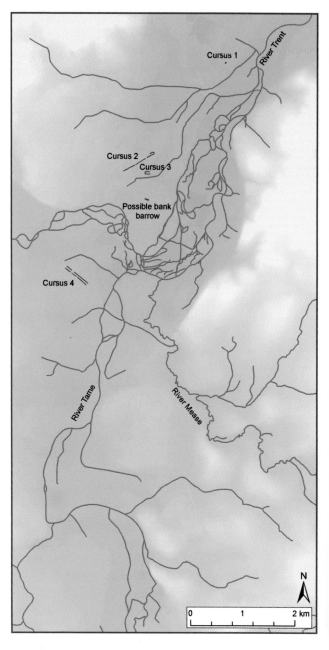

Figure 5.3 Linear monuments and cursus monuments within the study area

northern edge of the ceremonial complex (see below). Only the north-north-eastern section of the structure survives as it is cut obliquely by a road and has not been clearly recorded to the west of the road. The surviving section is 90m long, aligned north-north-east by south-south-west, similar to the first possible cursus described above. However, a possible extension of the southern ditch of this cursus is visible to the west, which would extend the full length of this feature to at least 670m. The ditches are about 35m apart, with the terminus forming a U-shape in plan, in contrast to the rectangular shape of the first example.

A third possible cursus in the Where Rivers Meet area (Cursus 3), perhaps the most convincing of the group, lies within the cluster of monuments that has been termed the 'Catholme Ceremonial Complex' (see below; Fig 5.4), and it is likely that this structure was in some way related to the other monuments forming the complex. The Catholme cursus (as we may term this example for convenience) is aligned east–west, with only the western terminus surviving as a cropmark nearly 100m long. The ditches are positioned about 45m apart and the terminus is rectangular in form. The position of the eastern end of this cursus is not known as it is cut by a road, beyond which is a small field that may have been less likely to yield cropmarks. However, as no cropmarks have been observed within a larger field yet further to the east, it is possible that the cursus was never more than about 150m long. In relation to cursus monuments identified elsewhere, this would make the Catholme cursus a very small example, the closest parallel probably being the example from Barford in Warwickshire, which measured just 185 by 40m (Loveday 2006). Indeed, the cursus monuments tentatively identified within the Where Rivers Meet area appear to belong to a distinct regional class of monument that has been referred to as the 'squat' cursus (Loveday and Petchey 1982).

The fourth possible cursus (Cursus 4) has been identified by aerial photography in the vicinity of Alrewas Quarry on the western edge of the National Memorial Arboretum (SAM ST220b). This feature was investigated by geophysical survey and excavation (Coates 2000). Fifteen trenches were excavated across this and other features in the vicinity but no evidence of earlier Neolithic activity was recovered. Neither the geophysical survey nor the excavation managed to reveal evidence of the possible cursus structure or other archaeological features. Given the aerial photographic evidence, it is possible that this structure has been ploughed away in recent years.

Beyond the immediate Where Rivers Meet area, another possible cursus has been identified as a cropmark some 8km further up the Trent at Hill Ridware (Barber 2007, 88). This possible cursus has a minimum length of 100m (neither end is clearly defined) and lies only about 800m north of the Mavesyn Ridware causewayed enclosure. Further afield in the Trent valley, two further cursus monuments, both large examples (each over 1.5km in length), have been investigated to the west of the confluence of the Rivers Trent and Derwent at Aston (Gibson and Loveday 1989) and Potlock (Guilbert 1996). The concentration of cursus monuments within the Middle Trent valley, together with the causewayed enclosures described in the previous section, emphasises the significance of this region during the earlier Neolithic period. As in other regions of Britain, the concentration and layout of the cursus monuments appear to be closely related to the courses of the rivers (Whimster 1989; Loveday 2006). As we will see in later chapters, the rivers themselves are likely to have had more than just practical significance to those who lived alongside them, travelled along them and exploited their diverse resources. It seems probable that whatever the ceremonial purpose of the processions which, we presume, took place along cursus monuments, water – the giver of life – played some role in the rituals performed.

Late Neolithic monuments of the Catholme Ceremonial Complex (c 3000–1500 BC)

New types of monument begin to appear in the later Neolithic, in the centuries following 3000 BC. Both in the study area and more widely in the region, these monuments are much more numerous than those of earlier periods, the causewayed enclosures and cursus monuments. One has the strong impression, at least, that this increase in monument numbers should reflect a real growth in population levels, associated with further woodland clearance and the opening up of the landscape. This may have allowed clearer sight-lines to and from monuments, and between them, influencing the way they related to the landscape and to each other. If any general themes can be detected in the diversity of new monument types, they are those of circular architecture and an association with human remains. By inference from monuments of the same period, by far the most famous of which is Stonehenge, we may also envisage that new religious significance and emphasis was given to the celestial bodies and their movements across the sky.

It is in this period, around 2500 BC, that what we have termed the 'Catholme Ceremonial Complex' takes shape (Fig 5.4). The two principal monuments of the complex comprise what we have described (perhaps somewhat fancifully) as the 'sunburst' monument and the 'woodhenge' monument. Both these monuments are situated close by the Catholme cursus, which would probably have been centuries old by the time the new monuments were built. This cluster of monuments became the apparent focus for what is the densest large-scale cluster of prehistoric burial mounds in the west Midlands, spreading for miles from the Trent/Tame confluence southwards up the Tame, north-westwards up the Trent and north-eastwards down the Trent. Before we describe these monuments in some detail – both the 'sunburst' and 'woodhenge' monuments and a fair number of the burial mounds have been subjected to excavation – we need to provide an outline sketch of some of the relevant developments that were taking place more widely in Britain at the time.

Stonehenge itself provides a familiar starting point but only the barest outline of its very complex development, spanning some 1000 years, can be provided here. It began, at around 2950 BC, as a circular ditch, with a low bank along its outer edge, about 110m in diameter, enclosing a ring of 56 substantial timber posts, each set within a pit. Cremated and excarnated human remains have also been found in some of these pits. The principal entrance across the ditch lay in the north-east, although there were other entrances to the south. In a second phase of development, a complex timber structure was erected just south of the centre of the enclosure, although later disturbance has rendered the surviving plan very incomplete. This timber structure appears to have comprised up to six concentric rings of timber posts, with an entrance feature to the south. It was only in its third phase, beginning around 2500 BC, that Stonehenge became a stone circle, comprising some 82 'bluestones' followed by 84 much larger grey 'sarcen' blocks, erected in a circle and horseshoe arrangement, and famously inscribing a solar orientation on the midsummer sunrise (and midwinter sunset).

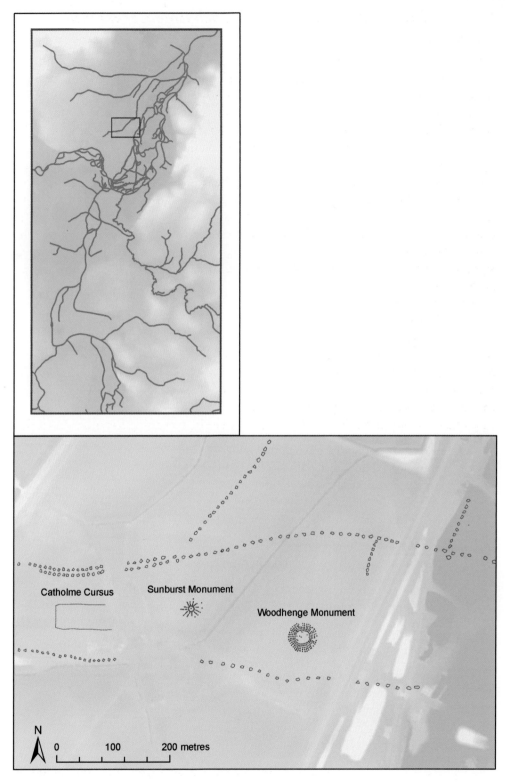

Figure 5.4
The Catholme
Ceremonial
Complex

Catholme Cursus

Sunburst Monument

Woodhenge Monument

N

0   100   200 metres

Subsequently, Stonehenge became the focus for numerous cemeteries of burials mounds (barrows) scattered across the surrounding landscape.

In the complex development of Stonehenge, many of the themes of later Neolithic monument construction can be discerned. Taking their name from Stonehenge, monuments comprising a roughly circular ditch and (usually) external bank, with one or more entrances, have been termed 'henges'. They are found throughout the British Isles and, like Stonehenge, some henges enclose stone circles. The survival of these stone circles (although many others have no doubt been destroyed) gives to these sites a contemporary importance that may not reflect their importance in the past. Elsewhere, stone circles are found in the absence of a surrounding ditch and bank – ie in the absence of a 'henge' – while henges are found without stone circles. The timber circle found within Stonehenge early in its constructional sequence, and the timber structure within its centre comprising multiple rings of timber posts, are also themes found elsewhere. Timber circles and circular structures may occur in a wide variety of sizes and constructional patterns (single or multiple rings, etc), with or without a surrounding ditch. Overall, it is the diversity of such monuments that should impress us. The range in size is enormous, from giants such as the henge at Avebury, Wiltshire, with its internal stone circles and associated processional avenues, to tiny monuments such as the remarkably preserved timber circle at Holme-next-the-Sea, Norfolk, dubbed 'Seahenge'. It would be absurd to infer unity of function for such widely diverse monuments, the largest monuments capable of forming the focus for huge gatherings, the smaller ones suggestive of use by just a single family. Such monuments defy easy classification – at best they are variations on some very broad themes – and many, especially the smaller examples, are often labelled with the unsatisfactory and virtually indefinable term, 'hengiform'. For want of a better alternative, it is to this category that the monuments recently explored at Catholme are best assigned. A detailed account of these investigations is provided in an academic report (Chapman *et al* forthcoming) so that only a summary need be provided here.

The 'sunburst' monument (pre-2500–2000 BC)

About 120m east of the cropmarks of the Catholme cursus is a cluster of features defined by cropmarks and referred to as the 'sunburst' monument (Scheduled Ancient Monument 21679–02; Fig 5.4). The cropmarks representing this monument consist of a ring-ditch, approximately 13m in diameter internally, comprising a ditch approximately 2m wide enclosing a central pit. Radiating outwards from the ring-ditch are twelve rows of pits or post-pits, each consisting of between three and five pits, covering an area approximately 40m across (Fig 5.5). The overall plan of the monument, a circle with lines of pits radiating out from it, suggested the name sunburst monument, but this is just descriptive and does not carry with it the implication that the layout of the monument was intended to represent the sun.

A trench measuring 20m by 10m was excavated over the central area of the

Figure 5.5 The
sunburst monument
and pit-alignments
at Catholme

sunburst monument by members of the Where Rivers Meet team in 2004 (Fig 5.6). The excavation encompassed the complete ring-ditch and internal features, in addition to at least one of the pits from the series of radiating alignments. This area was also intensively surveyed using a range of geophysical methods, and formed part of the geophysical 'ground truthing' exercise described earlier (see Chapters 1 and 3).

Sections excavated across the ring-ditch revealed that it had been recut at least once. The earlier ring-ditch was broadly continuous except for a distinct, though narrow, break in its western side. The recut of this ring-ditch, however, was evidently formed by the digging of a series of elongated pits. The fills of the ditch indicated that, following a period of natural silting up, material had slumped into the ditch from both sides, suggesting the partial collapse of both an internal and external bank. Profiles extracted from modelling of the ground-penetrating radar (GPR) geophysical data strongly indicated slumping on the outer section of the ditch, also suggesting that an external bank was present. A number of pieces of worked flint were recovered from different phases of the ditch construction, including two scrapers, a core and fifteen flakes. The dating of these pieces was inconclusive, although one of the scrapers may indicate a Beaker date (see below). Two small pits were cut into one of the terminals of

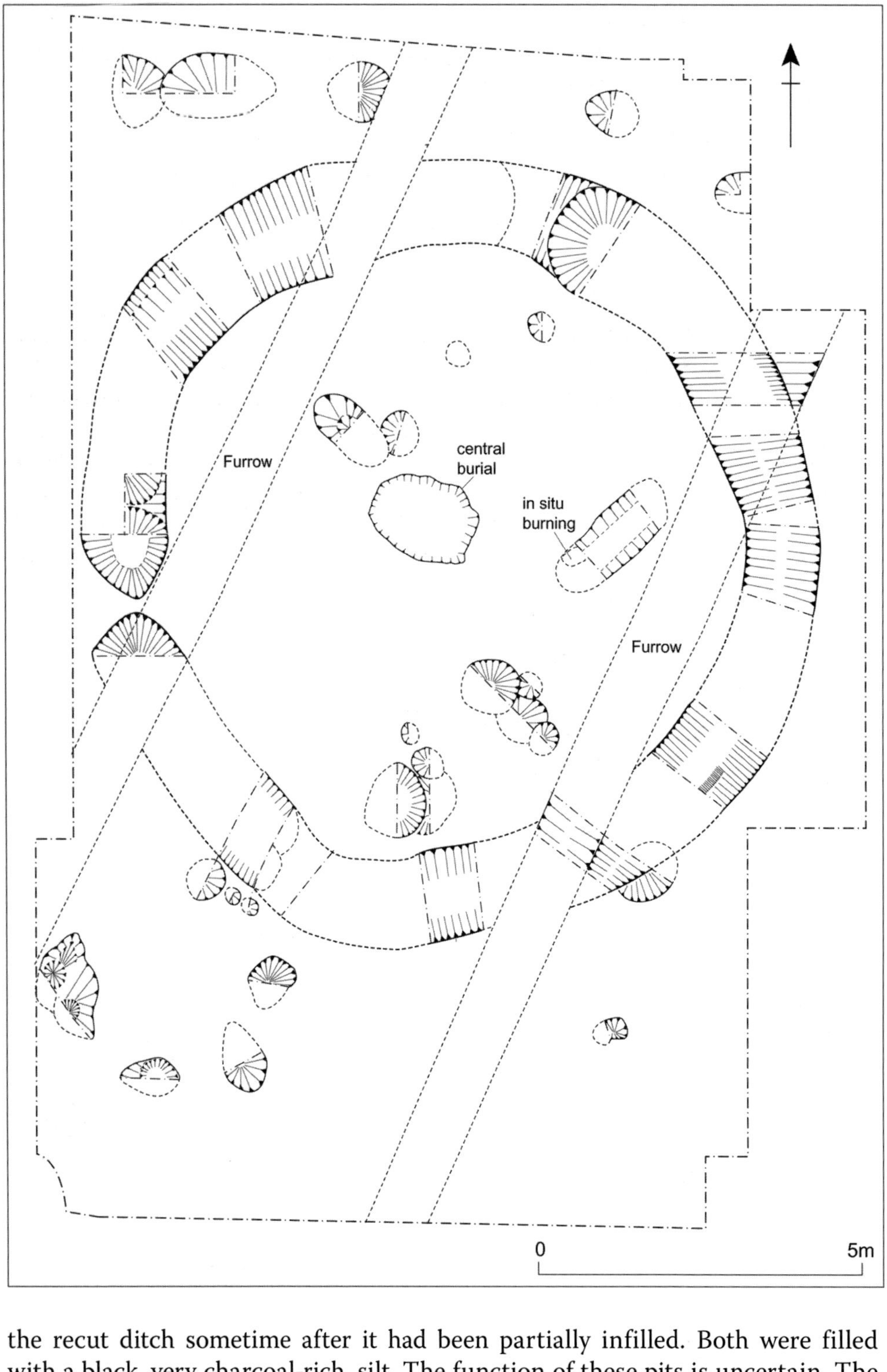

Figure 5.6 Plan of the excavated area of the sunburst monument

Furrow

central burial

in situ burning

Furrow

0   5m

the recut ditch sometime after it had been partially infilled. Both were filled with a black, very charcoal-rich, silt. The function of these pits is uncertain. The quantity of charcoal suggests they might have contained cremations, although burnt bone was absent.

Four samples of charcoal, two from the first phase of the ditch and two from its principal recutting, were dated using radiocarbon. The results, with the lab reference numbers, are given in the table below.

Primary fill	SUERC–11072	2580–2450 cal BC
Primary fill	OxA–16052	2620–2460 cal BC
Recut fill	SUERC–11071	2630–2460 cal BC
Recut fill	OxA–16051	2580–2460 cal BC

The samples were statistically consistent and suggested that the original cutting of the ditch and its recutting date to around 2500 BC. The modelling of the GPR data from the survey of the sunburst monument identified the shape of the elongated pits forming the recut ring-ditch. In addition to defining the construction of the ditch, the survey also indicated a number of pits beneath it (Fig 5.7). These pits may represent an earlier phase in the construction of the monument, and it is possible that the ditch was formed by joining these together. The arrangement of these modelled pit features broadly aligns with the radiating lines of pits or

Figure 5.7 Modelling of the GPR data revealed one segmented structure of the ring-ditch and possible pits beneath it

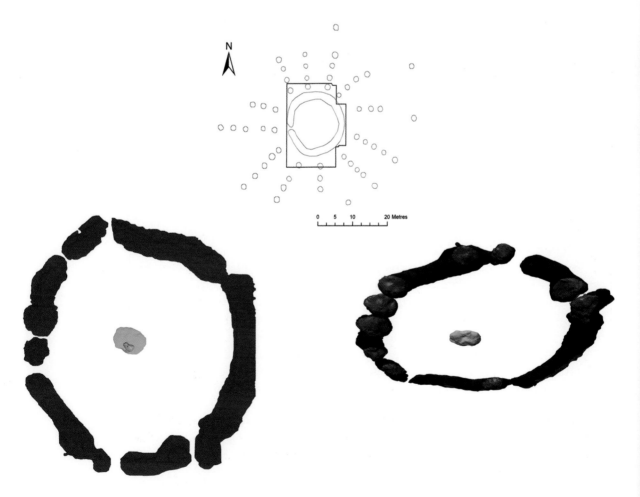

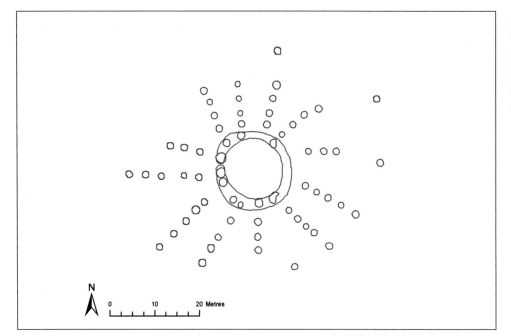

Figure 5.8 Plan showing how the pits within the ring-ditch of the sunburst monument align with the radiating rows of pits

post-pits that extend out from the ring-ditch (Fig 5.8) and it is therefore possible that the radiating pits were constructed at some time before *c* 2500 BC, being incorporated into the later monument. The excavation of at least one of these features directly adjacent to the ring-ditch revealed a flat-bottomed pit 1.3m in diameter and 0.6m deep. There was no evidence for a post within this pit, and there is no indication from the GPR modelling to suggest that the radiating pits ever contained posts.

Several features were found within the interior of the ring-ditch. The most clearly visible of these was a centrally positioned oval-shaped pit, orientated east–west and measuring 2.4m by 1.8m. This feature was also identified by aerial photography and geophysical survey. Despite the absence of surviving bone (due to the soil conditions), the shape of the pit, the colour and composition of the fill material, and the finds from the pit all suggested that it once contained a human inhumation. The shape in plan of the deposit suggested that the head was near to the eastern side of the pit and that the body would have been placed in a crouched position with the knees drawn up towards the abdomen. Thirty sherds of pottery, all apparently belonging to a single vessel (but which was not complete), were found in the pit, concentrated near the inferred position of the head. A discoidal scraper and seven flint flakes were also recovered from the pit.

The pottery sherds were from a type of vessel known as a Beaker, usually interpreted as a drinking vessel and ornamented with incised motifs in bands or zones, including filled triangles and chequers. Beakers often accompany crouched inhumation burials (see below), so this greatly strengthens the interpretation of the central pit as a burial. The specific style of the Beaker (the Northern/North Rhine group defined by Clarke 1970), suggests a date of around 2000 BC or later.

Additional pits and postholes were excavated within the interior of the ring-ditch, including a large rectilinear feature measuring 3.1m by 1.5m and 0.5m deep, which contained evidence for *in situ* burning. None of these features revealed any dating material. However, two pieces of unstratified pottery from the area of the sunburst monument were dated to the late Neolithic/early Bronze Age.

From the evidence assembled during the 2004 investigations, it appears that the sunburst monument comprises several phases of activity. The first phase appears to be represented by the construction of the radiating pits, which seem not to have contained posts, although further excavation would be required to confirm this. The inner circle of these pits then appears to have formed the basis for the construction of a ring-ditch with an external bank (and possibly an internal bank) around 2500 BC. Morphologically, this feature may be compared with hengiform structures which are found throughout Britain and which represent the final phase of Neolithic monumentality. This feature underwent at least one phase of recutting before finally forming the focus for a Beaker inhumation burial at around or shortly after 2000 BC.

The 'woodhenge' monument (*c* 2500 BC)

Some 160m east-south-east of the sunburst monument is a second circular monument identified originally from aerial photography (Whimster 1989; Fig 5.9). This structure consists of 39 radiating lines of post-pits forming five concentric rings, each ring separated by approximately 2.5m (SAM 21679–01; Fig 5.10). The structure is termed a 'woodhenge' or 'woodhenge-type' monument due to the similarity of its timber structure to that found at Woodhenge near Durrington Walls on Salisbury Plain (although the Catholme monument lacks the circular bank and ditch which surrounded the timber structure at Woodhenge). The total size of the monument is 51.5m by 50m externally, thus slightly oval in shape, enclosing a central area of approximately 24m by 23m. An area of the north-western section of the structure, measuring 20m by 10m, was investigated intensively using a combination of geophysical survey and excavation.

A sample of the post-pits was excavated in each of the five rings: seven in the innermost ring and four or five in each of the others. Each of the post-pits had near-vertical sides, was about 1m in diameter, and survived to a depth of between *c* 0.7m and 1.2m (there was no obvious pattern to the difference in depth of the pits, for example between rings). As a consequence of the arrangement of the posts in 39 radiating rows making up five concentric rings, the spacing between the post-pits in each of the rings naturally increased from the innermost ring (between 0.75m and 1.5m apart) to the outermost ring (between 1.5m and 3.0m).

In three instances excavation revealed evidence of former posts set within the post-pits. This comprised dark staining and charcoal flecks, indicating that the timber posts were typically about 0.6m in diameter. A particularly clear example was found in a post-pit of the fourth ring from the centre. This contained the

charred remains of a post 0.6m in diameter, its base packed around with stones; this was unique amongst the excavated sample. Evidently this post had burnt *in situ.*

A series of five radiocarbon determinations was obtained from five charcoal samples extracted from five of the post-pits. The results are summarised in the table below.

Figure 5.9 The 'woodhenge' monument. The sunburst monument and Catholme Farm are visible in the background

Ring 1 (innermost)	OxA–16050	2870–2500 cal BC
Ring 3	OxA–16049	2620–2470 cal BC
Ring 4	OxA–16048	2860–2500 cal BC
Ring 4	SUERC–11070	2580–2410 cal BC
Ring 5 (outermost)	SUERC–11069	2880–2500 cal BC
Estimated construction date 68% probability		2550–2480 cal BC
Estimated construction date 95% probability		2570–2470 cal BC

Statistical analysis of the radiocarbon dates was undertaken to assess whether or not the site represented a single phase of activity. The results from this showed

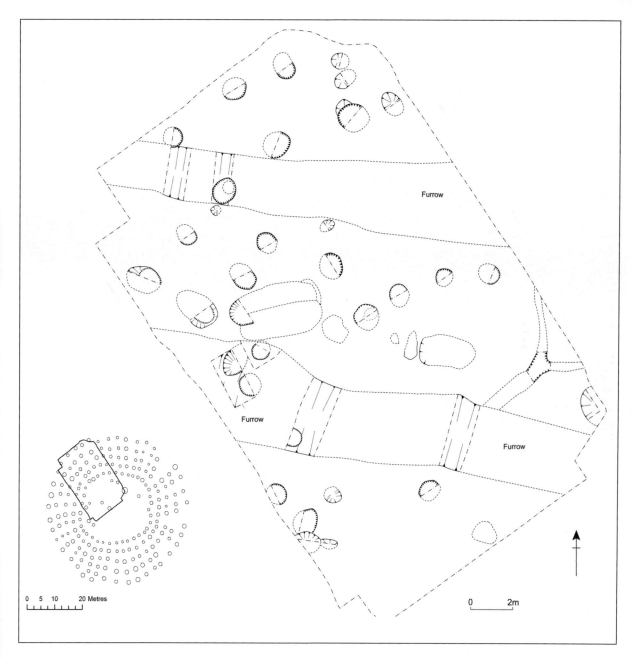

Figure 5.10
Excavation plan of
the 'woodhenge'
monument

that, whilst the date from the outer ring was not fully consistent with the other dates, the remaining four measurements indicated that these rings might have been constructed at the same time. The monument thus seems to have been of a single phase of construction and was built, like the sunburst monument nearby, around 2500 BC. The dating of the woodhenge structure suggests broad contemporaneity with well-known sites elsewhere, including the first phase of the construction of Silbury Hill and the initial stone settings at Stonehenge (Cleal *et al* 1995).

Analysis of the charred remains of the posts indicates that oak was chosen for construction, and the presence of heartwood suggests that this oak was structural, corroborating the archaeological interpretation of post-pits. Where it was possible to assess this, it also appears that the wood chosen for construction came from slow-grown trees.

Within the central area of the woodhenge structure two shallow, irregular pits were recorded but it is possible that these were natural features. No artefactual evidence was recovered from these features, from the excavated post-pits, or indeed from the investigation of the monument as a whole. Nevertheless, we know the probable date of the construction of the woodhenge monument with unusual precision and we have considerable evidence to help us reconstruct what it might have looked like. The depth of the post-pits and the diameter of the posts inferred from excavation suggests that the oak posts were substantial, and, with its 195 posts arranged in five concentric circles (39 × 5), it must have been an imposing monument, involving no small effort to construct. It must be remembered that each oak tree used in its construction had to be laboriously felled and shaped using only stone axes, and then had to be dragged to the site and erected. The post-pits were dug using the shoulder bones of cattle as shovels and deer antlers as picks (to judge from tools of this period found at other monuments, see for example Wainwright 1968). The initial laying out of the site betrays impressive skill in practical surveying, probably to some arcane ritual formula. The erection of each post – presumably using little more than muscle power, wooden levers and ropes woven of vegetable material or animal hide/sinew – demonstrates similar skill in practical engineering.

The end result must have resembled a small, but highly stylised and ordered, artificial forest. Perhaps to some extent it symbolised the forest tamed and controlled, its mysterious forces harnessed to human ends. From a distance one would see just a mass of huge posts but approaching more closely, regularities, sight-lines and highly contrived pathways would have opened up, controlling human movement and the experience of whatever rites were performed there. All focused on the central area, just a little more than 20m across – presumably a place of great mystery and power, an artificial clearing in an artificial forest.

Further possible 'hengiform' monuments

We define the principal monuments of the Catholme Ceremonial Complex as comprising the cursus, the sunburst monument and the woodhenge monument. Part of the reason for treating these as a distinct group is their close proximity to each other, and the similarity in date between the sunburst and woodhenge monuments. Another reason is that two pit-alignments, one to the north and the other to the south of the three monuments, appear to mark out this area and highlight its significance (see Fig 5.4). While it is unlikely that these pit-alignments are of Neolithic or early Bronze Age dates, because morphologically very similar pit-alignments investigated elsewhere in the Where Rivers Meet area have produced evidence of an Iron Age date (see Chapter 6), we believe nevertheless that these pit-alignments may well preserve boundaries that are earlier in origin.

A number of other possible 'hengiform' monuments have been identified within the study area (Fig 5.11). Located approximately 400m to the south of the ceremonial complex as we have just defined it, aerial photography has revealed a circular enclosure near Wychnor Bridges, some 60m in diameter and defined by a single ditch. The large size of this circular enclosure marks it out as something different from the general run of ring-ditches (ploughed-out burial mounds) to be described in the next section of this chapter. These are typically much smaller, ranging from *c* 10m to 30m in diameter.

Geophysical survey carried out as part of the Where Rivers Meet project revealed the enclosure ditch with good definition (notably the resistance data), and suggested the possibility of internal features of considerable complexity (Watters 2003). Subsequently, excavations were carried out over a short length of the ditch and an area within the interior of the monument (Bain *et al* 2004). In the excavated area the ditch survived to a width of *c* 2.2m and a depth of 0.8m, with a gentle U-shaped profile. This excavation was also positioned to investigate two linear ditches which appeared, from the aerial photography and geophysical survey data, to form a 'funnel entrance' into the enclosure. These linear ditches were found to be earlier than the enclosure ditch, which cut across them, and

Figure 5.11
Distribution
of hengiform
monuments in the
study area

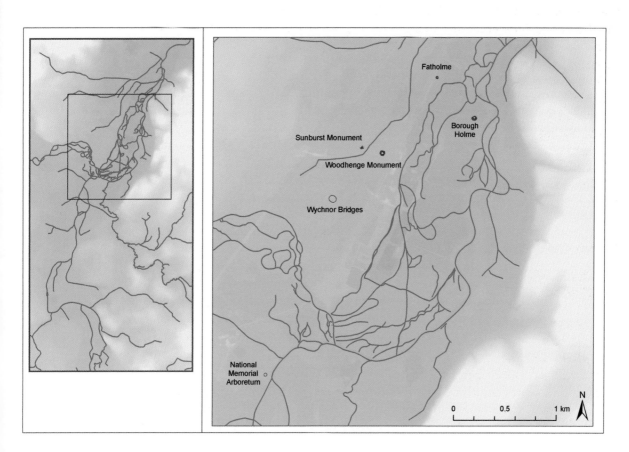

we mentioned earlier the tentative suggestion that they might relate to a 'bank barrow' dating perhaps to the earlier Neolithic (Evans 2006).

The excavation of an area measuring 20m by 10m within the enclosure revealed only a number of shallow, irregular features which did not appear to be of archaeological significance and may have been caused by tree roots or later agricultural activity. Indeed, all the archaeological remains in this field appeared to have suffered particularly badly from ploughing, and plough furrows obscured many of the features. The enclosure ditch, therefore, may have been very severely truncated and probably survived to only a fraction of its original depth. No artefacts or material suitable for radiocarbon dating were recovered from the excavation of the enclosure.

Despite the rather disappointing results of excavation, several lines of evidence suggest that the enclosure is most likely to be of Neolithic or early Bronze Age date. Perhaps of most significance are the two much smaller ring-ditches that are located in close proximity to the enclosure (about 40m distant in one case, 80m in the other) and appear to be sited with respect to it. Although neither of these ring-ditches has been tested by excavation, they measure about 10m to 15m in diameter. They are in all respects very typical of those ring-ditches within the Where Rivers Meet area that have been excavated and, where dating evidence has been forthcoming, shown to be of Bronze Age date. This area of the field is otherwise devoid of cropmark evidence of ring-ditches (or indeed other obvious archaeological features), so that the clustering of the three monuments – the large enclosure and two much smaller ring-ditches – is striking. If the two ring-ditches are correctly interpreted and were deliberately located adjacent to the circular enclosure, then of course the circular enclosure must be earlier in date than the ring-ditches. This interpretation is supported by the fact that the siting of Bronze Age burial mounds on the periphery of later Neolithic monuments – henges and stone circles – is a widespread phenomenon.

Finally, there is the question that if the enclosure is not a hengiform monument of some type, heavily plough-levelled, then what could it be? In the Where Rivers Meet landscape as a whole cropmarks of an archaeological character that are not earlier prehistoric in date are usually later prehistoric (Iron Age) or Roman period in date. However, as we will see in the next chapter, in this landscape Iron Age enclosures of circular form are unknown, the sub-rectangular enclosure being the dominant form. Furthermore, there is no evidence of Iron Age or Roman settlement in this field or the wider locality of the Catholme Ceremonial Complex (a fact of probable significance, as we will explore later), although it is abundant at Whitemoor Haye a few kilometres to the south of the complex as well as to the north, so that if the circular enclosure were Iron Age or Roman it would be an anomaly both in form and location. Added to this, the excavation of the enclosure yielded no cultural material of Iron Age or Roman date, which, although not always abundant on sites of these periods in this landscape, is more plentiful than earlier prehistoric material and might normally be expected in an excavation of the scale carried out on the enclosure. One needs to bear in mind that no artefactual finds were made during the excavation of the woodhenge monument, although the series of radiocarbon dates obtained puts its date beyond question, and had it not been for the central burial there would have been virtually no finds from the sunburst monument either. While such reasoning by a process of elimination is much less satisfying than positive evidence, it nevertheless lends weight to the arguments in favour of a Neolithic date for the circular enclosure, and its interpretation as a henge or something similar.

One problem with the interpretation of the circular enclosure as a henge monument, or similar, is the absence of apparent entrances. Henges usually have one or more entrances, their disposition being one of the criteria used in their sub-classification. However, without total excavation the absence of entrances cannot be confirmed, and even if there were no entrances, this would be a problem only for present-day typologists and not for the people who built and used the monument, although it may have altered the nature of associated ceremonies.

Lying about half a kilometre to the north-east and north-north-east respectively of the Catholme Ceremonial Complex are two further small monuments, at Borough Holme and Fatholme (see Fig 5.11), that would appear to be broadly contemporaneous with those of the complex and may be loosely described as 'hengiform'. Whereas the monuments of the ceremonial complex overlook the floodplain of the Trent, these two monuments lie within it. They are sited, no doubt significantly, on what would have been dry 'islands' – or 'holmes' – beside or amongst the numerous interweaving channels of the river.

The monument at Fatholme, on the western edge of the floodplain, was excavated in advance of quarrying in 1984 (Losco-Bradley 1984), although at the time of writing the full results have not been published but are in preparation (Guilbert forthcoming). The cropmark evidence for this site suggested a double ring-ditch 24m in total diameter, enclosing an area some 14m in diameter, and thus considerably smaller than the examples just described in the west of the study area. The excavation of the site revealed at least seven circuits of interrupted ditches, the lower fills of which contained early Neolithic flintwork, while late Neolithic Grooved Ware pottery and Beaker were also recovered.

Until full details of the excavation results are available, interpretation of this undoubtedly Neolithic monument must remain very speculative. The multiple circuits of interrupted ditches might suggest a causewayed enclosure but the enclosed area is much too small for the monument to fall into this category as normally defined. It might also be classified as a ring-ditch of the type normally believed to represent ploughed-out burial mounds (barrows), albeit one of very complex construction. It certainly falls within the typical size range for these. We prefer to describe it as a 'hengiform' monument (acknowledging the vagueness of this term), a small ritual monument with an assumed main constructional phase in the late Neolithic period, as suggested by the pottery.

The second monument lay approximately 500m to the south-east of the Fatholme site, on an island within the floodplain at Borough Holme (Evans 2006). From cropmark evidence this site appears to have consisted of two concentric ditched circles, with fragments of a possible third circle, enclosing a central area approximately 21m in diameter. Overall this monument measured approximately 50m in diameter. Unfortunately, the site was destroyed by quarrying without further investigation and so its interpretation must remain speculative. It has been interpreted as possibly representing a small causewayed enclosure (Evans 2006), but again the problem is the very small size of the enclosed central area compared with 'typical' monuments of this type. Again, too, an interpretation as a ploughed-out burial mound of complex construction is possible, but here the problem is its unusually large overall size for this monument type. We therefore prefer to interpret it as a potential hengiform monument, most likely to have been of later Neolithic date.

Some 2.5km to the south of the Catholme Ceremonial Complex, across the Trent and adjacent to the River Tame in the area of the National Memorial Arboretum, another large multiple ring-ditch monument has been identified from aerial photography (SMR 193, SAM ST199; Hughes and Hovey 2002), similar in many respects to those just described. Four concentric circuits of ditches or pits and a central pit have been identified from the photographs, the overall diameter being about 35m. The SMR records the site as a possible henge and this, or the more vague 'hengiform', is the designation we favour also.

This structure was designated as a Scheduled Ancient Monument in 1969. The area around it, which contained a cluster of smaller, simpler ring-ditches (characteristic of ploughed-out burial mounds) and other features, was quarried away with only minimal archaeological recording, but the site of the Scheduled Ancient Monument was preserved and now lies within the National Memorial Arboretum. During work at the arboretum in 1996, an engineering test pit was accidentally located within the scheduled area but outside and just to the south-east of the monument itself. This uncovered a large fragment and three smaller sherds of a late period Beaker vessel. Subsequent archaeological fieldwork in 1997 (Hughes and Hovey 2002) involved the recording of the location and the reinstatement of the test pit, including sieving of the disturbed soil. This resulted in the recovery of a further seven sherds attributed to the same Beaker vessel, allowing its reconstruction (Woodward 2002). It seems likely that the Beaker vessel was placed in a pit on the periphery of the monument; there was no trace of human bone to suggest a Beaker burial, similar to that inserted into the sunburst monument, but here too the soil conditions are such that unburnt bone is unlikely to survive.

The deposition of a Beaker on the periphery of the monument, whether accompanying a burial or not, indicates that the monument itself predates the deposition, suggesting a later Neolithic date for the monument on both chronological and morphological grounds.

Before we consider the interpretation and possible significance of the monuments of the Catholme Ceremonial Complex and the surrounding area in more detail, we need to trace the next stage in the evolution of this special place, which occurred between the end of the Neolithic and into the early Bronze Age.

A landscape of ancestors: the Beaker and early Bronze Age periods (c 2500–1500 BC)

Throughout Britain the majority of evidence for monumental activity during the last part of the Neolithic and the early Bronze Age is associated with funerary monuments. The construction of barrows as funerary monuments has a long tradition stretching back to the earlier Neolithic, with the construction of long barrows dating from perhaps between *c* 4500 BC and 3500 BC (although such monuments are conspicuous by their absence in the Where Rivers Meet area and indeed much of the west Midlands). These were normally associated with disarticulated burials, indicating that only the bones of previously defleshed individuals were buried, often without associated grave goods. By the end of the Neolithic and the onset of the Bronze Age (*c* 2500 BC) monument remains are typified by inhumation burials of individuals with associated grave goods under circular barrows and, slightly later, by cremation burials. Whilst this provides a somewhat simplistic overview, the landscape evidence in Britain for this period is significantly dominated by round barrows. In instances where these features have been flattened by agriculture, the circular ditch that once surrounded the upstanding barrow, and appears today as a cropmark, may be all that remains. This gives us one of the most characteristic monuments of the Where Rivers Meet area, the ring-ditch.

At the transition from the late Neolithic to the early Bronze Age 'proper' is what has been termed the 'Beaker phenomenon' (*c* 2500–1700 BC). Beakers are ceramic drinking vessels, generally flat-bottomed with a sinuous profile, probably used for a fermented beverage of some kind, and decorated with a range of characteristic abstract, often geometrical (triangles, lozenges, etc), incised designs (Fig 5.12). Different Beaker shapes and decorative schemes have been assigned to different dates within the long period during which they were in vogue. In Britain the 'textbook' association of Beakers is for them to be found accompanying single crouched inhumations under round barrows, where other associations might include characteristic barbed-and-tanged flint arrowheads, perforated stone plaques generally interpreted as 'wristguards' (to protect an archer's wrist from the bowstring when an arrow is released), copper daggers and trinkets (earrings, buttons, etc) of gold, copper, jet or amber. However, in reality Beakers are found in a wide variety of associations beyond this textbook stereotype. Furthermore, the so-called 'rich' Beaker burials including artefacts of copper and gold are very rare in the corpus as a whole, and virtually absent in the west Midlands, including the Where Rivers Meet area. Nevertheless, the first appearance of metalworking in copper and gold is closely associated in Britain with the Beaker phenomenon. The use of bronze, an alloy of copper and tin, comes a little later, and it is only at this stage that we can properly speak of a Bronze Age.

Beakers, 'Beaker burials', and the artefacts commonly associated with them, represent such a distinctive phenomenon in comparison to the types of monument and other archaeological remains that we have been considering up to this point, that for many archaeologists they would seem to represent the advent of a new

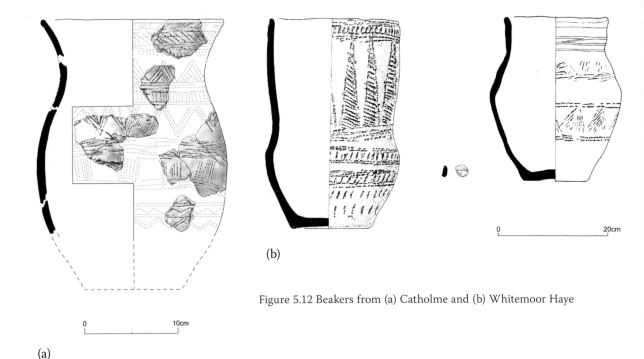

(b)

Figure 5.12 Beakers from (a) Catholme and (b) Whitemoor Haye

(a)

ideology, of new political and religious ideas. At the centre of that ideology is the 'warrior ethos' – flashy weapons, the conspicuous consumption of alcohol and showing off in general being amongst the essential characteristics of any self-respecting warrior.

A key aspect of the 'Beaker phenomenon' is that it is geographically very widespread. In Britain, Beakers are found from the Northern Isles to Land's End, but they are also found in Ireland and over much of central and western Europe. Furthermore, particular styles of Beaker pottery can be very widespread – we caught a glimpse of this when the Beaker accompanying the burial inserted into the middle of the sunburst monument at Catholme was described as belonging to the 'Northern/North Rhine group'. In the past, a popular interpretation of the Beaker phenomenon was that it represented the spread of a 'people', the Beaker Folk, across much of Europe. The Beaker Folk, it was argued, colonised and conquered large parts of Europe, including Britain, where they became a warrior elite, dominating the indigenous populations. Amongst the reasons which enabled them to achieve this dominance, it was argued, despite their relatively small numbers, were their warrior ethos, new weapons (which might have included the horse) and command over the arcane mysteries of metallurgy. Where the Beaker Folk might have originated was hotly debated, but Britain was not a serious candidate. While this idea has few supporters today, historical analogies, such as the conquistadors in America, are not difficult to find.

Today, most scholars prefer to view the Beaker phenomenon as reflecting the spread of an idea, cult or ethos, arising out of the growth of a network of contacts between communities, especially their elites. This new 'internationalism' would have been stimulated and maintained by the appearance of new 'prestige goods', such as weapons and jewellery of copper and gold, the raw materials for which were in limited supply, and limited in geographical location, promoting the development of new networks of trade and exchange.

Whatever interpretation of the Beaker phenomenon one prefers, the widespread appearance of round burial mounds across the landscape, with many of the earlier examples associated with Beaker burials, is undeniable. Archaeologists are fond of searching for and finding evidence of 'continuities', and a tradition of single burials under round mounds has been traced back into the Neolithic. However, the examples are relatively sparse, and, in many areas, including the west Midlands, the appearance of round barrows in the Beaker period (often directly associated with Beakers) is without precedent on current evidence, and represents a clear break with the past. Once established, the tradition of barrow burials continued, with variations in practice, well into the Bronze Age, long after Beakers themselves had gone out of fashion.

Beyond their specific cultural associations, the significance of round-barrow burials is essentially two-fold. Firstly, the prominence given to the individual buried below a barrow suggests that he or she had attained some level of prestige within the community, and perhaps a position of political power, particularly since such a low proportion of the assumed population is represented by these burials. Commonly, throughout the earlier and middle Bronze Age, these barrows become the focus for secondary and tertiary burials, both within the sides of the barrows and in the surrounding area. Secondly, as we have already noted in the context of Beaker burials, the associated grave goods occasionally highlight the importance of trade and exchange over great distances, for either the raw materials or for the finished items. It is likely that the Neolithic emphasis on the communal expression of control, power and difference, manifest in the construction of essentially communal monuments, was being replaced in the Beaker period and Bronze Age by more individual expressions of power and status, manifest in individual burials under burial mounds, and in the possession of elite status symbols obtained through trade or the practice of 'gift exchange'.

If the practice of round-barrow burial represents a new ideology and new religious ideas, then it might be expected that this new ideology would come into conflict with, or have somehow to be resolved with, the old ideology. We might be witnessing something of this conflict or resolution at Catholme, in the insertion into the very centre of the sunburst monument, presumably the most significant place within it, of an individual burial accompanied by a Beaker, as described earlier in this chapter. The radiocarbon dates relating to the construction or final elaboration of the monument, and the stylistic dating of the Beaker accompanying the burial, suggest that some 500 years may have separated these two events (roughly the time separating us from the first Tudors). It would appear that the old monument still held significance, and that the placement of the burial at its centre was a highly symbolic act, perhaps an act of symbolic 'conquest' and assimilation. In case this seems far-fetched, it is worth recalling that, in our age of much more rapid cultural change, the Investiture of the current Prince of Wales took place in Caernarfon Castle almost 700 years after its construction by Edward I as the ultimate symbol of the conquest of Wales.

The Beaker burial in the sunburst monument was, however, a one-off act. An even more powerful indication of the enduring significance of the Catholme Ceremonial Complex for later generations (or, going further back, of the special place that the Trent/Tame confluence had been for millennia) is the way in which it forms the apparent focus for literally hundreds of round barrows. In the Where Rivers Meet area a large number of these barrows – almost all surviving just as ring-ditches – have been subject to at least some degree of excavation, and it is to these monuments that we now turn.

The barrows of the Where Rivers Meet area

As is the case elsewhere, the majority of the evidence for Bronze Age barrows in the Where Rivers Meet area comes from aerial reconnaissance. There are two major concentrations of barrows on the Middle Trent, around the confluence of the Rivers Tame and Trent, and upstream of the Trent/Soar/Derwent confluence (Garwood 2007a, 2007b; Loveday 2004; Woodward 2007), reflecting the distribution of the earlier cursus monuments (Knight and Howard 2004). It is, however, the Tame/Trent confluence which is the focus of the largest of these concentrations within the Middle and Upper Trent basin (Vine 1982).

Within the Where Rivers Meet study area, the distribution of ring-ditches follows the line of the rivers closely, extending to the north-east and west of the 'ceremonial complex' along the Trent valley, to the south along the Tame valley, and to the south-east along the Mease valley (Fig 5.13). However, there is a distinct focus of activity on the higher areas overlooking the Neolithic ceremonial complex, indicating longevity of non-secular activity. This principal focus, to the north and west of the River Trent at its confluence with the Tame, is particularly striking when compared with the landscape to the east of the River Trent, north of the confluence. Here there are no recorded features indicative of early Bronze Age funerary activity. Whilst much of this area of the landscape is dominated by the less porous Mercia Mudstone geology, which restricts the formation of cropmarks, the lack of features compared with the density of ring-ditches to the west is clear.

A number of the ring-ditch monuments within the Where Rivers Meet area have been excavated (Fig 5.13). This provides some indication of the variety and complexity of their construction and the various dates of their use. We will briefly describe the results of some of these excavations, starting in the north of the area and working southwards. At the northern end of the study area, in the region of Tucklesholme Farm, one of a pair of ring-ditches revealed by aerial photography was excavated in 1991 on the edge of the gravel terrace overlooking the River Trent (Hughes 1991). The ring-ditch was found to be 29–31m in diameter and between 2.6m and 3.5m wide, with a V-shaped profile up to 1.7m deep. Internally, there were two concentric ring-gullies, interpreted

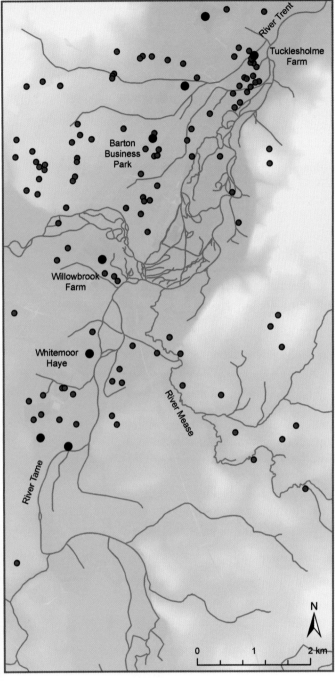

as post trenches. No evidence of a burial was found in the central feature (which had been part-excavated earlier, in 1975). The only small find directly associated with the monument was a flint flake from the ring-ditch. External to the ring-ditch was a sub-rectangular pit, the fills of which included substantial quantities of charcoal, tiny fragments of burnt bone, and elements of burnt wood, perhaps from a box or basket. The surprise came when radiocarbon dating of charcoal from this feature indicated a date in the 5th century AD. This raises the question of whether the whole monument is of post-Roman date, or whether (as we think is more likely) the prehistoric monument had retained significance as a locus for burial and ritual into the post-Roman period (see Chapter 8).

A ring-ditch was excavated in 2001 within the area of Barton Business Park, just to the north of the Catholme Ceremonial Complex (Nielson 2002). The ring-ditch, which formed part of a cluster revealed by aerial photography, was 20m in diameter, displayed evidence of recutting, and enclosed a central cremation. Externally, a number of other features were uncovered, including a possible boundary defined by bowl-shaped pits which predated the ring-ditch.

To the south of the ceremonial complex, in the area of Willowbrook Farm, on the southern side of the River Trent, another ring-ditch was investigated (Saracino 1990, 1991; Meeson 1991). The feature was 20m in diameter and up to 0.50m deep and, although no central burial was identified, a number of post/stakeholes were revealed predating the barrow structure, perhaps relating to a boundary feature as at Barton Business Park.

Figure 5.13 Distribution of barrows and ring-ditches within the study area. Solid black dots indicate excavated sites

Within the area of the Lafarge Whitemoor Haye Quarry, to the south of the National Memorial Arboretum and occupying the gravel terraces along the western side of the Tame, a large number of features have been investigated in advance of aggregate extraction. Three ring-ditches which had previously been identified from aerial reconnaissance were investigated within the northern part of this area (Martin 2001; Neilson 2001). One of these ring-ditches was 10m in diameter; the ditch was about 1m wide, with a U-shaped profile, and up to 0.33m deep. A central burial within this feature was indicated by an ovoid pit containing bone fragments within a charcoal-rich deposit. The other two ring-ditches were found to cut one another, the later one enclosing two cremation pits in the centre containing fragments of human bone, one within an urn. A possible inhumation burial with an associated *in situ* pot, charcoal, burnt bone and prehistoric pottery was identified within the vicinity of these ring-ditches. Other features in the area included an ovoid pit containing a number of sherds of prehistoric pottery. A cremation burial contained within an urn was also recovered from a small pit in this area of the quarry.

Some 500m further south within the quarry, excavations during the late 1990s failed to locate a ring-ditch identified from aerial photography (probably because by the time of excavation it had been completely ploughed away) but did manage to identify an oval pit which may have been the central burial within the ring-ditch. A large portion of a Beaker vessel was recovered from the pit although no traces of bone survived (Coates 2002). Further south again, still within Whitemoor Haye Quarry, excavations in 2002 investigated more ring-ditches and other prehistoric material. These features included part of a ring-ditch 21m in diameter which had been recut at least once, the fill of the recut containing sherds of Collared Urn (a characteristic type of burial urn, used to contain cremated remains) from the early Bronze Age. The primary fill also contained a single sherd of early Bronze Age pottery. The ring-ditch appeared to have a break in it and, at the terminal, a circular feature was found to contain the remains of a cremation burial with bone fragments. A possible second cremation was also found.

So far we have focused our attention on monuments whose apparent purposes involve ceremonial, ritual and death. At least insofar as the evidence is available to us, these monuments dominated the landscape. But the people who built these monuments lived somewhere and made a living somehow. What evidence do we have for settlement and domestic activities? We address this question in the following section.

The settlement question

As we noted earlier, except for a few regions (for example the Northern Isles), the evidence for farmsteads or villages in Neolithic and early Bronze Age Britain is generally slight. There have been two principal ways of interpreting this. According to one interpretation the houses and villages were there but their remains have only occasionally survived, perhaps because of the construction techniques used. Scatters of pits and postholes, and spreads of flintwork and pottery, are all that now remain of these settlements. The relatively few substantial houses that have been uncovered provide a model for what is largely missing but is assumed to have once existed.

An alternative viewpoint takes the evidence more at face value. Substantial houses and villages are scarce in the archaeological record because they really were scarce in the Neolithic and early Bronze Age. Perhaps an essentially nomadic lifestyle prevailed (inherited from the Mesolithic), with a range of insubstantial settlements occupied on a seasonal basis. Furthermore, in a variant of this interpretation, many of the finds of pottery or flintwork deposited in pits may not represent the vestigial remains of settlement sites but are to be interpreted rather as having a ritual purpose.

Within the Where Rivers Meet area, scatters of flint or pottery sherds dating broadly to the Neolithic/early Bronze Age are mainly concentrated within the eastern and north-eastern parts of the area, mostly on the higher areas overlooking the floodplain. The majority of these finds have been recovered during fieldwalking and are focused on the area to the east of the River Trent, outside of the ceremonial focus and concentration of ring-ditches to the west. This might suggest a separation of the landscape into areas devoted mainly to ritual activity and others devoted mainly to domestic activity: landscapes of the living and landscapes of the dead.

Structural evidence in the Where Rivers Meet area is provided by concentrations of pits, postholes and hearths, which may be interpreted as either 'domestic' or 'ritual' according to preference. Concentrations of pits and postholes were excavated in 1968 at Fisherwick towards the southern boundary of the area (Miles 1969). Neolithic flint tools including end scrapers and a discoidal knife were found associated with these features, in addition to a Peterborough Ware vessel in the Mortlake style. It was suggested that these features might indicate the remains of a possible house dating to the Neolithic period (Miles 1969; Coates 2002). A comparable site near Fatholme to the north was similarly interpreted as having a domestic function (Losco-Bradley 1984). Furthermore, at Whitemoor Haye, a pit excavated in 1995 within the region of a cluster of ring-ditches revealed four fragments of middle Neolithic Peterborough pottery, although here the large size of the fragments suggested a ritual purpose (Coates and Woodward 2002).

Interpreting the Catholme Ceremonial Complex (c 3000–1500 BC) (Fig 5.14)

Within the overall development of the cultural landscape around the confluence of the Trent, Tame and Mease, the area immediately around Catholme Farm increasingly became the focus of ceremonial and ritual activity. Specifically, there is evidence for continued use and reuse of this locality for ceremonial functions from perhaps as early as 3000 BC, continuing through to at least 2000 BC, a continuity of use that can be paralleled elsewhere, such as at Stonehenge.

The first phase of activity at this place appears to be the construction of a cursus monument within the area of the gravel terrace between the River Trent to the east and the higher ground to the west. This monument, 45m wide and perhaps 150m long, would have been constructed within a clearing in the

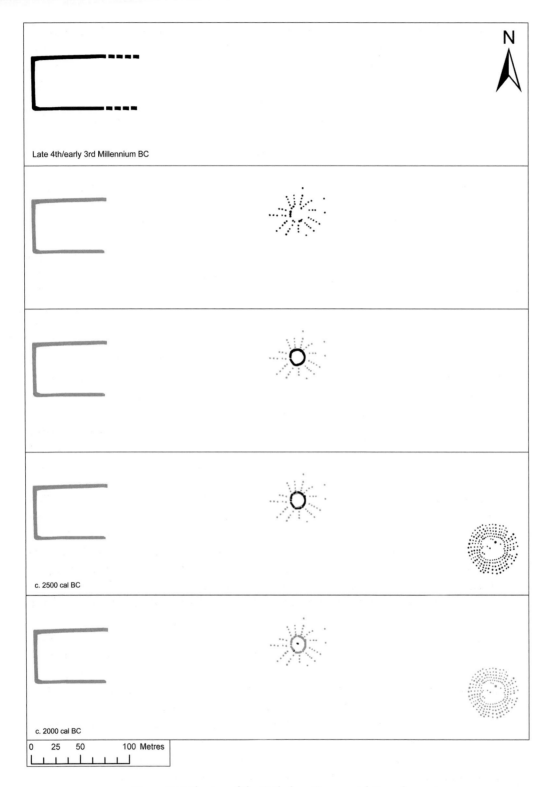

Late 4th/early 3rd Millennium BC

c. 2500 cal BC

c. 2000 cal BC

0   25   50   100 Metres

Figure 5.14 Phasing of the Catholme Ceremonial Complex

woodland. The northern and southern edges of the clearing may have marked the boundaries of the ceremonial area, while the river and the hills would have provided natural boundaries to the east and west respectively. The function of the cursus is a matter of some debate, as is its relatively short length. However, given its east–west alignment, the cursus would have framed views of the river, and processions would be directed along the path of the monument towards the river.

It seems likely that the radiating pits of the sunburst monument were constructed at some time before 2500 BC, following the construction of the cursus but predating the construction of the central ring-ditch or hengiform structure. The form of this structure is unique in terms of the overall plan of the site. The position of the sunburst monument places it slightly off-centre to the cursus to the west and so it seems unlikely that it formed an internal feature, as is seen on sites such as Springfield in Essex (Hedges and Buckley 1981). The structure defines a circular central space, quite different to the rectangular *temenos* of the cursus (*cf* Loveday 2006), which reflects changes in monumentality during the 3rd millennium BC. Activities taking place within this central area would have been visible to spectators positioned outside the monument, although if posts were ever present such activities would have been at least partially obscured.

At around 2500 BC the central circle of pits defined by the sunburst monument were cut by a circular ditch and then soon after recut into a segmented ditch formed from elongated pits. By this phase, even if posts had been present in the earlier structure, they would have now disappeared. Firstly, the ring-ditch overlies some of the pits, and secondly the external bank would have lain over the top of the second ring of pits. The morphology of this ring-ditch, with an external bank and possibly an internal bank also, in addition to its principal single entrance, is reminiscent of the hengiform structures that are relatively common in Britain (particularly the south) in the first half of the 3rd millennium BC. This structure is relatively small compared with many henges, which normally enclose an area in excess of 20m in diameter and often much more, although stylistic similarities indicate that this structure may have been a local variation of this national type. The length of time between the construction of the radiating pits and the hengiform ring-ditch is not likely to have been extremely long since the pits must have been visible at ground level to have been utilised within the later monument.

At the same time as the construction of the hengiform ring-ditch, at around 2500 BC, a second structure was erected to the east-south-east. This 'woodhenge' monument, comprising numerous upright oak posts, formed something of a simulation of the natural surrounding woodland within the clearing. Activities taking place within the central area would have been almost completely obscured from the view of any external spectators, which invokes the theme of exclusion which is so prevalent within monument construction throughout the later Neolithic period. The oak used for this construction is likely to have come from the floodplain area, where the conditions were not ideal for growth, since the tree rings were closely spaced which indicates slow growth. Given the probable height of the posts and their density within the structure, it is likely that these were relatively straight and may have come from managed woodland. The morphology of this monument shares some resonances with the sunburst monument in the use of radiating lines, although at the woodhenge structure the density of pits is much greater and the presence of posts has been demonstrated. Timber circles broadly similar to the Catholme 'woodhenge' have been found elsewhere, including its famous namesake near Stonehenge. A number of timber circles have been identified within henges and cursus monuments, and it is possible that these structures are an alternative manifestation of the henge structure (ie the ditch) itself. The function of these sites has been the subject of some debate. It has been observed that the positioning of the timbers may relate to a range of solar, lunar or cardinal alignments, or are aligned on the positions of other, earlier monuments within the landscape (Gibson 1998). Other interpretations include the idea that timber circles functioned as a type of calculator (Lees 1984), although this supposes a rather higher level of numeracy than is normally assumed for the period. The occurrence of burials within these structures appears not to explain their primary function. Rather, the most common interpretation is that these sites formed a focus for ritual, controlling the movement of people through them, generating themes of inclusion and exclusion, with both performance and observation.

The next phase of activity within the ceremonial complex at Catholme is the burial of an individual within the centre of the sunburst hengiform ring-ditch, probably *c* 2000 BC or shortly after. By this time, some 500 years after the construction of the sunburst and woodhenge monuments, any posts would have rotted, presenting a relatively flat local landscape. Perhaps it was only the ring-ditch and its accompanying bank, and possibly the cursus, that were now visible on the surface. It is possible that additional cremation burials were added to the western edge of the monument at this time, although the evidence remains inconclusive due to the poor survival of bone. This burial phase is reflected within the wider landscape through the construction of numerous burial monuments around the confluence of the Rivers Trent, Mease and Tame in the form of barrows and similar structures.

Whilst ceremonial activity certainly continued well into the Bronze Age, in the form of the creation of burial mounds, the construction of monuments within the Catholme complex ceased. However, it is likely that it was not until the end of the Bronze Age or into the ensuing Iron Age that the ceremonial area was defined by the pit-alignments dug to both its north and south (see Chapter 6). The layout of these pit-alignments in relation to the earlier monuments appears to be more than coincidental. The cursus and sunburst monument in particular lie centrally within the pit-defined area, which opens out in a funnel-like fashion towards the river, and connects the higher ground to the west with the river to the east. It seems likely, therefore, that at least some of the earthwork features of the monuments (ditches, banks and pits) were still visible on the ground at least 1000 years after their construction. Although the pit-alignments themselves are likely to be of late Bronze Age or Iron Age date, because this is the period of these alignments elsewhere in the Where Rivers Meet landscape and further afield in the Midlands where dating evidence has been forthcoming, they may well preserve or renew boundaries that are of much more ancient date, formerly marked out by hedge lines, for example. Such long-term preservation of boundaries, while the material means of marking them changes, is a very common phenomenon, being seen in our historic towns today, as well as in the countryside. Perhaps the boundaries of the ceremonial complex at Catholme were first marked by the edges of the woodland clearance created for them, and these boundaries were then preserved by a variety of means down to the Iron Age and beyond. Evidence for the long duration of a boundary at Catholme, marked out in different ways at different periods, is presented in the next chapter.

The Catholme Ceremonial Complex in its wider context

Whilst the individual monuments within the ceremonial complex and their particular combination are unique, there are a number of general parallels with other ceremonial complexes elsewhere. There are numerous examples of landscapes where monuments of successive periods cluster within the same area, often with features overlapping one another. The most famous of these landscapes is perhaps that around Stonehenge. Here, early Neolithic features, such as the Robin Hood's Ball causewayed enclosure and the numerous long barrows, are added to during the middle Neolithic by the cursus monuments and the first phase of the henge, followed during the later Neolithic and early Bronze Age by the stones themselves and the vast array of barrow groups (Cleal *et al* 1995).

The well-studied complex at Maxey, Cambridgeshire, on a gravel island adjacent to the River Welland (Pryor and French 1985), offers some particularly intriguing parallels with the Catholme complex. Here too is found a juxtaposition of ring-ditches, post-circles, mortuary structures and other religious monuments. The complex has its origin in the Etton causewayed enclosure (Pryor 1998), which stands apart from the complex of later monuments in a similar fashion to the relationship between the Alrewas causewayed enclosure and the later monuments in the vicinity of the confluence of the Rivers Trent, Tame and Mease.

However, we do not need to look so far afield to find general parallels for the Catholme Ceremonial Complex. Closest is the concentration of monuments found just some 20km further down the Trent, a little upstream of its confluence with the Soar and Derwent, which begins with the major cursus monuments at Aston and Potlock. Other examples, each a unique variant on the general theme, are found at Barford in Warwickshire, lying within a loop of the River Avon, and at Dorchester-on-Thames, Oxfordshire, lying within the confluence of the Thames and the Thame (Atkinson *et al* 1951).

In all these cases, a part of the landscape that formed the focus for early 'ceremonial' functions has been used and added to during later periods, indicating possibly unbroken use for over a thousand years. Generally, these are referred to as 'ritual landscapes', meaning that the features within these landscapes are not directly associated with settlement or mundane economic activities. An association with the disposal of human remains is common. The material excavated from the features within these landscapes is rarely utilitarian, but rather 'special' in one way or another. In some areas the relationship between monuments and settlement has been identified, as with the site at Maxey, but this is rare. It is uncertain whether these monuments formed the central places within communities or lay on the boundaries between different groups.

There remain many debates regarding both the function of each of the monument types and the way in which different monuments worked together, but it is clear that certain areas of the landscape became important for ceremonial activity. Furthermore the maintenance of these locales indicates how important these landscapes were to successive generations. Many of these ceremonial centres were located close to rivers or confluences of rivers. They are often placed in areas of natural boundaries, either to movement (such as rivers) or between different landscape types, such as on the edge of coastal saltmarsh (see eg Brennand and Taylor 2003).

The ceremonial landscape at Catholme reflects many of the themes, showing that the confluence of the Rivers Trent, Tame and Mease defined a regionally very important place throughout the Neolithic and into the Bronze Age.

CHAPTER SIX

Farms and boundaries
(*c* 1500 BC–AD 43)

A changing world 1500–450 BC

Between the early Bronze Age and the Iron Age one of the most profound transitions in the archaeological record – and in the nature of prehistoric society – took place, not just in south-east Staffordshire but across Britain and indeed in much of Europe. As we have seen in the preceding chapter, the archaeological record for the Neolithic and early Bronze Age is characterised by a range of ritual monuments and activity. Evidence for settlements, however, in our area and many other parts of the country, is elusive. By the Iron Age the picture is reversed: the record is dominated the remains of farmsteads and their associated field systems, and it is now the evidence for ritual activity that becomes more elusive.

When we compare these two periods, we seem to be looking at profoundly different worlds. On the one hand, we have the alien world (to us) of monuments such as the Catholme 'woodhenge', complex ritual structures whose purpose and meaning we can only guess at. It is the sort of world we might expect an 18th-century explorer to discover on some remote island in the South Seas, not just a little to the south of Burton upon Trent. On the other hand, by the Iron Age we are looking at a world that seems much more familiar. We find, for example, houses – typically roundhouses with roofs of thatch or turf – set within enclosures ('farmyards' might appear an appropriate term), themselves set within a pattern of fields and trackways, where crops were grown and cattle were pastured (Fig 6.1). With the help of the everyday items that are sometimes uncovered, such as pottery and querns for grinding the grain, we can readily conjure up a simple peasant existence. Although such a way of life has long disappeared from the British Isles, it is easily captured in the imagination. Look deeper, however, and there is much that is unfamiliar behind this familiar façade. Ritual and religion did not disappear from people's lives, but they took on different forms.

This transition did not take place overnight. Rather it was a process spread out over a period of about 1000 years, encompassing the middle Bronze Age (*c* 1500–1000 BC), the late Bronze Age (*c* 1000–800 BC) and the early Iron Age (*c* 800–450 BC). Only by the middle Iron Age (*c* 450–100 BC) is the new pattern clearly in place. Unfortunately, in our area, as in many other parts of the country (especially the Midlands), this long and important transitional period is poorly represented in the archaeological record. We might even go so far as to call it a 'dark age', at least from the perspective of its visibility in the archaeological record.

Figure 6.1
Reconstruction of
a typical Iron Age
farm (Bryony Ryder)

Before tracking these changes in the Where Rivers Meet area, we need to take a brief look at the wider picture. Because similar changes are found across much of the country, and are clearly related to changes also occurring in continental Europe, the transformation cannot be understood solely in local terms. One major aspect of this period, at least from the perspective of the archaeologist, is a transformation in the importance of metals, first bronze and later iron. In the early Bronze Age copper, bronze (an alloy of copper and tin) and gold tended to be used for relatively small, prestige items (eg daggers and ornaments), and although the craftsmanship was sometimes superb, both the range of techniques used and products made was narrow and the output was probably relatively small. In the later Bronze Age what amounts to a revolution in metalworking took place. A much wider range of products was made, using a variety of techniques (including the 'lost wax' method and sheet-metal working), and evidently much more metal was in circulation. Two aspects of this revolution are striking. First, the way in which the styles of the metalwork and the products themselves can be traced across wide areas of Europe, indicating networks of trade and exchange (and in some cases perhaps the actual movement of peoples), which drew regional populations into wider social formations and trends. Second, how much of the metalwork – swords, spearheads, shields, body armour, horse equipment – has a military connotation (Fig 6.2).

Brandishing such weapons and dressed up in such armour, the late Bronze Age warrior would have resembled one of Homer's heroes. This is not altogether surprising because the couple of centuries from *c* 1300–1100 BC were years of turmoil in the Mediterranean, with repercussions much further afield, into which Homer's story of the Trojan War historically fits. Cities around the eastern Mediterranean were destroyed, the great civilizations of Mycenaean Greece and Hittite Anatolia (Turkey) collapsed, and Egypt was permanently weakened by attacks from the mysterious 'Sea Peoples'. Like the much later 'Dark Age' which followed the collapse of the Roman Empire, this 'dark age' was probably also a time of widespread migrations affecting much of Europe (although, lacking historical evidence, many archaeologists tend to play this down).

In continental Europe, two further changes are also apparent in this period. The first, also found in Britain and clearly linked to the other evidence for increased warfare, is the development of many more overtly fortified sites than can be recognised from earlier periods. In their initial stages, forts often consisted of no more than a timber palisade erected around a defensible location, perhaps a hilltop, but through time these fortifications developed into elaborate timber-framed constructions, infilled with rubble and earth, and with the addition of a

Figure 6.2 Middle Bronze Age rapier recovered during quarrying at Langford Lowfields, Nottinghamshire. Length of rapier, 470mm

sloping revetment bank. Eventually, these developed into the great hillforts, with their earthen banks and ditches, which are such a characteristic feature of the British Iron Age.

The second change apparent in continental Europe (but much less clear in Britain, where the situation is more varied and complex) is an almost universal transition from burying the dead in graves to cremating the remains and placing these in pits in the ground or in funerary urns, creating so-called 'urnfields' from which the period often takes its name – the 'Urnfield period'. This was part of a number of changes to the spiritual dimension of life and death, which also includes what is evidently the ritual deposition of metalwork in rivers and other 'watery places'.

A fundamentally important aspect of the transformations which took place during the later Bronze Age and the earlier part of the Iron Age is the issue of 'ethnicity'. Following the collapse of the Mycenaean civilization and the ensuing Greek 'dark age', by around 800 BC the Greek city states were beginning to emerge from obscurity and the development of what was to become classical Greek civilization was underway. This was followed several centuries later by the inexorable rise of one Italian city state, Rome, to create an empire which encompassed the whole Mediterranean world and much of Europe north of the Alps, including, of course, much of Britain. The development of the Greek and Roman civilizations had a huge impact even upon those lands and their inhabitants which remained, temporarily or permanently, beyond their direct influence through colonisation or conquest. Furthermore, the Greeks and Romans were literate, and their historians and geographers wrote at length on the barbarian lands beyond their frontiers. From this it emerges that during the Iron Age much of Europe including the British Isles came to be occupied by peoples known collectively as the Celts. These peoples spoke closely related Celtic languages, which in Britain is known as British (or Brythonic) and is ancestral to modern Welsh. (Irish, or Goidelic, was a different but closely related language, ancestral to modern Irish, Scots Gaelic and Manx.) British was the language spoken by most of the inhabitants of Britain at the time of the Roman Conquest and throughout the 400 years of Roman rule, and we would presumably still be speaking a descendant of it (something akin to modern Welsh) were it not for the Anglo-Saxon settlements that followed the end of Roman Britain.

The question is, where did these Iron Age Celts, including the inhabitants of the Trent valley, come from? There are broadly two possible answers to this question. The first, favoured by an earlier generation of archaeologists (eg Piggott 1965) saw the adoption of Celtic languages and culture as the result of the spread, through migration and conquest, of an original Celtic people from central Europe, perhaps to be identified with an 'Urnfield Folk' (see above). This idea does not involve presuming that the inhabitants of the conquered areas were wiped out, but only that, in time, they came to adopt the language of their conquerors. Roman authors, notably Livy, documented some of the Celtic migrations, for example the settlement of northern Italy.

The second answer, more popular amongst the recent generation of archaeologists (eg Renfrew 1987), is that no major movement of population – no conquest of Celtic warriors – was involved. Instead, both the Celtic languages and Celtic 'culture' (eg distinctive art styles, religious beliefs and patterns of behaviour) emerged over wide areas of Europe in a process which is sometimes known as 'cumulative Celticity'. In this view the first speakers of Indo-European (the language family to which most European languages, including the Celtic languages, belong) were the first farmers who spread into Europe from the east, arriving in Britain around 4500 BC. Then, 'the Celtic languages are seen to emerge, by a process of differentiation or crystallization, from an undifferentiated early Indo-European language which was spoken in Europe north and west of the Alps' (Renfrew 1987, 249).

Although these two answers to the question of where the Celts came from involve radically different interpretations of the archaeological and linguistic evidence, the important point to emerge is that, either way, regional populations, such as those living in the Trent valley, cannot be treated in isolation, but their lives were shaped (knowingly or unknowingly) by processes and historical developments that operated at a variety of scales up to that of Europe as a whole.

One aspect of this period that may well have contributed to some of the social changes that are documented, although with much regional and local variation, is a general deterioration of the climate, which from around 1500 BC became wetter and cooler. In Britain much of the evidence for this has come from the environmental interpretation of cores extracted from peat bogs (Knight and Howard 2004, 80). How this might have affected the Where Rivers Meet area is debatable but, especially at the confluence of rivers, increased rainfall may have led to more frequent flooding and the development of floodplain wetland. The downturn in the climate may have adversely affected the growing season for crops and caused a shift in emphasis from arable to pastoral activity.

The Trent valley 1500–450 BC

With this background, we may now turn to look at developments in the Trent valley and the Where Rivers Meet area during the later Bronze Age and early Iron Age. The great expansion of metalworking during this period, and the frequent deposition of metalwork in hoards or as votive deposits in watery places was noted above. The River Trent is no exception to this pattern and has yielded substantial quantities of bronze weapons and tools of middle and late Bronze Age type (Knight and Howard 2004, 82–3). Rather surprisingly, given the amount of archaeological excavation and quarrying that has taken place, no examples have been recorded from the area around the confluence of the Trent and the Tame, which one would anticipate to have been a prime location. However, because of the way in which these items were generally deposited, as what were evidently ritual 'offerings' cast into water, they tend not to turn up on the sites of settlements and burials, which were located on the drier ground, but to be found by chance during fishing or dredging or, especially, quarrying for gravel buried under alluvium. At the time of writing, the sub-alluvial gravels at the Whitemoor Haye quarry have yet to be extracted.

Important concentrations of metalwork have been discovered downstream from the Where Rivers Meet area, however, around Aston-upon-Trent near the confluence of the Derwent and Soar with the Trent. Here, at Shardlow Quarry (where metal detectors are used on the conveyor belts) twelve middle to late Bronze Age spearheads, rapiers, palstaves (a type of axe) and socketed axes have been discovered (*ibid*). They appear mainly to have been deposited at the edges of former lakes. Quarrying at Aston-upon-Trent has also revealed the fragmentary waterlogged remains of a wooden trackway, part of which comprised a brushwood layer on a foundation of sandstone blocks, held in place by sharpened posts driven into the underlying gravel (*ibid*, 58). Trackways such as this one may have been built across wet and boggy ground to link dry 'islands' within the floodplain. At Flag Fen, Peterborough, a post-built causeway of this general nature has been extensively excavated, and has produced nearly 300 metal objects, mainly of the period between 1300 and 700 BC, which were deposited in the water around the posts and along one side of the causeway (Pryor 1992). Near to the trackway at Aston-upon-Trent, a largely intact log boat (one of several found along the Trent) has also been uncovered during quarrying (Garton *et al* 2001; Knight and Howard 2004, 58–9). It was carrying a cargo of sandstone blocks, which it is tempting to suppose might have been intended for use in the construction of the foundation of the trackway. Radiocarbon determinations indicate a date of 1440–1310 BC for the boat. Similar discoveries from the area around the confluence of the Trent and the Tame are perhaps just a matter of time.

The ritual deposition of metalwork in water (the quantities involved are simply too great for these to be accidental losses by very careless people!) is one aspect of changes in spiritual life at this time, although it should be noted that the practice started earlier, in the early Bronze Age, but on a much smaller scale. Another aspect is changes in burial customs. As we saw in the previous chapter, by the early Bronze Age the principal burial rite was either inhumation or cremation under a round barrow, numerous examples of which have been discovered and excavated in the Where Rivers Meet area. Mirroring trends on the continent, the so-called 'Urnfield' phenomenon, there is a shift in the middle Bronze Age to flat cremation cemeteries, with the burials either contained just in pits or placed within cinerary urns in the pits. The style of pottery generally used for these urns is the so-called 'Deverel-Rimbury ware', which is characteristic of the middle Bronze Age in midland and southern Britain. These flat cemeteries are much more rarely found than are barrows but this may be in considerable part a consequence of their lower archaeological visibility.

A good example of one of these flat cremation cemeteries was excavated in the Where Rivers Meet area at Tucklesholme Farm, Barton-under-Needwood, in 1996 (Martin and Allen 2001). It was found in 1996, by chance, during the excavation of a pair of ring-ditches (ploughed-out round barrows) in advance of quarrying. The flat cemetery lay just beyond one of the two ring-ditches and comprised a group of 21 cremations along with the remains of five cinerary urns of Deverel-Rimbury type (Fig 6.3).

The association of later flat cremation cemeteries with earlier barrows is not uncommon. At the simplest level, the old barrows would provide a convenient 'marker' for the new cemeteries, but it is also likely that the barrows retained significance. If there was direct continuity of the local population, these barrows would be the burial places of the ancestors, and perhaps the memory of these ancestors and their exploits was retained through poetry and song, even elaborated down the centuries into legend and myth, much in the manner of

Figure 6.3 Deverel-Rimbury urns from the flat cremation cemetery excavated at Tucklesholme Farm

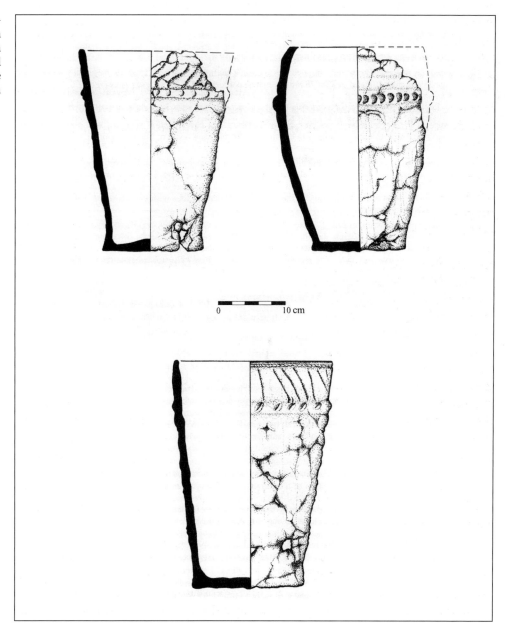

0   10 cm

the Homeric poems. Even if there was no such direct continuity, the remains of barrows and other ritual monuments would have been prominent features of the landscape, and, along with natural features such as rivers and hills, would have been imbued with spiritual significance. Such continuities from the past, and the way the past influenced the present, are an important aspect of the evolution of the landscape, and a theme we will meet again when we consider the persistence of boundaries.

Although many flat cremation cemeteries probably await discovery and many more have already been destroyed by ploughing or quarrying, it is unlikely that these burial places account for the whole of the dead of the population. The same is true of the earlier barrows, which, although more numerous, still only account for the burial of hundreds whereas many thousands must have died over the millennia. What happened to these people? The problem is even more acute by the time of the late Bronze Age and Iron Age, during which very few burials of any kind are found in Britain, and none in our area. However, as ethnographic research shows, there are many ways of 'disposing of the dead' other than burial. For example, bodies may be burnt on pyres and the ashes simply scattered, they may be exposed on platforms and in trees for nature to take its course, or they may be placed in bogs, rivers and other 'watery places'. Intriguing evidence for the latter possibility has come from excavations at Langford Lowfields, further down the Trent in Nottinghamshire. Here excavation (Garton *et al* 1996; 1997) revealed several hundred bones of animals and humans, together with timbers and brushwood, collected in what appeared to be a log-jam in an abandoned channel of the river. At least thirteen human skulls were present, along with the skulls of sheep, wild and domesticated cattle, deer and dog. Possibly the humans and animals were the victims of a catastrophic flood but, more intriguingly, they may be remains from riverside mortuary rituals. A radiocarbon determination suggests a Neolithic date for this event, but mortuary rituals such as this may provide one context for some of the numerous deposits of later metalwork found along the river.

While evidence of burial decreases as the Bronze Age progresses into the Iron Age, evidence for settlement increases, although it remains sparse until the middle Iron Age. Within the Where Rivers Meet area and more widely along the Trent valley, a general trend can be discerned whereby unenclosed settlements in the later Bronze Age and early Iron Age (*c* 1500–450 BC) give way to enclosed settlements by the middle Iron Age (*c* 450–100 BC). In parallel with this development, what appears to be an essentially open landscape transforms into a highly organised landscape divided up by territorial boundaries and sub-divided into fields. It seems probable that these developments reflect, at least in part, a real growth in population rather than differences in archaeological visibility.

The traces of settlement in the earlier period are few and far between, and the remains are often ephemeral. They are usually found by chance during the excavation of more substantial remains of later periods. In the Trent valley, the association of settlement remains with Deverel-Rimbury pottery (the middle Bronze Age pottery style used for the urns at the flat cremation cemetery at

Tucklesholme, described above) is particularly rare (Knight and Howard 2004, 86). One example within the Where Rivers Meet area is at Fisherwick in the south of the area. Here a series of cropmark features was excavated in 1973 (Smith 1976). These turned out to be the casts of ice-wedges, the product of freeze-thaw processes during the period of the Devensian glaciations. However, by chance, less substantial archaeological remains were also encountered, comprising a cluster of gullies, postholes and stakeholes associated with burnt daub, charcoal and a small assemblage of pottery sherds. The style of the pottery was consistent with a middle Bronze Age date, broadly within the Deverel-Rimbury tradition, and this was supported by two radiocarbon dates from charcoal. It would appear that the remains as a whole relate to part of a roughly circular building, perhaps a house, but the very limited extent of the excavation makes it impossible to determine much about this building, or whether it was an isolated structure or part of a larger settlement.

Associations of structural remains with post-Deverel-Rimbury pottery (PDR) plainwares, dating roughly to the late Bronze Age, are more common. A particularly important example of an unenclosed settlement of this date was excavated in the Where Rivers Meet area at Catholme, where it was uncovered during the excavation of the Anglo-Saxon settlement to be described in Chapter 8. Widely distributed across the site were the remains of at least eight roundhouses, mainly constructed of rings of posts but also including one example of post-in-slot type (Losco-Bradley and Kinsley 2002). There were also several four- and six-post structures. Such structures, consisting of either a square defined by four postholes or a rectangle defined by six postholes, are usually interpreted as 'raised granaries', the idea being that by raising the grain store off the ground on posts the grain would be protected both from damp and vermin. There was no direct dating evidence for these structures but as they are relatively common on late Bronze Age and Iron Age settlements elsewhere and are rarely found in the Anglo-Saxon period, it is likely that they were associated with the unenclosed settlement of timber roundhouses.

The progression from unenclosed to enclosed settlement during the Iron Age may be documented within the Where Rivers Meet area at Fisherwick, on the gravel terrace to the west of the Tame in the south of the area, although the argument is rather convoluted. Rescue excavations of a series of enclosures with associated field systems, of Iron Age to Roman date, were carried out here in the 1970s (Smith 1979). At one of the locations investigated (SK 187082) the principal features, revealed as cropmarks through aerial photography, consisted of a sub-rectangular enclosure containing two ring-gullies representing roundhouses.

At Fisherwick, only the more substantial of the two roundhouses and the entrance terminals of the enclosure surrounding them were investigated by excavation. Upon excavation it transpired that the ring-gully of the roundhouse cut into and partially destroyed an earlier 'ring-groove' with traces of stake settings in its bottom. This ring-groove was interpreted as the foundation for the wall of an earlier roundhouse, of different construction method to the later one. There was no direct dating for the earlier house, but as the later house could be dated to the middle/late Iron Age on the grounds of the associated pottery and radiocarbon dates, then an early Iron Age date seemed reasonable for the earlier house. Fragments of other ring-grooves of similar construction were also found during the excavation of the entrance to the enclosure, and appeared too close to the enclosure ditch (ie they would have lain beneath the associated enclosure bank) to be contemporary with the enclosure and therefore were considered to be earlier. On this basis an early Iron Age settlement consisting of several unenclosed roundhouses was hypothesised.

The evidence from Fisherwick is hardly compelling, but when combined with the evidence of unenclosed settlement at Catholme and similar evidence from further afield (Knight and Howard 2004, 86–7) a period of scattered open settlement during the later Bronze Age and early Iron Age, followed by the development of enclosed settlement from the beginning of the middle Iron Age (c 450 BC) begins to look like a convincing pattern.

Analysis of pollen and other plant remains from waterlogged deposits at a number of sites along the Trent valley provides another perspective on the changing landscape (*ibid*, 83–4). As might be expected, the picture is complicated but a general trend of increased clearance of woodland through the later Bronze Age and into the Iron Age is apparent. Along with woodland clearance (with local episodes of regeneration), there is increased indication of pasture and arable cultivation. Although the evidence is sparse, emmer and spelt wheat and barley were amongst the crops grown in the later Bronze Age.

Pit-alignments – territorial boundaries?

From the little evidence that is available to us, we can envisage the middle Bronze Age landscape in the Where Rivers Meet area as a largely open landscape, with scattered unenclosed settlements of roundhouses and perhaps communal, unenclosed grazing on the pastureland. The old round barrows, still foci for burials, together with the remains of other ritual monuments from an earlier age, will have been familiar features of the landscape, of continuing spiritual significance and also perhaps acting as markers for the organisation of the landscape and for territorial rights for the use of resources.

From this apparent starting point an enclosed landscape came into being, which appears to have achieved its most complete form by the end of the Iron Age and into the Roman period. One key element of this enclosed landscape is the long boundaries known as 'pit-alignments'. Both the date of pit-alignments and their function are unclear, but their importance is not in doubt: revealed as cropmarks through aerial photography, and sometimes strikingly clear, they can stretch for over a kilometre across the landscape and their construction must have involved a very considerable investment of labour (see Fig 1.6). Both single-row and double-row pit-alignments are found, the latter consisting of two parallel rows of pits, the rows close to each other. What was their purpose?

Several examples of pit-alignments have been sampled by excavation within the Where Rivers Meet area. The example excavated in Area S at Whitemoor

Figure 6.4 Excavation of double pit-alignment at Whitemoor Haye Area S

Figure 6.5 Plan of the double pit-alignment at Whitemoor Haye Area S (the overlying enclosure is of Roman date)

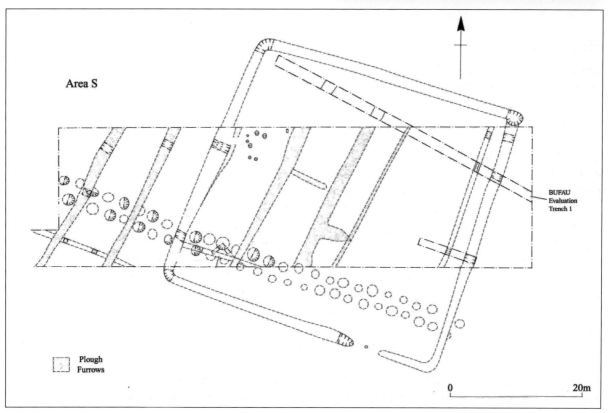

Area S

BUFAU
Evaluation
Trench 1

Plough
Furrows

0   20m

Haye Quarry (Coates 2002, 13–15) provides some idea of the character of these constructions as well as some of the complexities, and a rare indication of the date of construction (Figs 6.4 and 6.5). This is an example of a double-row pit-alignment, a 25m-long stretch of which was excavated. The two rows were staggered, such that the pits in one row were opposite the gaps between the pits in the adjacent row. The pits were roughly circular, and when excavated measured between 2.2m and 1.0m in diameter; they were bowl-shaped in profile and were spaced anything from about a metre down to 20cm apart. However, the size and depth of the pits as they survived cut into the sands and gravels is probably not an accurate indication of their size and depth at the time they were originally dug because the original topsoil had been removed and the archaeologists were seeing only the bottom part of each 'bowl'. Taking account of this, it is possible to envisage each row of pits as originally dug as perhaps forming a more-or-less continuous string, like beads on a necklace.

The pits were filled with both primary and secondary 'silting', suggesting they had filled up naturally over a fairly long period of time. Furthermore, each pit had been 'recut', that is, dug out again, at least once but to a slightly shallower depth.

The most curious thing about pit-alignments as boundaries is their discontinuous nature. To us, a continuous ditch seems a rather more obvious, and familiar, way to mark out a boundary, and the earth excavated from the ditch can be piled up on one side to form a bank, upon which, if something yet more substantial is required, a hedgerow might be planted. Of course, it is quite possible that the earth dug out from each of the pits was formed into a continuous bank in the manner just described but unfortunately because of centuries of ploughing no evidence for this survives. But why pits? One possibility is that the construction of these boundaries, remembering that some of them stretched for kilometres so the work involved was substantial, was a communal enterprise for which each participating member (or family?) in the community was individually expected to dig a certain number of pits. By constructing the boundary in this way it was possible to monitor how much work each participating individual was contributing, which is more difficult with a continuous ditch – perhaps there was even something of a competition for who could dig the most pits.

We will never know, but looking at the matter from this perspective usefully focuses our attention on the actual act of constructing the boundary and digging the pits (and later redigging them). Perhaps this was the most important part. Perhaps it was the act of communal participation in the marking out, or reinforcing, of the boundary that was symbolically significant – the resulting construction may have been secondary. This was, of course, a prehistoric period, before maps or charters or similar 'proxy' methods of remembering and recording what was what. If boundaries were to be remembered and their importance to be recreated and reinforced, then physical participation was the most powerful way of achieving this. The basic idea survived much later in the concept and action of 'beating the bounds', although the physical effort of digging or redigging pits makes the point much more forcibly. Viewed from this perspective, the double-row pit-alignments may simply have had double significance.

The communal, symbolic act of marking out or recalling boundaries (as in 'beating the bounds') may well have involved other rituals and celebrations, such as feasting. Most of the time, in the Where Rivers Meet area as further afield, little or nothing in the way of finds is recovered from the pits of pit-alignments, which is not surprising. However, in the stretch excavated in Area P at Whitemoor Haye, evidence was found which does suggested other, associated, activity. Here, the fills of many of the excavated pits contained some burnt or heat-cracked stones (Coates 2002, 13). These were probably 'pot-boilers'. Before the extensive availability of sheet-metal cauldrons (heavy, expensive items), the use of pot-boilers was a common method of boiling water for cooking (and other purposes) without having to apply a flame directly to the water container. The water container can take a variety of forms: a large wooden vessel or a suitably lined pit in the ground, for example. The stones are heated up in a fire and then tossed into the water, which often causes them to crack or shatter. This is actually a remarkably effective method of boiling water.

As well as the burnt stones, some of the pits (all in the northern row) of the pit-alignment in Area P at Whitemoor Haye produced sherds of Iron Age pottery (*ibid*, 15). Only one pit produced pottery from the primary deposit, but three others produced pottery from the recuts of the pit. One of these recuts also contained a stone rubber, made from a glacial 'erratic' deriving from Scottish or Lake District granites, and another produced a fragment of flint core. A radiocarbon date from one of these pits, with a range within the middle Iron Age, confirmed the dating evidence provided by the pottery (*ibid*). Furthermore, c 15m to the north of the pit-alignment, a group of small postholes was uncovered. There was no definite pattern in the layout of these postholes, but they may have formed some kind of curved structure or wind-break. Interestingly, from the deepest of these postholes a large collection of pot sherds was recovered, all fragments of a single large middle Iron Age globular jar, similar in type to sherds found in one of the pits of the pit-alignment. It seems that the broken fragments of the jar had been deliberately deposited in the posthole. An associated radiocarbon sample produced a similar middle Iron Age date (*ibid*).

Taken together, the burnt stones, the pottery, the postholes and the evidence for deliberate deposition of a smashed pot all point to feasting, possibly of a ritual nature, associated with the digging or redigging of the double pit-alignment here. (The absence of animal bones is simply a consequence of the acidity of the soil; except in palaeochannels, bone very rarely survives in the Where Rivers Meet area.) They also provide rare good evidence of the date at which this pit-alignment was laid out and, as the overall layout of many of the pit-alignments in the Where Rivers Meet area form a coherent pattern, it seems unlikely that the other pit-alignments will be of a radically different date, even if direct dating evidence is rarely forthcoming.

One of the most intensively investigated stretches of pit-alignment within the study area, which also indicates something of the longevity of these boundaries, was at Catholme, where it was examined in the course of the excavation of the Anglo-Saxon settlement (see Chapter 8; Losco-Bradley and Kinsley 2002).

This boundary ran not east–west but broadly north–south, marking the edge of the terrace overlooking the River Trent. In a broader perspective, it can be seen as part of the series of boundaries which divides up the land around the Catholme Ceremonial Complex. A 90m stretch of the boundary was excavated, and it turned out to be a long-lived and complex feature with several periods of renewal. In brief, the boundary began in the prehistoric period (although direct dating evidence was only provided by three small sherds of not very diagnostic handmade pottery), and comprised 'a pit-alignment, an apparent bank, and a post-line, replaced and redefined by a series of ditches with approximately the same extent and alignment into the Anglo-Saxon period' (Losco-Bradley and Kinsley 2002, 15; Fig 6.6). Such longevity has also been demonstrated by the study of pit-alignments in Warwickshire, where several have been seen to correspond to the boundaries of medieval parishes (Stuart Palmer, pers comm).

There are over twenty examples of pit-alignments within the Where Rivers Meet area, from Tucklesholme Farm in the north to Whitemoor Haye in the south. The predominant, but not exclusive, trend of these pit-alignments is broadly east–west, and they effectively divide the landscape into a series of blocks along the western side of the river, with boundaries perpendicular to the river. Although today these pit-alignments seem to stop short of the river, this almost certainly just an illusion, both because the river has migrated eastwards and because the land near the river has become buried under alluvium.

Each of these blocks will have contained a 'cross-section' of the resources available in the landscape – the resources of the river itself, and of the floodplain wetland (reeds, fowl), water meadow (hay), and then, moving away from the river and onto the drier ground, land with potential for pasture, arable farming and settlement. Perhaps, moving onto the higher ground, they also contained woodland. The pattern is not dissimilar to 'linear parishes' of the medieval period, which cut across the grain of the landscape in a similar way and for a similar purpose.

The two very distinct pit-alignments which mark off the Catholme Ceremonial Complex from the land to the north and south were described in Chapter 5. It is very difficult not to see these boundaries as related to the monuments of the Neolithic and early Bronze Age, yet all the dating evidence we have, both in the Where Rivers Meet area and further afield in the Midlands, points to the pit-alignments themselves being dug in the later Bronze Age or Iron Age. How is this apparent contradiction to be resolved? A clue is provided by the stretch of pit-alignment excavated at Catholme described above. Here the boundary itself was shown to be very long-lived, although the pit-alignment phase of the boundary may have been comparatively short-lived and in later periods the boundary was marked in different ways. Could the boundary have been in existence *before* the digging of the pit-alignment but marked in such a way that it is archaeologically invisible in these earlier periods? This would resolve the contradiction.

When we consider the boundaries in the overall context of the evolution of the landscape, a possible scenario emerges as to how these boundaries were perhaps

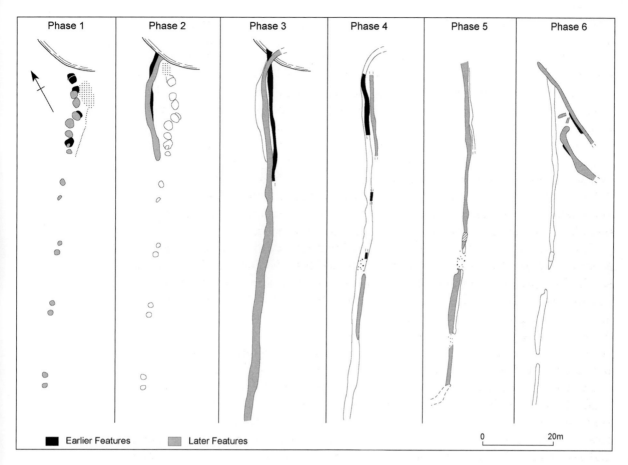

Phase 1	Phase 2	Phase 3	Phase 4	Phase 5	Phase 6

■ Earlier Features   ▨ Later Features

0   20m

Figure 6.6 Multi-phase boundary at Catholme, beginning as a pit-alignment and lasting through to the Anglo-Saxon period

first marked out in the Neolithic or early Bronze Age and were, thousands of years later, renewed by the digging of pit-alignments. At the beginning of the Neolithic, around 4000 BC, the landscape across which the pit-alignments were later to cross would have been heavily wooded. Clearances would have been created in the forest for the cultivation of land and for the erection of monuments, but most of the land would have remained forested. The overall character of the landscape, a pattern of woodland clearings, pathways and routeways (most importantly the rivers), would have been very different from today. Boundaries between cleared land and forest, between the 'wild' and the 'domesticated', would have been physically and spiritually important, but of course will have left no archaeological trace.

We may imagine the monuments of the Catholme Ceremonial Complex, perhaps at first just the cursus monument, aligned perpendicular to the river and opening towards it, set within such a clearing. If the clearing followed the lines of the later pit-alignments it would have been a dramatic setting, creating a sort of funnel opening out towards the river. Later, within this clearing, which was presumably maintained, the 'woodhenge' monument was constructed, a small artificial 'forest' of massive oak posts, with its own clearing in the centre – a forest within a forest, the forest 'domesticated', as it were, and given ritual form.

Although the environmental evidence is still too coarse-grained to reveal the pattern clearly, the general trend during the later Bronze Age and Iron Age was towards progressive clearance of the landscape until, by the middle Iron Age, the gravel terrace along the Trent and the Tame had evidently been almost entirely cleared, and a network of fields, tracks and enclosures had been laid out. A critical point in this clearance process will have occurred when the old boundaries between woodland and clearing disappeared with the widespread clearance of the woodland. Now boundaries, hallowed by centuries of tradition and maintenance, would have to be physically marked out in new ways, and this may be the context for the creation of pit-alignments as a widespread phenomenon. They are associated with, and are indeed a marker of, the final stages of woodland clearance. Their broad date range in the Midlands, from the Bronze Age through to the Iron Age, may simply represent the local progress of major woodland clearance. By the time the last pit-alignments were dug, they were already an ancient, traditional way of doing things, many generations old.

When we look at the overall pattern of pit-alignments in the Where Rivers Meet area (Fig 6.7), we can see that it makes broad sense with respect to the ancient landscape of Neolithic and early Bronze Age monuments and barrows. For example, the double-row pit-alignment at Whitemoor Haye Area S, described above, seems to serve to divide the area to the north, where intensive evidence of Neolithic and early Bronze Age ritual activity has been found, from the area to the south, where the pattern of Iron Age 'farmstead' enclosures is much more prominent, occupying the southern two-thirds of the Whitemoor Haye quarry area and continuing south into Fisherwick. Thus, on the broad landscape level, one may envisage a coarse division between an 'ancestral landscape of the

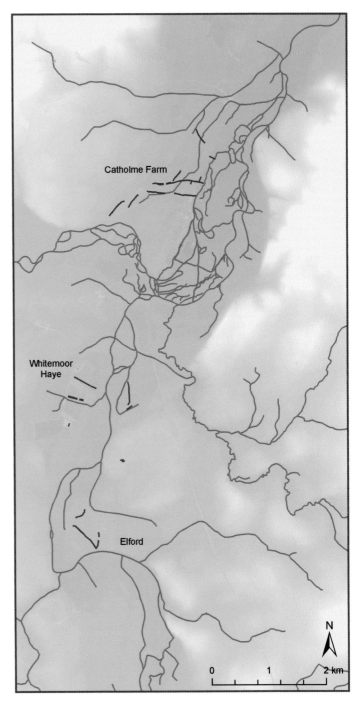

Figure 6.7 Pit-alignments in the Where Rivers Meet area

dead' around the confluence of the rivers and a 'landscape of the living' to the south (and perhaps to the north also, although here the data are more scanty). This division is not clear-cut, however, and even if valid it will obscure both chronological and spatial complexity.

If boundaries may survive for thousands of years so too, perhaps even more resiliently, may trackways, possibly originally cut through woodland. There is intriguing evidence for this in the section of pit-alignment excavated in Area T at Whitemoor Haye (Coates 2002, 15–18). The double pit-alignment here is very similar in character to the pit-alignment some 300m to the north, investigated in Area S, to which it runs parallel, but no dating evidence was found. A curious aspect of the pit-alignment in Area T is that there is a marked break in it at the point where a Roman-period trackway, defined by ditches on either side, passes through it (Fig 6.8). This implies that the trackway, although its ditches were dug only in the Roman period, followed a much more ancient route, a fact also suggested by the way that the Iron Age enclosures, described in the next section, are clearly related to it.

Figure 6.8 Plan of double pit-alignment and later trackway at Whitemoor Haye Area T

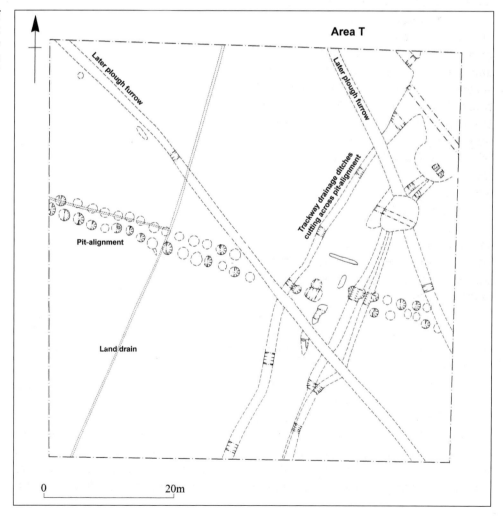

Iron Age farmsteads

By the middle Iron Age (*c* 450–100 BC) the landscape comes clearly into focus, and is characterised by enclosed farmsteads, often set within a system of trackways and fields. Typically, each farmstead comprised a ditched enclosure, sub-rectangular in shape with rounded corners and a single entrance, and in the range of 50m to 100m across. Inside the enclosures roundhouses were often found, from one to six in number, usually defined by a circular 'eaves-drip gully', in the range of 7m to 13m in diameter. The eaves-drip gully served to collect water draining from the conical roof (thatched with reeds or straw, or possibly turfed) and prevent it from draining back into the building. The actual size of the building was therefore somewhat less than the diameter of the ring-gully. A gap in the ring-gully marked the position of the entrance, which nearly always faced to the east. Although in other parts of the country a ring of postholes may be found within the ring-gully, marking the position of the roundhouse wall, this was not found in our area. The method of wall construction must have been different – perhaps mud walls or stacked turfs were used – leaving no archaeological trace. However, a variety of pits and postholes are often found within the ring-gully. Although these seldom form a clear pattern and their function is generally unclear, in at least a couple of cases paired postholes at the entrance suggest a door frame. In a few cases remnants of a central hearth have been found.

Five examples of these farmstead enclosures have been excavated in advance of quarrying at Fisherwick in the 1970s (Smith 1979) and at Whitemoor Haye from 1997 to the time of writing (Coates 2002; Hewson 2007). The example from Fisherwick is worth describing in some detail, because the waterlogged conditions in the enclosure ditch preserved not only plant and insect remains, allowing environmental reconstruction, but also wood and animal bone. These are rarely found in the Where Rivers Meet area and enable reconstruction of aspects of the farmstead that are not possible elsewhere.

Fisherwick

The Fisherwick site lies in the extreme south of the Where Rivers Meet area, close by the River Tame, and the excavations described below were carried out between 1973 and 1976 in advance of quarrying in the area of Blue Circle Aggregrates' Elford Quarry (Smith 1979). The Fisherwick farmstead enclosure can be seen from the cropmark plot produced by aerial photography to have contained at least two roundhouses. Only one of these, the more prominent, was excavated, along with several sections of the enclosure ditch and the entrance to the enclosure. We described in an earlier section how these excavations revealed traces of possible earlier roundhouses attributed by the excavator to a phase of unenclosed occupation. Here we are concerned only with the main phase of occupation (Fig 6.9).

The enclosure measured about 52m by 48m, surrounded by a ditch 3m wide and up to 1.75m deep. The bottom of the ditch was waterlogged and

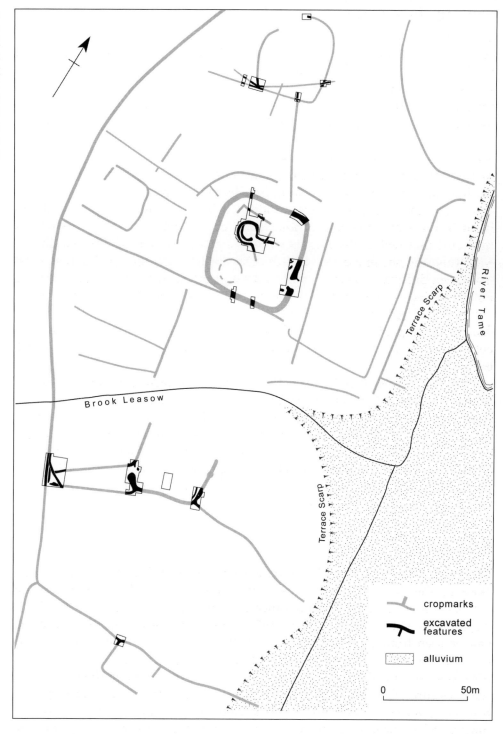

Figure 6.9 Iron Age enclosures and associated field systems at Fisherwick showing the farmstead at the centre, with the partially excavated north and south enclosures either side of it

Brook Leasow

Terrace Scarp

Terrace Scarp

River Tame

cropmarks

excavated features

alluvium

0   50m

contained preserved seeds, insects, wood and animal bone, as well as Iron Age pottery (Fig 6.10). It is likely that the bottom of the ditch would have held water throughout most of the year in the Iron Age, so it was presumably

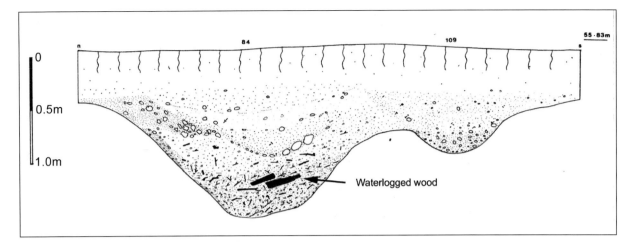

0

0.5m

1.0m

Waterlogged wood

Figure 6.10 Section through the enclosure ditch at Fisherwick, showing organic deposits preserved in lower fills

dug out in the late summer. There was no clear surviving evidence of a bank but this is likely to have been on the inside of the ditch (its presence reducing the usable space inside the enclosure considerably), with perhaps some upcast dumped on the outer side of the ditch also. The discovery of waterlogged hawthorn and blackthorn twigs, some of which had been deliberately cut and were presumably hedge trimmings, amongst other species commonly found in hedges, suggested to the excavator that the bank had been surmounted by a laid thorn hedge.

While the ditch-bank and hedge would have formed a considerable barrier, keeping animals in or out, there is no sense in which the enclosure at Fisherwick – or any of the other enclosures along the valley – could be considered defensive in a military sense. After it had silted up naturally (a process which would have been accelerated by its waterlogged state) the ditch was recut (cleared out), but this time to a shallower depth, stopping just short of the water table, so that there would now only have been standing water in the bottom of the ditch in the winter months, although it would have been muddy and damp throughout most of the year.

The entrance to the enclosure was positioned off centre in the eastern arm of the enclosure ditch. Groups of postholes either side of the ditch terminals indicated a substantial and perhaps imposing passage-like timber gateway into the enclosure, and a worn patch suggested the trampling of animals.

The roundhouse inside the enclosure was surrounded by a substantial ring-gully (an 'eaves-drip' gully), with a 5.5m-wide gap at the south-east, marking the position of the entrance. Although the ring-gully was about 11m in diameter, the house that it surrounded would have been only about 9m in diameter, to judge from the location of two large postholes that seem to have marked the doorway. A hearth, comprising a scoop containing burnt pebbles packed into scorched clay and earth, occupied the centre of the house. There were also numerous postholes and stakeholes of various sizes scattered about the interior of the house, presumably associated with internal divisions, fixtures and fittings but forming no clear pattern. In the absence of a ring of posts forming the framework for a wattle-and-daub wall, it was suggested that a mud-wall construction was used. The evidence for this came from the recovery of significant quantities of mud walling – a dried mud with an admixture of grits, small pebbles, charcoal and fragments of fired clay – from the ring-gully (Samuels 1979). A mud wall, bound together with pebbles and other materials, built up in layers, would have been quite strong enough to support the roof.

The area just outside the entrance to the roundhouse was also excavated, and it seems that much of daily life must have taken place here. The area was defined by two gullies, perhaps for drainage, fanning out from the terminals of the ring-gully. A large part of the area was occupied by a shallow hollow, presumably caused by wear, in the centre of which was an external hearth. Clusters of stakeholes and postholes may indicate windbreaks or screens.

From the cropmark plot it can be seen that the farmstead enclosure at Fisherwick sits in the midst of a complex of ditched boundaries, including two other enclosures, one to the south and one to the north. Both were sampled by excavation in the 1970s before the site was lost to quarrying. Unfortunately, due to the shortage of time and resources, the excavations were on a very small scale and the conclusions are therefore tentative. The southern enclosure, only three sides of which were evident, may have started out as a settlement enclosure. There were traces of an internal ring-gully on aerial photographs, although there was no time to excavate it before this part of the enclosure was quarried away; there were also sufficient quantities of Iron Age pottery in the ditch to suggest domestic occupation. However, at this stage the enclosure had two entrances, at its south-east and south-west corners, and this is more suggestive of stock control; entrances are often positioned at the corners of stock enclosures because the sides of the enclosure then act to funnel the animals towards the entrance. The enclosure ditch was recut in a second phase of use, at which point the south-east entrance went out of use and two parallel ditches, forming what is almost certainly a droveway, were dug leading up to the south-west entrance.

The northern enclosure was less substantial than the southern enclosure, and was tentatively interpreted as an arable field. It produced only three finds – the lower stones of a rotary quern and a saddle quern, and a sherd of Iron Age pottery, suggesting, although hardly conclusively, a date broadly contemporary with the homestead enclosure.

The remainder of the ditches visible on the cropmark plot include a long boundary ditch that surrounds the three enclosures just described on their western and southern sides to form a defined plot of land, which would have been bounded on the eastern side by the River Tame. Within this plot of land, which it is tempting to call a farm, further ditches divide the plot up into a series of fields or enclosures, which appear from their layout to be clearly related to the enclosures. Not all these ditches need be Iron Age, however; at least one was dated by pottery to the Roman period.

The results of the Fisherwick excavation enabled a fairly rounded picture of the Iron Age farm and its landscape to be tentatively sketched (Greig *et*

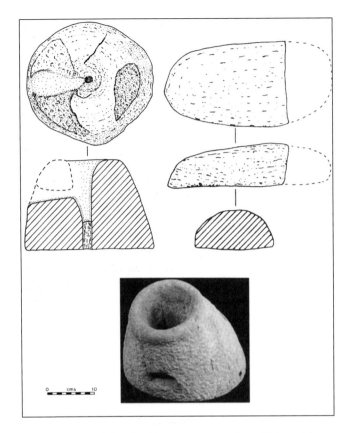

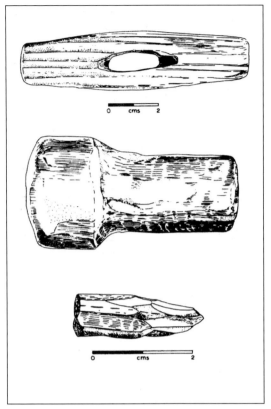

Figure 6.11 Top left: a beehive rotary quern from Fisherwick; top right: a rubbing stone (for a saddle quern) from Fisherwick; bottom: a beehive rotary quern from Whitemoor Haye

Figure 6.12 Top: a possible toggle, perhaps for securing clothing, made of ash; middle: a peg made of hazel; bottom: a fragment of a shaft made of hazel (perhaps a fragment of arrow shaft, the sharpened point fitting into the iron head)

al 1979). The pollen from the farmstead enclosure ditch indicated that the surrounding land had been almost entirely cleared, with very little primal woodland remaining, perhaps only on the valley sides beyond the river terrace. The seed and beetle remains indicated, not surprisingly, a typical farmyard environment in the immediate vicinity of the ditch, with weeds of broken ground and a high proportion of beetles of genera that live in the dung of large herbivores, presumably mainly cattle. Although only 63 identifiable animal bones survived, cattle predominated, with pig, sheep, horse and deer also represented. The deer bone is a reminder that hunting would have still played a role in daily life, and one of the pig bones was so large as to almost certainly belong to wild boar. No doubt fish and fowl were also taken, despite the lack of evidence for them. Arable farming and the processing of grain were indicated by cereal pollen, the saddle and rotary querns (Fig 6.11), and impressions of threshed emmer wheat and spelt spikelets on fragments of oven daub. A single pollen grain suggested that beans may have been rotated with the cereals. There was insufficient evidence to allow firm conclusions to be drawn regarding the relative importance of arable and livestock farming, although the feeling was that the rearing of livestock may have been the principal activity.

An infield-outfield system of farming was postulated, with ditched and hedged fields for arable and stock located close to the farmstead (and accounting for the cropmarks), and rough pasture, perhaps used in common with other farmsteads, beyond. There is little to suggest that Fisherwick represents much more than an essentially self-sufficient peasant farm.

Craft activities would have included woodworking, and the finds from amongst the waterlogged wood in the farmstead enclosure ditch included a spade or paddle, a toggle for fastening clothing and a pointed shaft, possibly an arrow (Fig 6.12). Most of the pottery used, mainly of simple jar forms, was probably made from local clays, although there was no evidence of potting on site (Fig 6.13). There was no evidence for ironworking either, and the iron tools necessary for everyday life (not found during the excavation) were probably manufactured by specialists, although again probably locally. Something equally essential to everyday life, salt, used to preserve and flavour meat, was however an import. The evidence for salt at Fisherwick comes from fragments of very coarse ceramic

Figure 6.13 Iron Age pottery from Fisherwick (1–3) and Whitemoor Haye (4–8) farmstead enclosures

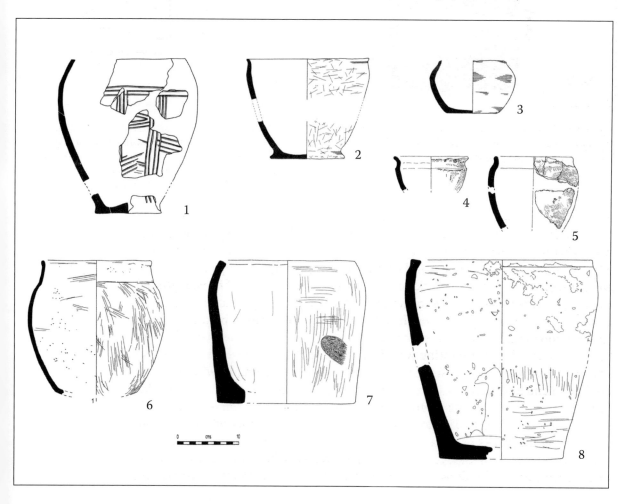

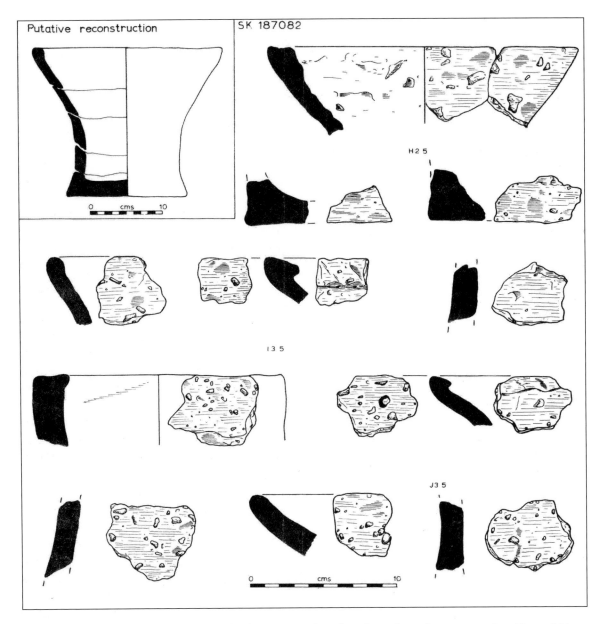

Putative reconstruction SK 187082

0 cms 10

H2 5

I 3 5

J3 5

0 cms 10

containers, known as briquetage, which were used to dry the salt and transport it (Fig 6.14). The salt itself came from inland brine springs, and the rock inclusions in the fabric of the Fisherwick briquetage is now recognised as deriving from the area of the Cheshire Plain around the brine springs at Nantwich, Middlewich and Northwich (Morris 2002). The production and distribution of salt from these sources was evidently a major enterprise, with the characteristic containers being found from north Wales in the west to the Trent and Soar valleys in the east Midlands.

Figure 6.14
Briquetage from
Fisherwick

Whitemoor Haye

The excavations at Whitemoor Haye Quarry, from 1997 onwards, have been much more extensive than those at Fisherwick and enable us to take a broader view of the Iron Age landscape (Fig 6.15). Whitemoor Haye lies just to the north of Fisherwick, in a similar situation on the western terrace of the Tame, and forms part of the same landscape.

The principal feature of this landscape at Whitemoor Haye is a trackway that, from the cropmark aerial photographic evidence, can be seen to follow a broadly north–south route along the gravel terrace parallel to the river, which it meets at its southern end. Along most of its course this trackway is defined by ditches on either side. Excavation of these ditches at several points along the route of the trackway has shown them to be of Roman date. However, there is little doubt that the trackway is of more ancient origin than this, perhaps starting out as a pathway through the woodland on the terrace before this was cleared. There are several lines of evidence which suggest this. First, as was noted earlier, the east–west-orientated double pit-alignment that was excavated in Area T has a gap in it where the trackway passes through, suggesting that the trackway was already in existence when the pit-alignment was constructed. Second, further to the south, a short stretch of double pit-alignment was revealed during a watching brief on topsoil stripping in the quarry (Hewson 2007) that corresponds precisely with the (projected) line of the trackway at this point, which is unlikely to be coincidental. Third, several of the Iron Age enclosures, most notably those excavated in Areas A, B and J, are clearly related to the trackway and orientated on it.

The best-preserved and most completely excavated Iron Age enclosure at Whitemoor Haye was that investigated in Area A (Coates 2002), situated close by the trackway and opening towards it (Fig 6.16). In size and shape the enclosure was closely comparable to the main enclosure at Fisherwick, and also had its entrance on the eastern side, although the V-shaped ditch was not as deep. Four roundhouses, also with the entrances facing east, were found within the enclosure. These were defined by ring-gullies but lacked evidence for an internal post-wall, so presumably the method of construction was similar to that conjectured for Fisherwick. The excavator argued that it was unlikely that all four roundhouses were in use at the same time, and suggested that they formed two pairs of houses, each pair consisting of a larger building and a smaller one (the largest house, in terms of the diameter of the ring-gully, measured c 14m across and the smallest c 6m). The suggestion is that the larger building would have been the house and the smaller one an ancillary building for stock, crafts or storage. When the first pair of buildings needed to be replaced – whether because they were beyond repair or because a new house was wanted (eg a son inheriting from his father) – a new pair was built adjacent to the old one. As at Fisherwick, the enclosure ditch had been recut some time after it had silted up, but to a shallower depth, and it is tempting to suppose that this may have occurred at the same time as the new buildings were constructed. After the life of the second pair of buildings had come to an end it was perhaps time to move on to a new site altogether and start over again. The old enclosures could be reused for non-domestic purposes.

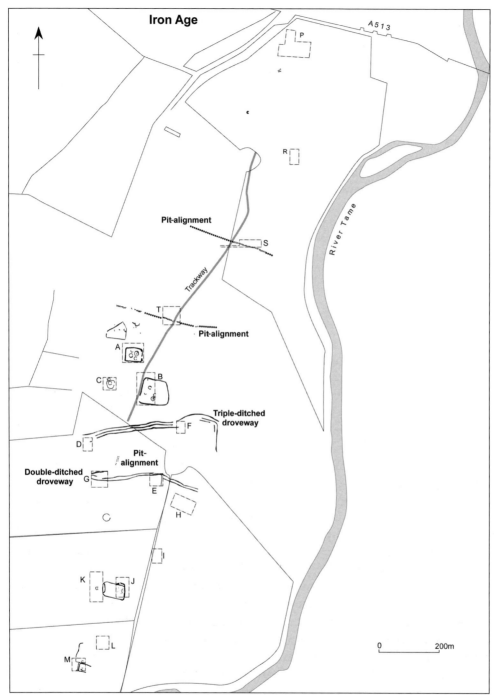

Figure 6.15 Plan of Iron Age enclosures, trackways and boundaries at Whitemoor Haye identified from aerial photographs and in excavation. Note the isolated roundhouse to the south of Area G. It is likely that many of these features originally continued further towards the River Tame, but have become concealed beneath alluvium

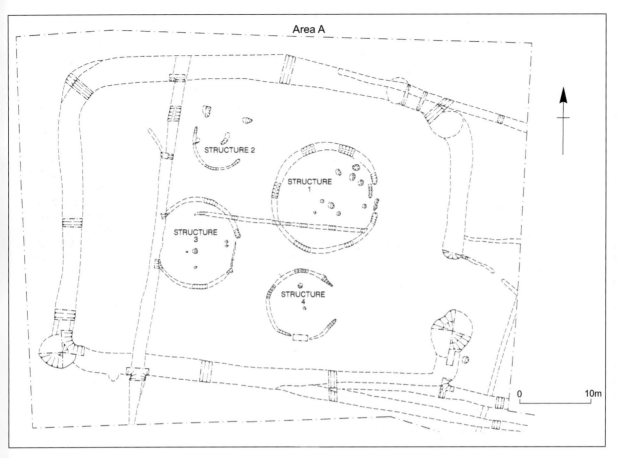

Area A

STRUCTURE 2

STRUCTURE 1

STRUCTURE 3

STRUCTURE 4

0   10m

Figure 6.16 Plan of Iron Age enclosure at Whitemoor Haye Area A. Note the late Iron Age/Roman period pits at the south-west corner and the southern terminal of the entrance (see p.137)

The Area B Iron Age enclosure, just 50m to south of the Area A enclosure, was larger and, although only part of it was excavated, it contained no fewer than six roundhouses of various sizes. Here it was clear from stratigraphic relationships that not all the buildings were contemporary, and again a succession of paired structures was proposed by the excavator (*ibid*). This enclosure was situated hard up against the trackway, on the opposite side to the Area A enclosure, with its entrance at the corner of its western side opening directly onto the trackway. Indeed, when the trackway was provided with ditches along either side in the Roman period, the eastern ditch of the trackway precisely followed the line of the western side of the enclosure. However, despite the fact that the enclosure entrance (or one of them – there may have been another in the unexcavated eastern half of the enclosure) opened to the west, the doors of the roundhouses conformed to the general pattern of opening to the east.

The enclosures in Areas A and B are just two of several that were dotted along the line of the trackway at Whitemoor Haye, and which have been excavated or part-excavated in the course of archaeological work in advance of quarrying. Not all enclosures conformed to the rectilinear pattern of Fisherwick or Whitemoor Haye Areas A and B; nor were all roundhouses set within enclosures. In Area C, for example, a typical pairing of two roundhouses, one larger and one smaller, with entrances to the east, was found (Fig 6.17). The 'enclosure' surrounding these buildings, however, was irregular in shape and marked only by shallow ditches, which appeared to have been excavated later than the buildings. They may have been mainly for drainage or, if accompanied by a fence or hedge, may have served to keep animals away from the buildings and stop them damaging the walls or eating the thatched roof! Only four sherds of undiagnostic Iron Age pottery were found associated with the Area C buildings, so it is possible that they might belong to the early Iron Age phase of unenclosed settlements that was tentatively advanced earlier.

Not all the unenclosed roundhouses necessarily date to this early phase. An apparently isolated roundhouse to the west of the trackway was uncovered during the watching brief in 2001, the ring-gully containing sherds of middle Iron Age

Figure 6.17 Plan of Iron Age roundhouses at Whitemoor Haye Area C

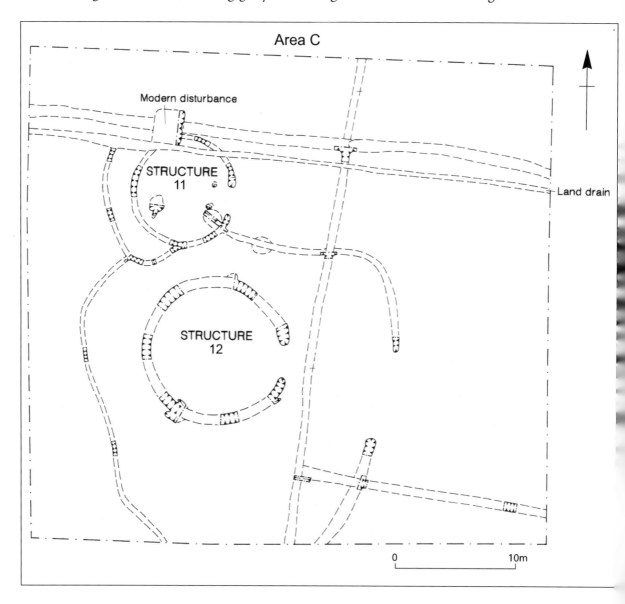

pottery, making it broadly contemporary with the enclosures (Hewson 2007). An unusual feature of this roundhouse is that in addition to its main eastern entrance it also had a smaller west-facing entrance. A central hearth contained heat-shattered stone and a substantial amount of charcoal.

The final archaeologically visible element of the Iron Age landscape at Whitemoor Haye comprises two trackways, defined by ditches, which run east–west across the landscape, crossing the north–south trackway that seems to have been the principal focus for settlement. These are interpreted as droveways. Extending the infield-outfield model proposed at Fisherwick, the function of these droveways would have been to move stock from meadowland down on the floodplain of the river, through the 'infield' area around the settlements, where the arable fields are likely to have been, and out onto the rough pasture beyond, which may have been communally held.

The northernmost of the two droveways comprises three parallel ditches, and the purpose of this, if each ditch was accompanied by a fence or hedge, may have been to allow 'two-way traffic' of animals along the droveway. At its eastern end the droveway ditches become lost under the alluvium that has built up on the floodplain, but just before this point the cropmarks (some of which were sample excavated during a watching brief in 2004) become more complicated and could be associated with an enclosure. This may be part of the arrangements for corralling the animals before herding them up the droveway. The more southerly droveway is a simpler, two-ditch affair.

The finds from the excavation of the Iron Age enclosures and roundhouses at Whitemoor Haye compare well with those from Fisherwick, although animal bone and waterlogged wood was lacking, and paint a similar picture of what would appear to be relatively low-status, largely self-sufficient farming communities, perhaps with a greater emphasis on rearing livestock than on arable farming (Coates and Woodward 2002). The pottery used was simple, mainly medium and large jars that would have served for storage and cooking. Judging from the fabrics, most of it was probably produced locally, although the occasional vessel was brought in from further afield. Also providing evidence of these communities being engaged in networks of trade and exchange were finds of briquetage (salt containers) from the Cheshire Plain, identical to the examples from Fisherwick noted above. As at Fisherwick, querns of Millstone Grit would have been imported from the Pennines; both the rotary and saddle type were represented. Although the farmsteads were of Iron Age date, a lack of iron or bronze tools and ornaments is not surprising as valuable items would have been retained when a farm was abandoned.

Society, religion and change

The excavations at Fisherwick and Whitemoor Haye enable a fairly rounded impression of the everyday life of peasant farming communities to be built up. The impression is not so very different from what might be found elsewhere along the Trent valley or more widely in the Midlands. Taking the evidence at face value there might appear to be little more to life than the daily farming round, the tasks changing, as always, with the seasons. But these people were Celts, who we know had a rich and complex social, artistic and spiritual life, and were noted for their warlike tendencies. What can be inferred about these dimensions of life?

One monument that hints at a hierarchy of settlement in the Where Rivers Meet area, and of the existence of a noble, warrior class, is the possible Iron Age hillfort at Borough Hill, near Walton-on-Trent (Challis and Harding 1975; Fig 6.18). It occupies a defensive hilltop site, c 3ha in area, on the eastern edge of the valley, directly overlooking the Trent and the ancient ritual complex around Catholme, just north of the confluence with the Tame. Earthworks are evident on the hill top but their original plan cannot be determined, and human remains have been found at Borough Hill Farm. Without excavation, however, the identification of the site as an Iron Age hillfort is far from certain (Guilbert 2004).

An unequivocal indicator of the existence of a wealthy noble class in the Where Rivers Meet area is provided by the discovery of a hoard of three gold torcs at Alrewas, just over the river from Borough Hill (Fig 6.19). This was a metal-detector find declared Treasure Trove in 1996. Torcs were neck rings – there are several depictions on statues and metalwork of warriors and even gods wearing them – and were clearly a symbol of status and power, both sacred and secular. They were made of a variety of materials – silver, bronze and even iron – but gold, as at Alrewas, was presumably reserved for the most important people. They were made in several ways, one of the most common being to twist together strands of gold wire in a rope-like fashion (the word 'torc' comes from the Latin *torquere*, to twist). This is the way that many of the fantastic torcs found in 1990 in a hoard at Snettisham, Norfolk, were made, and it was also the method used for the Alrewas torcs. Torcs do not form a complete circle, but the two ends of the 'rope' are twisted back to form terminals – sometimes elaborately decorated – so that their shape is penannular. This allowed them to be fitted around the neck, although this must often have been difficult and painful for the wearer; perhaps, like wedding rings, they were seldom taken off. The Alrewas torcs were damaged in antiquity, before their burial, and appear to be unfinished.

On stylistic grounds the Alrewas torcs can be dated from the late 2nd century BC to the 1st century AD, the last part of the Iron Age. This is the date of comparable torcs from elsewhere in Britain, for example the remarkable concentration around Snettisham in the territory of the Iceni tribe. Staffordshire can now also claim an important concentration of torc finds, with single examples having been found earlier at Glascote (Tamworth), also of course on the Tame, about 10km to the south of Alrewas, and at Needwood, a similar distance to the north (Fig 6.20).

In Britain, torcs are found not in graves but on their own, singly or in a hoard, deliberately buried in a hole in the ground; this is why they are most often found by metal-detectorists rather than during archaeological excavations. This may have been simply to hide them in times of trouble, the unfortunate individual

Figure 6.18 Plan of
possible hillfort at
Borough Hill

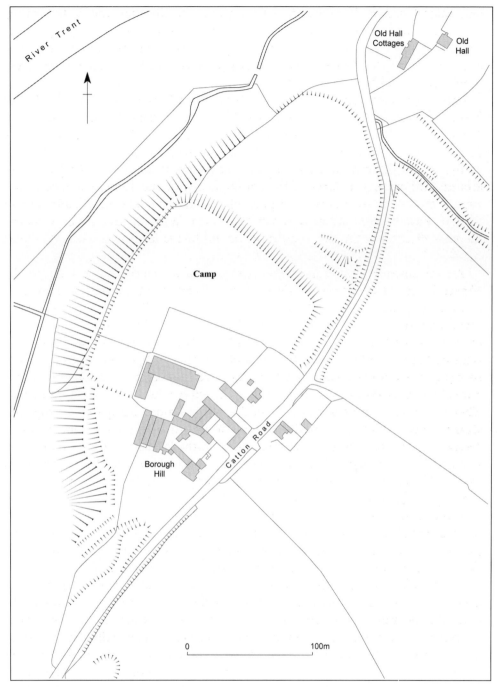

who hid them presumably not surviving to recover them. However, from what we now know about ritual deposition in the Bronze and Iron Ages, it is much more likely that they were buried as ritual offerings. Not infrequently the metalwork ritually deposited in rivers and other places was deliberately broken or bent,

Figure 6.19 The three Iron Age gold torcs from Alrewas Overall length: 310mm

perhaps symbolically 'sacrificed', and it is tempting to imagine that this might have been the case with the Alrewas torcs also.

At a stroke, the cluster of gold torcs from south-east Staffordshire make us rethink our impression of the Iron Age in the region, so sharply does it contrast with the image of simple farming communities gained from the excavations at Fisherwick and Whitemoor Haye. It stresses what we do not know about the

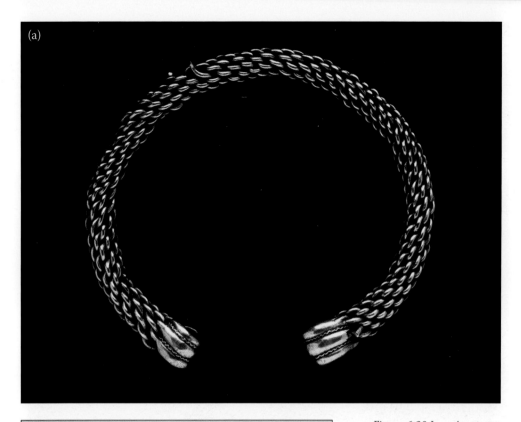

Figure 6.20 Iron Age torcs from (a) Glascote (Tamworth) and (b) Needwood

archaeology of the area, and how much more there is to be learned. If Borough Hill is correctly interpreted as an Iron Age hillfort, was it the local centre of tribal power, residence of the powerful men and women for whom skilled craftsmen made such finery as the Alrewas gold torcs? One implication of the existence of an elite – nobles, warriors and priests, and their followers, craftsmen, servants and slaves – is that they had to be fed and supported by the mass of the population, the farmers. As in all pre-industrial societies, the land and its produce – for the Celts, perhaps, particularly cattle – were the roots of wealth.

In this light we might see the farming families occupying simple farmsteads such as those excavated at Fisherwick or Whitemoor Haye as working not just to feed themselves, but also to produce a surplus, and provide other services, to support an elite. From this perspective, the intensification of farming, the formalisation of boundaries, and the laying out of fields and droveways, may be viewed as aspects of the development of an increasingly stratified society. It is not necessary to view the nobility as owning large estates, as in later periods of history. In the Iron Age the land may have been held communally by the tribe, or by subdivisions of the tribe, with grazing rights and plots for growing crops being allocated to families or individuals. It is not who owns the land but who takes possession of the surplus it produces that matters. All the indications are that during the Iron Age what is called an 'embedded economy' prevailed. This means that social and economic life were closely intertwined and that goods mainly changed hands not through impersonal buying and selling and taxation as today, but through the fulfilment of obligations of kinship, clientage and hospitality. The elite earned their status through feats of bravery in battle, through displays of their wealth (largely 'portable' wealth such as jewellery, elaborate weapons and armour, and cattle), through conspicuous consumption and largesse in feasting, through the giving and receiving of gifts, through their offerings to the gods and spirits, through arcane religious knowledge, and in other ways only partially familiar today.

Much of our knowledge of such things comes from the writings of classical authors about Celtic peoples as well as from archaeology. We know too from these sources that religion permeated every aspect of life, and the Celtic world was full of gods and spirits and forces, often inhabiting or associated with natural places, such as springs, lakes, rivers, caves and forests. The rites carried out at such places only occasionally leave an archaeological trace. There is even, as we have noted, a religious dimension to torcs, seen both in their depiction on images of gods and in their ritual deposition in pits. They must have possessed a potent, perhaps life-protecting, mystical force, and their deposition may have been accompanied by great ceremonial.

Torcs were the preserve of the elite; the common mass of people had no such offerings to make. However, archaeologists have begun to recognise what may be the ritual deposition of more everyday items, such as pots. We encountered one possible example of such 'structured deposition' earlier, when we noted the large chunks of pottery that had been disposed of, presumably deliberately, in pits of one of the pit-alignments, and associated pits nearby, at Whitemoor Haye. We suggested that this deposition was possibly associated with feasting (from the evidence of 'pot-boilers' found in several of the pits) but in the Celtic world 'feasting' and 'religion' are not disassociated activities. It is easy to dismiss such accounts and to come up with 'practical' alternatives but this is likely to be an anachronistic approach, from an age and society where religion has been set apart from everyday life; this was not the case in the Iron Age.

Something else that we noted earlier was the way in which, with very few exceptions, the doors of the Iron Age roundhouses faced eastwards. Perhaps this was just a practical measure, for protection against the prevailing winds, but it has been noted very widely throughout Britain and it may instead have been of religious and cosmological significance. The entrances face the rising sun (not, note, the sun at the warmest part of the day, in which case they would face south). There may be an association here with birth in the east and death in the west, and so, following this, a whole range of symbolic implications in the way that space was used in roundhouses. Again, this is easy to dismiss, but only if we take a modern, western view of things, where life, religion and the symbolism of architecture have ceased to be closely intertwined. We know, from countless studies of architecture in 'traditional' (what used to be called 'primitive') societies, that this is an unwise position to take.

The Alrewas torcs date to the late 2nd century BC–1st century AD, that is the closing stages of the Iron Age, when contact with the literate civilisations of the Mediterranean increased, culminating in the Roman invasion of Britain in AD 43. This late Iron Age period was a time of major change in the Iron Age societies of Britain, especially those of the south-east. The social inferences that can be drawn from the existence of these torcs cannot be projected back into the earlier stages of the Iron Age. Indeed, what we appear to be witnessing in the Where Rivers Meet area, as elsewhere in the Trent valley, is a long-term trend of intensification of use of the landscape, with increased woodland clearance, landscape division and organisation, and settlement from the middle Iron Age onwards. A real and substantial growth in population is probably signified. The stratified society that emerged towards the end of the Iron Age was a product of both this long-term trend and external factors, including the indirect impact of the growth of Roman power and influence.

An interesting feature to emerge from the study of the Iron Age pottery from both the Fisherwick and the Whitemoor Haye excavations is that obvious late Iron Age forms are rare. It is highly unlikely that the intensity of use of the landscape diminished and this may signify a reorganisation of settlement, with the farmsteads on the gravel terrace being abandoned as year-round settlements and the area increasingly given over to the rearing and management of stock. Occupation was now on a temporary basis, seasonal stock-herders huts perhaps, with the main focus of human settlement now relocated elsewhere, and currently undiscovered. This certainly appears to be the situation in the Roman period (see next chapter) but perhaps this change began earlier, in the late Iron Age. Without excavation, it is impossible to assess the role of the possible Iron Age hillfort at Borough Hill in such changes, but hillforts are frequently associated with a centralisation of settlement, together with providing a defended, centralised storage facility for the community.

Aspects of these changes are evidenced at the Iron Age enclosures excavated in Areas A, B and C at Whitemoor Haye. By the late Iron Age the enclosures in Areas B and C may have been abandoned completely, but the enclosure in Area A was modified, apparently for use by stock. Four large pits were dug into the silted-up ditch of the enclosure, and were recut on several occasions. The largest of these pits, dug into one of the entrance terminals of the old enclosure ditch, was evidently a watering hole for stock. This was clear from the analysis of the beetle remains found in the waterlogged basal deposit of the pit (Smith 2002). Few species associated with human occupation were present, but there were species associated with standing water, frequent species associated with rough and scuffed grassland, such as one would expect to find around a watering hole, and very large numbers of dung beetles.

The late Iron Age was, therefore, a time of change, although the precise nature of this change remains elusive in the study area. By the time of the Roman conquest, Britain was divided up into a number of major tribal groupings. The areas occupied by each tribe can be roughly reconstructed by scholars based on such sources as accounts of the Roman military campaigns and inscriptions of the Roman period. From such evidence it appears that the Where Rivers Meet area lay somewhere near the boundary between two of these tribal groupings, the Cornovii to the west and the Corieltauvi (or Coritani) to the east. Indeed, as a major natural boundary running approximately north–south, the Upper Trent and the Tame may well have formed the boundary between these two tribes. Such a boundary may have been very ancient, and this would again emphasise the importance of the Where Rivers Meet area as a meeting place of peoples.

CHAPTER SEVEN

The impact of Rome
(*c* AD 43–410)

Introduction

As we saw in the last chapter, Rome had an impact on the British tribes long before the invasion of AD 43. Naturally enough, this influence was felt most strongly amongst the tribal groupings of the south and east, those in closest proximity to Roman-occupied Gaul, which from after 100 BC minted their own coinage. In the north and west the influence was least felt, while the tribes of the Midlands, the Corieltauvi in the east (who also minted coins) and the Cornovii in the west (who did not), occupied an intermediate position, geographically and culturally (Fig 7.1). From Roman historical sources and from the coinage we know something of the power politics and personalities of the period between Julius Caesar's expeditions of 55 and 54 BC and the Claudian invasion of AD 43, in the south-east at least. These are dominated by the expansionist policies of the Catuvellauni, a tribe originally centred on what is now Hertfordshire, one of the southern neighbours of the Corieltauvi. From the very early years AD through to around AD 40 the High King of the Catuvellauni was a powerful and highly successful leader called Cunobelin, who ruled his kingdom from his capital at Camulodunum (Colchester), which he had captured from one of his eastern neighbours.

It is clear from both historical and archaeological evidence that in the early decades AD the British tribes of the south and east were engaged in significant trade and diplomatic relationships with the Roman Empire, as well as politicking and warfare amongst themselves. British exports included slaves and raw materials; imports included wine and other luxury goods. A 'treaty relationship' with Rome was one more card to play in a complex political game. Around AD 40 Cunobelin's expansionist ambitions culminated in the Catuvellauni over-running the territory of the Atrebates to the south, whose king, Verica, fled across the Channel to seek the support of the Roman Emperor, Claudius. This was the pretext for the Roman invasion of Britain in AD 43, although Claudius's need for a major conquest to enhance his prestige at home was probably more fundamental (modern analogies are not hard to find).

Such power politics and inter-tribal warfare will have affected the Corieltauvi and Cornovii, although we lack historical evidence. The slaves which were a major British export will have been mainly the captives of inter-tribal warfare and raiding, and in this context it is easy to imagine the Catuvellanuni, for example, turning their attention to the north and west. From this perspective the archaeological picture of quietly self-sufficient farming communities in the Where Rivers Meet area may be misleading and the apparent disruption and

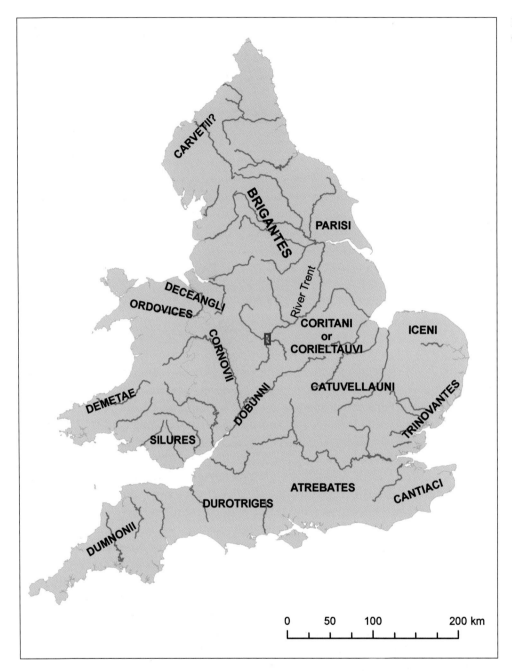

Figure 7.1 The tribes of Roman Britain

reorganisation of settlement in the late Iron Age may find some explanation. It is in this general period too that the burial of gold torcs at Alrewas, Glascote and Needwood took place and, whatever the circumstances of their deposition, they can perhaps be seen as a sign of troubled times. Both stylistically and as a phenomenon these torcs and their burial provide a link with the eastern neighbours of the Corieltauvi, the Iceni of Norfolk, also on the northern border of the Catuvellauni.

This rich mixture of tribal power politics and economic and diplomatic relations with Rome and her provinces provides the background and context for the Roman invasion of AD 43. Broadly speaking, tribes had the option of collaboration or resistance, although there were clearly differently minded factions within tribal groupings, and effective resistance would involve fragile alliances with rival tribes. Although Claudius himself led the Roman army into Camulodunum in AD 43 and accepted the surrender of eleven British kings, the Roman conquest was a drawn-out affair, with major setbacks such as the rebellion led by Queen Boudica of the Iceni in AD 60, and it wasn't until around AD 80 that the subjugation of Wales and northern England was completed.

The west Midlands played a pivotal role in both the Welsh campaigns and those into northern England, although few historical details are available and most inferences are based on archaeological evidence, principally the locations of fortifications of various types. The vast majority of 1st-century Roman forts are found in the west and north of the country and provide eloquent testimony both to the extent of resistance and to the subsequent need for military occupation. The south-east provides a very different picture.

Conquest and occupation

The response of the Corieltauvi and the Cornovii to the Roman invasion is not known, but if the distribution of temporary camps and later, more permanent, forts is a guide, then the Cornovii may have put up some resistance while the Corieltauvi acquiesced more easily. The Roman legions advanced into Cornovian territory in the late 40s. Whilst on campaign the army built temporary marching camps, but, once a territory was subdued, forts were established at strategic locations, linked by military roads. From the distribution of temporary camps and later forts it is clear that the main advance into Cornovian territory and on into Wales was along the line of what was to become Watling Street, which linked the provincial capital (initially Colchester and later London) with the legionary fortress at Wroxeter (Shropshire), established some time in the mid-50s.

A series of forts was built at regularly spaced intervals along Watling Street on the way to Wroxeter, and one of these was sited about 10km to the south-west of the Where Rivers Meet area at Wall (Letocetum – Fig 7.2). Just to the east of Wall, another road, almost certainly somewhat later than Watling Street, crossed Watling Street, following a roughly south-west–north-east route. This was Ryknield Street, which ran from the West Country to Yorkshire, and which, north-east of Wall, runs through the Where Rivers Meet area, its line now followed by the modern A38, heading for the fort at Littlechester. It is the most significant Roman feature in the study area.

The course of the road through the Where Rivers Meet area runs roughly parallel to the Tame past Whitemoor Haye, then crosses the Trent just upstream of its confluence with the Tame and follows the Trent valley on its north-eastern course past Catholme, Fatholme, Borough Hill and Tucklesholme towards Burton

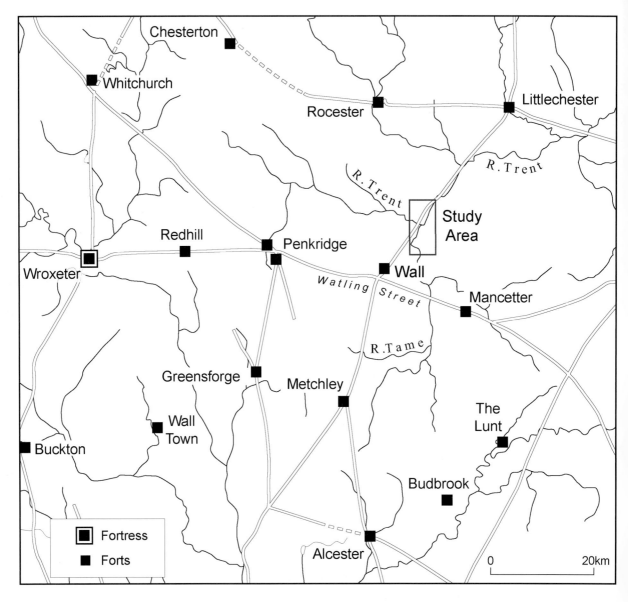

upon Trent. It passes within a kilometre or two of each of these sites, and its construction and use cannot but have had an impact on the inhabitants of the area.

Roman roads were built by the army for the military purposes of troop movement, communication and supply. The construction of these roads was a major engineering enterprise. Following survey, the route of the road and the land to either side was cleared of trees, bushes and other obstructions. Then a shallow trench was dug and filled with stone to form the foundation, which was generally capped with a layer of gravel. Drainage ditches were usually provided either side of the road and where necessary bridges were built to cross narrow streams.

Figure 7.2 The regional Roman period context to the Where Rivers Meet area, including roads and forts/towns

The construction of the road will have changed the character of the landscape of the Where Rivers Meet area and, as the major thoroughfare, perhaps replaced the ancient trackway, described in the previous chapter, which followed a roughly parallel course across what is now Whitemoor Haye quarry, closer to the river. This trackway did not go out of use, however, but (as will be described below) was renewed and itself provided with drainage ditches along its sides during the Roman period.

The generally accepted view is that a fort was established at Wall around AD 60 and that the original fort was large enough to house a large legionary vexillation (detachment) (Wardle 2003, 11). This fort appears to have been replaced by a second, smaller fort built at the same location in the last quarter of the 1st century, which was occupied up until the middle of the 2nd century, although the sequence of forts and the chronology is not clear (*ibid*). The existence of this fort, with its requirements for materials for construction and subsequently for maintenance and supply, must have had a profound effect on those living in the vicinity, especially those who lived in close proximity to the road system, such as in the Where Rivers Meet area. In addition to their primary military function, forts also acted as depots for locally gathered resources and for supplies brought in from further afield, as well as being centres for recruitment.

Towns and villas

It was very often the case in Roman Britain that places that started off as fortresses (for legions) or forts (for smaller army divisions) subsequently developed into towns. This is the case, for example, at the legionary fortress of Wroxeter (Viriconium), which became the tribal capital of the Cornovii under Roman rule, and it is the case also for all five of the small towns in Staffordshire, including Wall (Wardle 2003). The stimulus for the development of these towns was the needs of the garrisons in each fort, and they started off as informal settlements known as *vici* just outside the forts. Here would live traders, craftsmen and others who would help to supply both the official requirements of the garrison in terms of goods and services, and the individual needs of the soldiers. Here too would live the unofficial wives and families of the soldiers. Whether intentionally or not, these *vici* became a major force in the 'Romanisation' of the surrounding populace (but see below), and when the forts were eventually abandoned when the military need for them was over, the towns and their markets often survived, sometimes taking on local administrative functions.

The *vicus* at Wall was extensive, stretching along Watling Street for at least 1km, and included both industrial activity and high-status buildings, as revealed by numerous small-scale archaeological excavations and by metal-detector finds (Wardle 2003, 12). Two buildings are on public display today, one a bath house and the other a courtyard house, generally interpreted as a *mansio* (a guesthouse for travellers on official imperial business) (Fig 7.3). These date from the late 1st century through to the late 2nd or early 3rd century. There is also a large late Roman enclosure that is interpreted as one of a series of

Figure 7.3 The baths and *mansio* at Wall (Letocetum). The baths buildings and baths basilica are in the foreground, the *mansio* is behind, on the other side of the street

burgi, or strongholds, established along Watling Street in the late 3rd or 4th century. However, the overall plan and organisation of the *vicus* at Wall is not clear (*ibid*).

In addition to forts, roads and towns, the fourth archetypical monument of the Roman period is the villa. Villas were farms where the residence and other principal buildings were built in a Roman style of architecture, often including mosaics and ancillary buildings such as bath houses, although they vary in size from not much more than a cottage to the palatial. They are generally interpreted as the farms of the members of the native elite who had 'bought into' the Roman lifestyle, although the ownership of villas is very seldom known. Villas tend to cluster around the major towns, especially along the roads leading to and from them.

There are only seven definite villa sites in Staffordshire, three of which have been excavated to some extent, but the other four are readily identified from the quantities of characteristic building materials that have been collected during fieldwalking (Wardle 2003). A similarly sparse number has been identified in neighbouring Derbyshire (Taylor 2006) but there are probably more in both counties that have not been identified. All but one of the villas in Staffordshire are situated close to a Roman road (Wardle 2003, 18) and three of these are strung out to the west of Ryknield Street between Wall and the Where Rivers Meet area. One of the unexcavated villa sites, identified from the large quantity of finds, including tesserae (pieces from mosaics), recovered during fieldwalking, lies within the study area, just to the west of Barton-under-Needwood.

Rural life

It is against this background that the evidence for Roman period activity uncovered by excavation within the study area needs to be assessed. As for the Iron Age, the principal excavations have taken place at Fisherwick (Miles 1969; Smith 1979) and at Whitemoor Haye Quarry (Coates 2002; Hewson 2007). This means that it is possible to follow the development of the landscape from the Iron Age through into the Roman period. The description will progress from the southern extreme of the study area northwards.

The excavations at Fisherwick carried out in the 1970s (Smith 1979), and described in the previous chapter, produced very little in the way of Roman period material, just nine sherds of Romano-British pottery. This clearly indicates that the Iron Age settlement had been abandoned by the Roman period. However, the ditch of the main enclosure (SK 187082) was recut following abandonment, but only to a shallow depth and not apparently all the way round, with the base of a Romano-British vessel being found in the silting. Another stratified Romano-British sherd was found in an adjacent field boundary ditch. The excavator suggested that the former settlement enclosure was transformed into an arable field, taking advantage of enrichment of the soil that would have resulted from the muck associated with the former settlement (*ibid*, 22). It would appear, then, that although settlement had relocated by the Roman period, use was being made of the Iron Age field system for agricultural purposes.

Just under 2km to the north of this site there was a further complex of cropmarks at Fisherwick (SK 183098), which included a pentagonal enclosure attached on one side to a north–south track or droveway, and which was interpreted as a stock enclosure. It is undated, but the similarity to Roman period enclosures also attached to a trackway at Whitemoor Haye (described below) suggests a similar date for this Fisherwick example.

The trackway just mentioned at the Fisherwick site headed northwards towards a ford across the River Tame. Some 0.5km further north along the line of this trackway, shortly before reaching the ford, is the most northerly of the sites explored at Fisherwick, which was excavated in advance of quarrying in the 1960s (Miles 1969). This site (SK 185102) is rare amongst the Roman period sites in the Where Rivers Meet area in producing evidence of buildings.

The site comprises a series of D-shaped enclosures associated with further field boundaries and the track or droveway leading to the ford across the Tame (this ford last appears on maps in 1809). Within the enclosures was a series of huts, four of which were excavated. They seemed insubstantial affairs, marked by depressions, slight gullies and postholes (Fig 7.4). This and the general paucity of finds, principally Romano-British pottery of the 2nd to 3rd centuries AD, suggested to the excavator that the huts may have been only seasonally occupied. The layout of the enclosures indicated that the function of the site was stock rearing and control, possibly of cattle and horses. The excavator concluded that the 'evidence from [this site at] Fisherwick ... suggests a group of poor people, either slaves or nominal freemen, working on the land of a richer master' (Miles 1969, 11).

Moving northwards again, the landscape at Whitemoor Haye essentially forms a continuation of that at Fisherwick. Indeed the trackway just described may link up with the major north–south trackway identified at Whitemoor Haye, cutting off a meander loop of the Tame, which was perhaps forded at two places. The Whitemoor Haye trackway was described in the previous chapter, where it was noted that it formed the main focus for a number of Iron Age homesteads, none of which may have been very long lived, distributed along its length.

In the Roman period, probably around the end of the 1st century AD to judge from the pottery evidence, the trackway was provided with ditches, presumably principally for drainage, on either side. Several sections of this trackway have been examined during formal area excavations and watching briefs at the quarry since 1997. In the various excavated portions the shape and size of the ditches were found to be variable, there was sometimes evidence of recutting, and in places there was a double ditch to one side of the trackway. Such variation

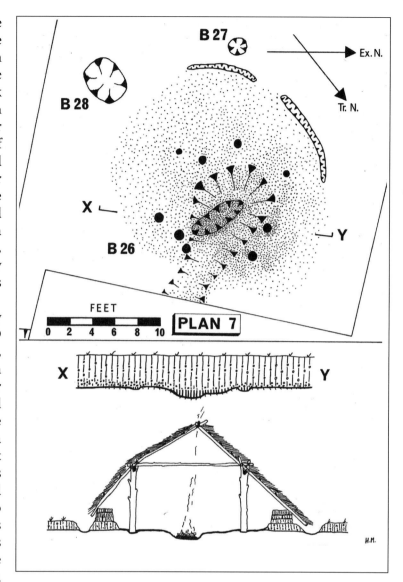

Figure 7.4 Plan and reconstruction of a hut at the Fisherwick Roman site

simply suggests that the ditches were renewed and maintained in an *ad hoc* fashion over a long period, perhaps up to the late 3rd century, again judging from the pottery evidence (Coates 2002; Hewson 2007).

Roman period enclosures are strung along the trackway in a similar fashion to the Iron Age enclosures, and in at least two cases were remodelled versions of the Iron Age enclosures (Fig 7.5). There are two principal differences, however. The first is that more of the Roman period enclosures are directly attached to the trackway, such that one side of the enclosure corresponds with a stretch of the trackway. The second is that structural evidence of buildings is absent, although generally very small quantities of Roman pottery suggest occupation of some sort, perhaps only short lived or seasonal.

Some of the Roman period enclosures along the trackway may be briefly

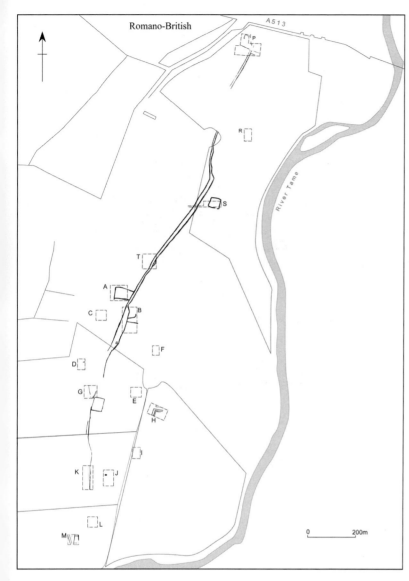

Romano-British

A513

River Tame

R

S

T

A

C

B

P

F

D

G

E

H

I

K

J

L

M

0   200m

Figure 7.5 Overall plan of Roman period trackways and enclosures at Whitemoor Haye

described, from south to north. In Area M, near the southern end of the quarry concession at Whitemoor Haye, a rectilinear Iron Age enclosure ditch was partially cleared out with a shallow U-shaped recut, the silting of which contained a few sherds of Romano-British pottery (Hewson 2007). This recalls the course of events at the main Iron Age enclosure at Fisherwick, mentioned above.

Further north, just to the south of Area G, a complete rectangular enclosure, measuring about 53m by 42m, was excavated during a watching brief in 2002 (*ibid*). It seems to have been laid out *de novo* hard against the east side of the trackway in either the late Iron Age or Roman period. The V-shaped ditch, up to 1.6m wide by 0.9m deep, was waterlogged and had been recut on one occasion. Finds were restricted to two abraded sherds of late Iron Age pottery, indicating that it was not a settlement enclosure but served some other function, probably as a stock enclosure.

Further north again, an enclosure of similar proportions was attached to the west side of the trackway in Area A. The Iron Age farmstead enclosure in Area A, one of the best preserved at Whitemoor Haye, was described in the previous chapter, and contained four roundhouses, interpreted as a succession of two pairs of two. A late phase in the use of this enclosure, after it had been abandoned as a settlement, was marked by the digging of four large pits into the enclosure ditch (see Fig 6.16). The largest of these pits was interpreted as a watering hole for stock (as the others may have been), an interpretation strongly supported by beetle evidence from the primary fill of the pit, which had been recut on no fewer than five occasions. The final silting of this pit contained a sherd of Romano-British pottery, suggesting use into the Roman period (Coates 2002, 27). In the Roman period this enclosure, its ditches now largely silted up, was apparently remodelled by the addition of new ditches to connect it up with the trackway. A small assemblage of sixteen sherds of Roman pottery, dating to the mid-2nd century AD, provides an approximate date for this remodelling, but the small quantity of pottery argues against domestic occupation, and the primary function of the enclosure at this time was probably the management of stock.

Northwards once more, in Area S, was another rectilinear enclosure of Roman period date. This differed from the enclosures thus far described in being detached from the trackway, but its eastern and western sides were laid out parallel to it. An interesting feature of this enclosure is that it overlay the roughly east–west-orientated Iron Age double pit-alignment which ran through Area S (see previous chapter – Fig 6.5). Thus it clearly did not 'respect' this ancient boundary, which ran across the southern part of the enclosure, and which had presumably fallen into oblivion by this time (it would have been at least several centuries old). Nevertheless, the layout of the enclosure precisely follows the orientation of the earlier pit-alignment and, even more remarkable, subsequent medieval plough furrows (exposed during the excavation) precisely follow the orientation of the enclosure. This indicates that however much structures and features of particular periods may come and go, the basic 'grain' of the landscape is preserved over millennia, a strong indication of a fundamental continuity in the evolution of the landscape. A small assemblage of 76 sherds of Romano-British pottery was recovered from the (few) excavated sections of the enclosure ditch and associated features, suggesting a broadly late 2nd-century date.

Finally, in pursuit of the trackway and its associated enclosures northwards, mention may be made of rescue excavations in advance of quarrying that were undertaken by the Trent Valley Archaeological Research Committee in 1974, although they have only been published in summary note form (O'Brien 1974). The site was located in what is now the National Memorial Arboretum, immediately to the east of Alrewas and north of Whitemoor Haye Quarry. Aerial photographs showed cropmarks of a number of enclosures here, covering an area of c 2ha. Sections of the ditches of some of these enclosures were excavated, and foundation trenches and postholes were also uncovered, the pottery suggesting a 2nd- to 3rd-century AD date. As the precise location of these enclosures lies along the projected route of the trackway, and there are cropmarks suggestive of a trackway leading up to them, it is possible that this site forms part of the same system recorded more fully at Whitemoor Haye.

Overall, then, a string of enclosures connected by a north–south trackway or trackways can be identified running along the western terrace of the River Tame for a distance of c 5km, from Fisherwick to the confluence of the Tame with the Trent. A significant proportion of these enclosures has been sampled by excavation, and the dating evidence, provided by Romano-British pottery types, suggests a consistent date-range from the late 1st century through to the early 3rd century, with the majority of the material datable to the 2nd century.

The enclosures and the trackway have all the appearance of a coherent 'system', which was perhaps only in use for a fairly limited period, devoted to the breeding, corralling and movement of stock, presumably principally cattle and horses, which were probably pastured on the adjacent land. Evidence of human habitation is slight, most enclosures producing no structural evidence for buildings, and where there was some such evidence, as at Fisherwick, nothing more is implied than insubstantial huts. Most telling is the very small quantity of pottery involved. For example, the whole of the Whitemoor Haye excavations from 1997 to 2004 produced only 642 sherds of Roman period pottery from the trackway and associated enclosures (Hancocks 2002, 53; Evans 2007). This is a very small quantity for Romano-British sites, and can imply little more than occasional, temporary occupation; the enclosures were for animals not people. Moreover, the pottery is overwhelmingly utilitarian in character, dominated by types associated with food preparation (mortaria, cooking pots, bowls) and storage (jars) (Hancocks 2002, 58) (Fig 7.6, 1–17). Imported fine tableware is represented by just sixteen sherds of samian (Fig 7.6, 18–20).

It is quite possible that this 'system' of what seems to be intensive and organised animal husbandry was geared mainly to meeting the needs of the fort and associated *vicus* established at Wall, just 10km (or a couple of hours' walk) away down the new road. Those who actually tended and herded the stock were evidently of the lowest social stratum, but whether they worked for themselves or, as Miles (1969, 11) suggested, they were 'slaves or nominal freemen, working on the land of a richer master', cannot be determined. The latter seems the more probable. Hints of where the richer class lived, if not in the *vicus* at Wall, is provided by the evidence for three (unexcavated) villa sites strung along the road from Wall to the Trent crossing, one of these in the study area. These may have been the residences of members of the native British elite, whose existence in the late Iron Age is so dramatically suggested by the Alrewas gold torcs described in the previous chapter. Alternatively, good farm land like that in the Where Rivers Meet area, close to a road, may have been allocated to Roman army veterans from nearby Wall (Coates and Woodward 2002, 87).

Whatever the case, it is clear from the excavations that the trackways and enclosures were not laid out *de novo* in the Roman period but developed from the system already in place by the middle Iron Age. What we appear to be witnessing is an intensification of stock-rearing activity, perhaps in fact beginning in the late Iron Age, accompanied by a shift in the location of settlement, although perhaps only a slight local shift.

A clue to where those who actually worked the land lived during the Roman period is provided by one of the most recent excavations to be carried out at Whitemoor Haye, in Area H (Hewson 2007). Here, only *c* 250m east of the trackway, towards the river, aerial photography revealed cropmarks of what seems to be a large triple-ditched rectilinear enclosure (Fig 7.7). Only part of the western side of this enclosure was visible as a cropmark, the majority of the enclosure being buried by alluvial silt deposited by river floods some time after it had gone out of use.

Unfortunately, the excavations were restricted to the north-west corner of the enclosure, encompassing just the three ditches and a very small part of the interior. The ditches of the enclosure were not particularly substantial, conforming to the

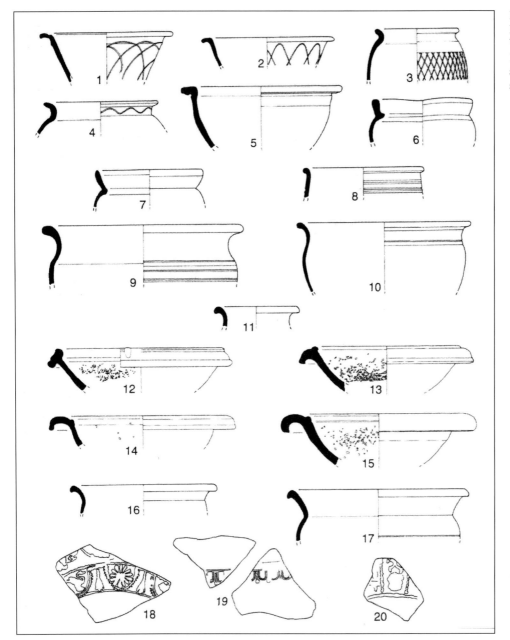

Figure 7.6 Romano-British pottery from Whitemoor Haye: 1–17, coarsewares and mortaria; 18–20, samian

general range of width and depth found at the other enclosures at Whitemoor Haye. It could not be ascertained whether the three ditches were contemporary – which would make the enclosure very distinctive in this landscape – or whether they had been excavated in a sequence, perhaps progressively enlarging the enclosure over the period of its use. What is most striking about the excavation in Area H, however, is that even though only a few short segments of the ditches were excavated, an assemblage of 1015 sherds of pottery were recovered, over 700 of these coming from just one, 1m long, excavated segment of the inner ditch (Evans 2007). This is more Roman period pottery than from the rest of the excavations at Whitemoor Haye and Fisherwick put together, and clearly suggests domestic occupation. The pottery assemblage, dating to the mid-2nd century, was dominated by utilitarian forms, principally storage jars and cooking vessels of regional manufacture, although amphorae (for oil) and a samian cup were also present.

The very limited excavation of the triple-ditched enclosure in Area H raises the possibility that the principal focus of settlement in the Roman period (and perhaps earlier) lay closer to the river than those parts of the landscape that have received the most attention from excavation, primarily due to the presence

Figure 7.7 Roman period triple-ditched enclosure at Whitemoor Haye Area H

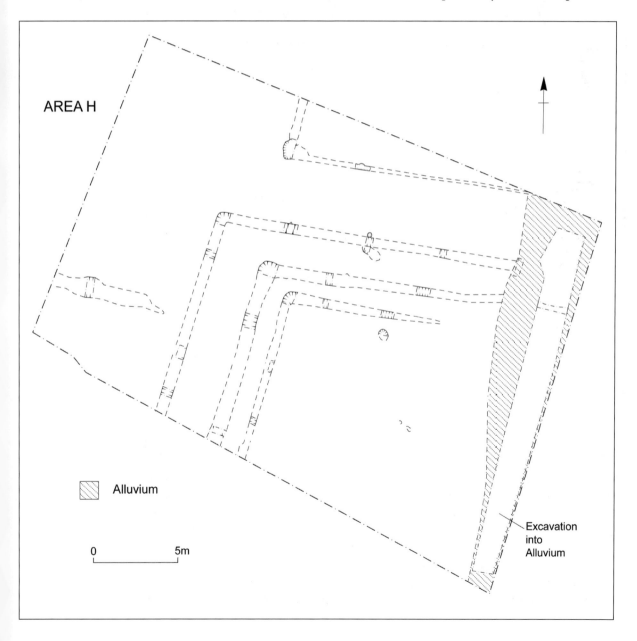

AREA H

Alluvium

0   5m

Excavation into Alluvium

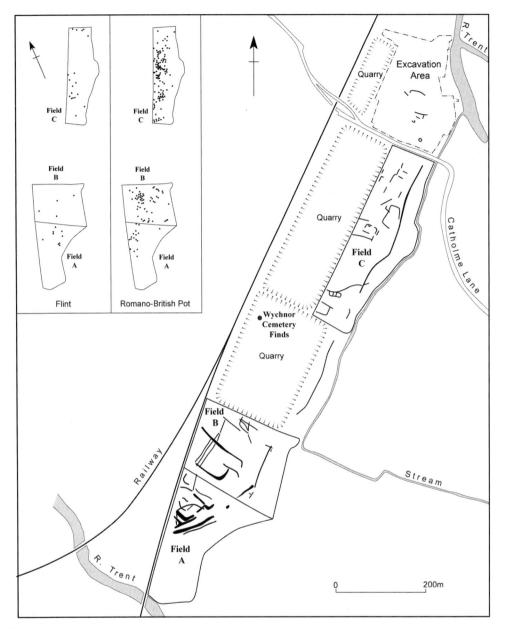

Figure 7.8 Cropmarks and distribution of flint and pottery recovered by fieldwalking to the south of the excavated area of the Anglo-Saxon settlement at Catholme. The approximate location of the Wychnor Cemetery finds is also shown

of cropmarks. However, the strip of land closest to the river has been covered by a deposit of fine silt alluvium from river floods, which both masks the ditches and other features that would otherwise produce cropmarks and makes excavation much more difficult. On the positive side, the alluvium provides a protective blanket so that archaeological remains may be better preserved, with the possibility of waterlogging. This is a challenge for the future: at the time of writing, sand and gravel extraction at Whitemoor Haye Quarry has not extended substantially into the alluviated zone.

Study of the cropmarks revealed by aerial photography indicates that the triple-ditched enclosure was not an isolated feature. There are other enclosures and features nearby which can be seen disappearing under the alluvium. These include a single-ditched rectilinear enclosure immediately to the north of the triple-ditched enclosure and sharing an alignment with it (the south-west corner of this enclosure was also sampled in the Area H excavations, and the small assemblage of pottery recovered suggested a similar date). Further east towards the river, in the alluvial zone, an apparently isolated length of ditch with an attached enclosure may be sited on a gravel ridge.

A suggestion of something similar is found further north at Catholme, close to the Anglo-Saxon settlement to be described in the following chapter, which is also situated at the edge of the alluvium. Here, in three fields to the south-west of the Anglo-Saxon settlement, cropmarks have been recorded running along the edge of the alluvium, and comprise enclosures and possible trackways morphologically typical of the Iron Age and Roman periods. They are bounded on their eastern side by a major linear boundary running along the top of the terrace-edge slope, which was partially excavated and turned out to have a very long life, being remodelled on at least six occasions (see previous chapter). These fields were fieldwalked as part of the Catholme investigations and a substantial quantity of Romano-British pottery, 209 sherds, was recovered, mainly from the field immediately to the south of the Anglo-Saxon settlement (Losco-Bradley and Kinsley 2002; Leary 2002) (Fig 7.8). The pottery ranged in date from the 1st to the 4th century, but was mainly of the 3rd and 4th centuries (Leary 2002, 21). A concentration such as this is strongly suggestive of settlement on the terrace edge, which may have been a favoured location.

The late Roman period

The date of the Romano-British pottery from Catholme raises an interesting question because elsewhere in the Where Rivers Meet area, at both Whitemoor Haye and Fisherwick, the pottery recovered dates from the late 1st century through to the mid-3rd century at the latest, with the bulk of material considered to be 2nd-century, and 4th-century pottery conspicuous by its absence. Given the extent of the excavations that have taken place at Whitemoor Haye, this strongly suggests that the landscape we have described – principally the track or droveway with its associated stock enclosures but including the probable settlement associated with the triple-ditched enclosure in Area H – belongs only to the earlier part of the Roman period. This, in turn, may be seen to support the association of the intensive use of the landscape for stock rearing with the military presence at Wall, which appears to date from the mid-1st century through to the mid-2nd century. After that, from the 3rd century into the 4th century, we have a gap in our record and no indication, with the exception of the hint provided by the Catholme fieldwalking results, of what form settlement took or how the landscape was exploited.

This is part of a more general phenomenon noted throughout Staffordshire.

In a recent survey of the Roman period archaeology of the county it is noted that 'in general excavation on the county's *vici* and villas tends to suggest that activity began in the latter half of the 1st century, and reached a peak in the middle or latter half of the 2nd century' (Wardle 2003, 25). It is highly improbable that there was a major population crash, so some other explanation must be sought, one related to changes in settlement patterns, lifestyle, material culture and perhaps cultural attitudes.

It has long been recognised that the archaeology and history of Roman Britain falls into two broad periods, an earlier period from the invasion in AD 43 to around the end of the 2nd century and a later period comprising the 3rd, 4th and early 5th centuries (see eg Esmonde Cleary 1999). In terms of the broader Roman Empire, what separates these two periods is an interval of about 50 years in the middle of the 3rd century – often termed the '3rd-century crisis' – which saw major political and military upheavals, such that the empire appeared at times on the verge of collapse. These upheavals included new and more potent barbarian incursions on the empire's border; huge political instability marked by intrigue, assassination and civil war, with a string of short-lived emperors and usurpers temporarily holding sway over this or that part of the empire; and financial turmoil.

These broader events affected Britain also, which faced raids from the northern tribes beyond Hadrian's Wall and seaborne piracy and raiding from Saxons and others along its coasts. Indeed, towards the end of the 3rd century the man appointed to protect the Channel coast from raiding (Marcus Aurelius Carausius) seized control of Britain and, for a period of around a decade, Britain, together with part of northern Gaul, formed an independent kingdom that had to be recovered by force. The net effect of these upheavals was that the Roman Empire and Roman Britain in AD 300 were very different places – socially, politically, militarily and culturally – than they had been in AD 200.

Although the change is clear enough, it is difficult to characterise the differences between early and late Roman Britain. In both periods there were fundamental differences between the south and east of the country, on the one hand, and the north and west on the other, with our area lying at the divide. Indeed by AD 312 Britain had been divided into four provinces that to some extent reflected these differences. In the early period the Roman army was a dominant presence in the north and west, and much of the 'Romanisation' of the native population seems to have been either directly or indirectly stimulated by the military presence. Thus we have seen how all five 'small towns' in Staffordshire, including Wall, developed as *vici* associated with forts of the Roman army, while the handful of known villa sites in the county are closely related to the road system. A coarse assessment of 'Roman find-spots' shows notable concentrations around the forts/*vici*, especially Wall (Wardle 2003, 23–4).

'Romanisation' is, however, a slippery and perhaps misleading concept. Archaeologically, other than the development of towns and villas, 'Romanisation' is primarily recognised through the presence of items of Romano-British material culture, mainly pottery, on native settlements that are otherwise essentially indistinguishable from their Iron Age predecessors (and possibly their post-Roman successors also). This indicates engagement in aspects of a market economy stimulated by the Roman invaders. Thus in the Where Rivers Meet area, for example, during the Iron Age most of the pottery used was probably locally produced, with the main evidence of participation in wider trade/exchange networks being provided by salt containers (briquetage) from the Cheshire Plain and Millstone Grit quernstones from Derbyshire. These networks, insofar as they are archaeologically visible, are only regional in scale. By the early Roman period however, and peaking in the 2nd century, we witness the use of pottery, presumably bought at markets such as that which would have existed at Wall, obtained through trade networks operating at the regional, provincial and inter-provincial levels. The large (in a local context) assemblage of Romano-British pottery from the probable settlement associated with the triple-ditched enclosure at Whitemoor Haye can be taken as typical in this respect. The majority of the pottery, *c* 86%, was probably produced fairly locally, including Derbyshire coarsewares, but the remainder came from further afield (Evans 2007). This included mortaria (grinding bowls) from the Mancetter-Hartshill potteries, just a short way south-east down Watling Street, and 'Black-Burnished' ware from south-east Dorset. Imported wares accounted for *c* 5% of the assemblage and included two sherds of amphora (of a type used to transport olive oil) from southern Spain and fragments of a samian (fine tableware) cup from central Gaul.

The question is, to what extent does the use of new types of marketed pottery indicate that people had become 'Romanised' in any meaningful sense? This, and the limited adoption of Roman coinage (although none has been found on the excavations in the study area and only five chance finds are recorded in the Historic Environment Record), need represent no more than a relatively temporary, in part imposed and ultimately perhaps superficial, adjustment to a new political and economic order. Culturally, and deeper down, the changes may have been less profound. Thus, when the stimulus provided by a substantial military presence was removed, insufficient momentum had developed for 'Romanisation' to have taken root. Social, cultural and economic development took a different path, in part showing continuity from the past and in part an adaptation – but a distinctive local or regional one – to the realities of living within a province of the Roman Empire.

The Roman period landscape extensively excavated at Fisherwick and Whitemoor Haye, and sampled on a smaller scale to the north of the confluence of the Tame and the Trent, may therefore represent a relatively short-term response to the huge demand of the Roman army for, particularly, meat and leather. Once this stimulus was removed, the landscape and its people disappear from archaeological view, at least at the current state of knowledge, for several centuries until they re-emerge in the Anglo-Saxon period, explored in the next chapter.

It is important to stress that this picture cannot be generalised to other parts of Roman Britain. In many senses and in many parts of the country, notably the south and east, the 4th century AD was the 'golden age' of Roman Britain, marked particularly by a revival of villa construction in the countryside, not infrequently on a lavish scale. Different regions and peoples responded differently to what is sometimes described as the 'Roman interlude' and it is only through studies of the type attempted in the Where Rivers Meet area that these regional patterns can begin to be understood. At present, however, this study has highlighted as much what we do not know as what we know – for example, about developments in the late Roman period – and points to some of the directions that need to be taken in future research.

CHAPTER EIGHT

The Anglo-Saxon legacy
(*c* AD 410–900)

The end of Roman Britain and the Anglo-Saxons

The end of Roman Britain is a complex issue that cannot be separated from the wider history of the Roman Empire. It is sufficient to say here that the closing years of the 4th century and the opening years of the 5th were a time of great turmoil, with increasing barbarian incursions across the frontiers of the empire, in Britain as more widely. Although Britain was suffering attacks from Saxons and other barbarians, troops had to be withdrawn from Britain to defend Italy itself. The situation was complicated by revolts and usurpations against the 'legitimate' government of the empire led from Britain. In AD 410 the Emperor Honorius apparently turned down an appeal for help from Britain and ordered the Britons to arrange for their own defences. This event (although the historical source is ambiguous) is generally taken to mark the political and administrative end of Roman Britain as part of the empire. Of course, life did not change overnight as a consequence, but the political and administrative 'end' must have entailed an economic 'end' as the imperial fiscal system broke down, leading to a military 'end' as the means to pay and supply the remaining troops disappeared (Esmonde Cleary 1999, 173). An end to the general use of Roman-style material culture followed within a generation, by the middle of the 5th century.

In essence, Roman Britain eventually fell apart into numerous small kingdoms, some (especially in the north and west) led by indigenous war lords and some (especially in the south-east) led by invaders. The principal invaders were the Angles and Saxons from Germany, who began to settle parts of eastern and southern Britain around the middle of the 5th century and to develop their own petty kingdoms. By this time Britain had been officially Christian for more than a century but the early Anglo-Saxons were pagans. Archaeologically, the spread and influence of the Anglo-Saxons is best seen through the distribution of their pagan cemeteries (Fig 8.1). These comprise either cremations in distinctive urns, inhumations in graves, or both (with chronological and regional variation, inhumation replacing cremation everywhere *c* AD 600). Men were buried with weapons and women with brooches and necklaces. In the east, including the east Midlands (the 'Anglian' region), the women favoured cruciform brooches, while in the south (the 'Saxon' region) round brooches were preferred.

Although there are problems of interpretation, the overall extent of early Anglo-Saxon settlement is provided by the distribution of these typical burials. Barring the occasional outlier, the stretch of the Middle Trent from Catholme to Burton marks the western limit of their distribution in the Midlands, with an

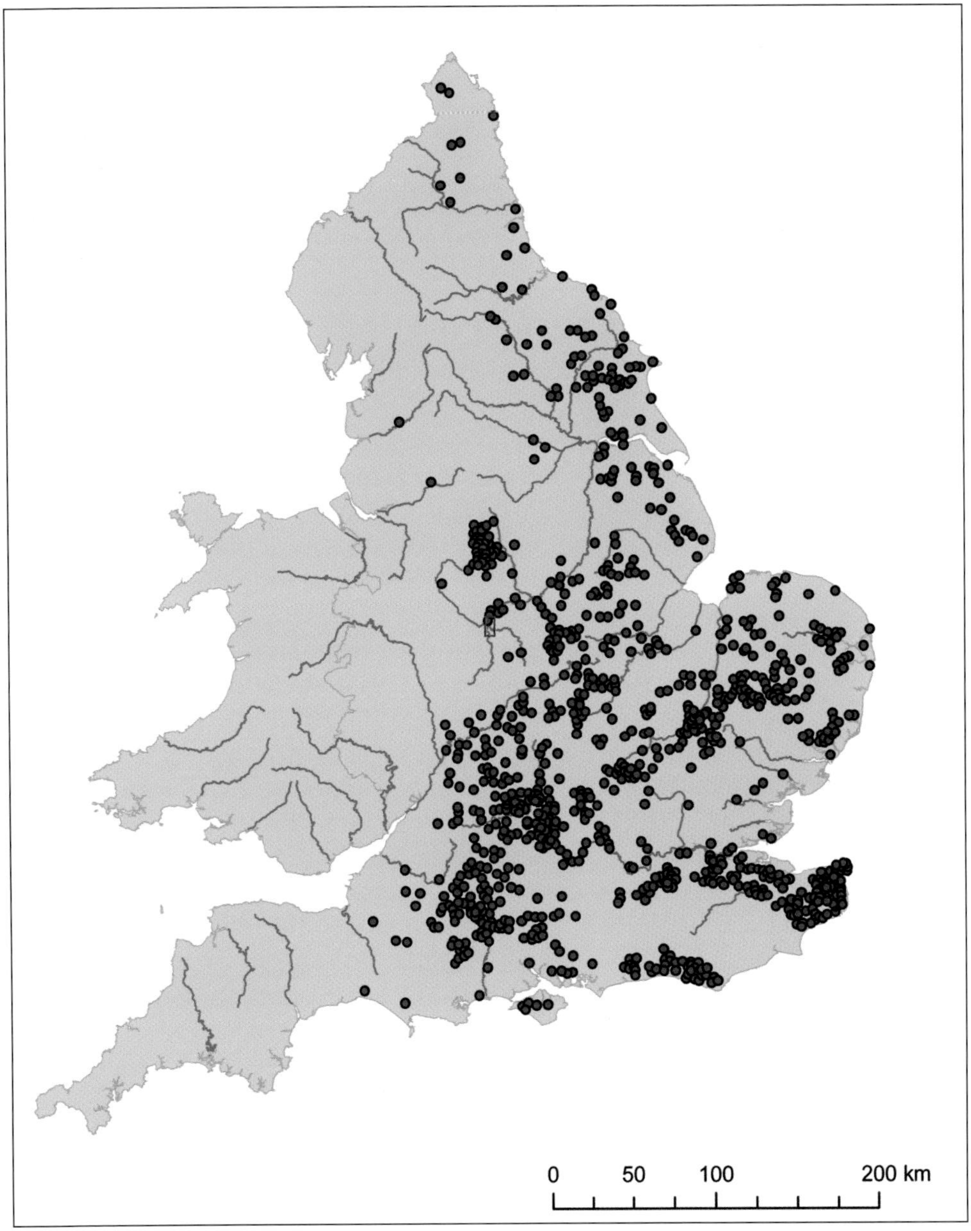

Figure 8.1
Distribution of
Anglo-Saxon
cemeteries in
England

important grouping of (later) barrow burials to the north in the Peak District. Thus the Where Rivers Meet area emerges once again as lying at a significant boundary, this time between 'Anglo-Saxon' lands to the east and 'British' lands to the west (recalling the division between the Corieltauvi and the Cornovii in the Iron Age and Roman periods). The inverted commas are needed, however, because the Germanic origins of all those buried in 'Anglo-Saxon' graves cannot be automatically assumed and, more importantly, because the existence of such graves cannot be taken to indicate the ethnic origins and orientation of the majority of the population in a given area, especially in a boundary zone such as the one we are concerned with here. These are issues we will consider later, but first the Anglo-Saxon remains from the study area need to be described.

The Tucklesholme and Wychnor Anglo-Saxon cemeteries

Two Anglo-Saxon cemeteries have been discovered in the Where Rivers Meet area. Both were uncovered during quarrying in the 19th century and our knowledge of both is scanty. The first was found in 1851 near Tucklesholme Farm in the north of the area, close to Ryknield Street, during the digging of a ballast pit in a field containing a mound. From the sketchy description it seems that cremations and possibly inhumations were uncovered; many urns containing human bones are mentioned, and knives and 'weapons' were also found (Losco-Bradley and Kinsley 2002, 3). All this material has since been lost.

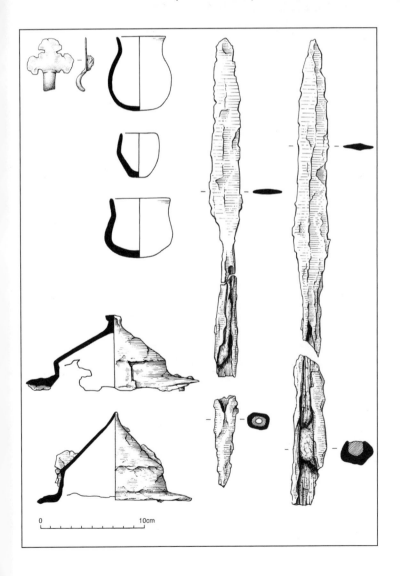

Figure 8.3 The gilded cruciform brooch from the Anglo-Saxon cemetery at Wychnor

Figure 8.2 Finds from the Anglo-Saxon cemetery at Wychnor. Clockwise from top left: headplate and bow of a copper-alloy small-long brooch; three small pottery vessels; two iron spears; two iron shield bosses

Rather more is known about the second cemetery, which was found at Wychnor during the digging of a sand pit in 1899, and was located immediately to the south-west of the Catholme Anglo-Saxon settlement excavated in the 1970s (described below). Further finds were made in the same pit at an unknown date after the initial discovery and again in 1926. The extant finds have now been catalogued, described and illustrated (Kinsley 2002) (Figs 8.2 and 8.3). They comprise six iron spearheads, five iron shield-bosses, three small pottery vessels, the fragmentary remains of a wooden bucket, and the headplate and bow of a bronze trefoil-headed 'short-long' brooch. The most important item, however, found in 1926 in association with part of a human jaw, is a 'florid' gilded bronze cruciform brooch, decorated with highly stylised animal ornament (known as 'Style I'), characterised by disjointed heads and limbs of animal- and human-like figures (Fig 8.3). Other finds, now missing, included further urns, iron knives and an iron buckle. The 'urns', which did not contain bones, are clearly accessory vessels with inhumation burials rather than cremation urns. Given the varied dates and locations within the sand pit at which the finds were made, this was evidently an extensive inhumation cemetery, typically Anglo-Saxon, containing both male and female burials, as indicated by the weapons and brooches respectively. Based on the typology of the finds the cemetery can be dated to the 6th, possibly into the early 7th, century (*ibid*).

The Catholme Anglo-Saxon settlement

In England as a whole, pagan Anglo-Saxon burials are numerous and more than 1500 have been investigated in whole or in part, although to very variable standards, dating from the early 5th century to the early 8th century (Campbell 1982, 27). In sharp contrast to this, relatively few Anglo-Saxon settlements have been located and fewer than ten have been excavated on a large scale. In large measure this is because settlements are much more difficult to locate and recognise. Unlike graves, the settlements do not produce large amounts of jewellery, weapons and intact pots, so they can easily escape attention. The remains of the buildings largely comprise postholes and beamslots, too insubstantial to produce cropmarks and usually only recognisable in the context of formal archaeological excavation. Furthermore, the principal category of find, handmade pottery, is much more difficult to recognise than, say, Romano-British ceramics, and is more fragile and readily destroyed in the soil. In short, unlike a grave, there is little that will catch the attention of the farmer or quarryman, and unlike the ring-ditch of a barrow, say, such settlements do not produce diagnostic cropmarks which will be easily recognised by the aerial archaeologist.

The one feature typical of Anglo-Saxon settlements that may produce a potentially 'diagnostic' cropmark is the *Grubenhaus*. This German term translates as 'pit house', denoting the rectangular sunken floor that is the defining feature of these small buildings. In 1973 the Trent Valley Archaeological Research Committee decided to investigate one of three large pit-like marks at Catholme, which looked like they might be *Grubenhäuser*, located in an area threatened by quarrying (Salisbury 2002, xi). Stuart Losco-Bradley excavated a trial trench across one of the potential *Grubenhäuser* and indeed it turned out to be a Saxon sunken-floored building. Given the rarity of Anglo-Saxon settlements and therefore their importance, a campaign of archaeological rescue excavations, led by Stuart Losco-Bradley, was carried out from 1973 through to 1980, uncovering no fewer than 65 buildings together with trackways and enclosures (Fig 8.4). However, more than a bit of good luck was shown to be involved in the initial trial excavation because the other two cropmarks interpreted as potential *Grubenhäuser* turned out to be periglacial features (that is features caused by

Figure 8.4 Overall plan of the Catholme Anglo-Saxon settlement

Houses

0   50m

repeated freezing and thawing of the gravel during the Ice Age). Had one of these been the chosen for the trial excavation the Anglo-Saxon settlement at Catholme might never have been discovered.

The Catholme Anglo-Saxon settlement is important both because such sites are rare and because it is one of only a handful to have been extensively excavated. A full report on these excavations has been produced (Losco-Bradley and Kinsley 2002) and only a brief summary of the findings, based almost entirely on the published report, is necessary here.

The settlement was long-lived. Diagnostic, closely datable finds were scarce on the excavation, so that dating the settlement had to be based on a combination of radiocarbon dating and stratigraphic inference. This indicated that the settlement was in use from at least the early 7th century through to the late 9th century. It may well have begun earlier; the presumably associated cemetery at Wychnor to the south is probably 6th-century in date, and handmade Saxon pottery was found during fieldwalking between the excavated area of the settlement and the cemetery. This suggests that the settlement extended south of the excavated area and here, adjacent to the cemetery, may have been the location of the earliest phase of the settlement. Indeed this field also produced substantial quantities of 3rd- to 4th-century Romano-British pottery (see previous chapter). To explain the totality of the evidence the excavators developed a model of continuity and migrating settlement, moving slowly north-westwards along the terrace edge over the centuries. Such evidence includes the long life of the terrace-edge boundary, which seems to have been first laid out in the Iron Age but to have been maintained and redefined in different ways through to the Saxon period (see also Chapter 6). If correctly interpreted, such evidence of continuity has potential implications for answering the question as to who built the settlement, native or intruder; this issue will be pursued later.

Although 65 buildings were identified within the excavated area of the Catholme settlement, the long life of the settlement means that only a few of these will have been in contemporary use. This was demonstrable in several instances where the plans of buildings overlapped. Unfortunately, there are too few such stratigraphic relationships to provide secure phasing of the settlement as a whole (eg to produce plans of 'early', 'middle' and 'late' phases of the settlement). This was attempted in a preliminary report (Losco-Bradley and Wheeler 1984) but in the final report (Losco-Bradley and Kinsley 2002) it was decided to err on the side of caution, and no general site phasing was offered.

Nevertheless, a feature of the layout of the site is that it comprises apparent groups of buildings, some of which lie within distinct ditched enclosures. It may be imagined that such groups represent individual households or families, each household comprising a dwelling and associated ancillary structures such as barns, storehouses, workshops and so forth. On each 'ancestral plot' these buildings would be replaced over time as required. If we take this view, there might have been only half a dozen or so households represented within the excavated area at any one time, so we are dealing with a small village. The most long-lived features of the settlement were ditched trackways, which were probably used for stock control, several of these converging on the terrace edge where cattle may have been led for watering.

The buildings uncovered at Catholme fell into two broad types, 'wall-post buildings', which were the most numerous, and *Grubenhäuser* (Figs 8.5 and 8.6).

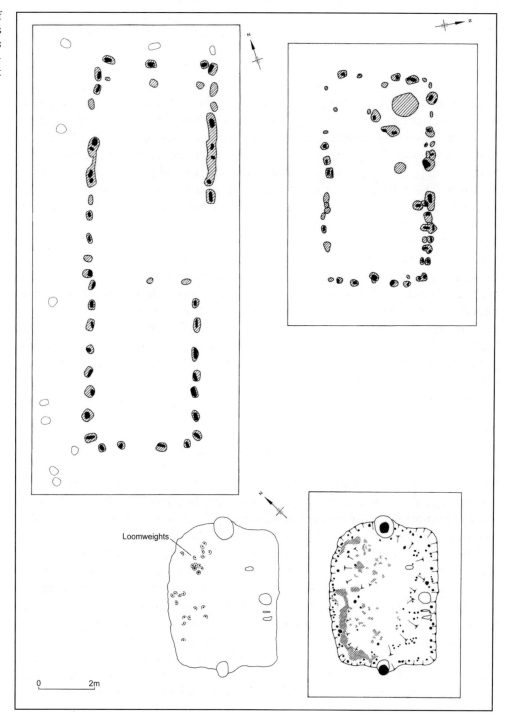

Figure 8.5 Plans of wall-post buildings and a *Grubenhaus* at Catholme Anglo-Saxon settlement

Loomweights

0   2m

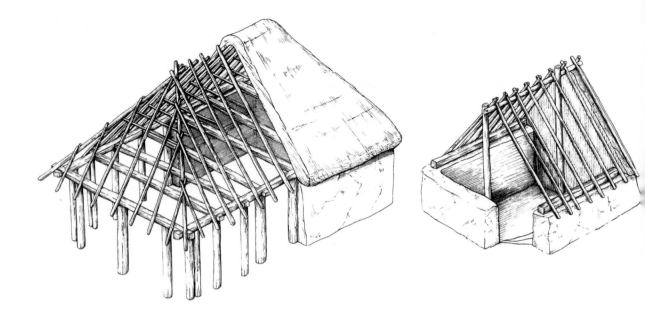

Figure 8.6
Reconstruction of a
wall-post building
and a *Grubenhaus*
at Catholme Anglo-
Saxon settlement

Archaeologically, the wall-post buildings were represented by parallel rows of postholes indicating the long side walls of rectangular buildings; direct evidence of the end walls survived more rarely. In some cases the postholes were located within a shallow trench, giving a 'post-in-trench' form of construction. The wall-posts would have supported a 'wall-plate' (a timber beam or beams running the length of the top of the wall) and these would in turn have supported tie-beams running at intervals across the width of the building, giving rigidity to the structure. A thatched (straw or reeds) gabled roof, possibly with hipped ends (Dixon 2002, 99), was supported on the wall-plates. There was no direct evidence of the material from which the walls were made. It is likely that a mass of clay or mud was used, perhaps half a metre thick or so, given support by the wall-posts (buried within it) and perhaps by horizontals between the posts also. The location of entrances (indicated for example by gaps in wall trenches or pairs of particularly deeply set posts) was difficult to determine in most cases but where this could be done they were placed roughly opposite each other in the long walls of the buildings.

A notable feature of the wall-post buildings at Catholme was the irregularity of the spacing of the wall-posts, so that they would have had a distinctly 'rickety' appearance prior to the construction of the mud walls. In large measure, such irregularity may have been a consequence of using irregular timbers for the construction of the buildings, the way the irregular timbers fitted together determining the spacing and location of the posts (*ibid*, 94–5). The buildings were also relatively small, ranging in length from *c* 4m to 12m and less than 6m in width (*ibid*). A few of the buildings had evidence for an annexe attached to one end, although whether these were actually roofed was seldom clear. One of the larger buildings, evidently late in the sequence, had a distinctive L-shaped plan.

The second type of building found at Catholme was the *Grubenhaus*, of which thirteen examples were recorded (eighteen if rebuilds are included). The characteristic feature of these buildings is of course the subrectangular pit or hollow that defines the type. Both the depth and dimensions of the pit were very variable, with lengths ranging between *c* 2m and 5m, and thus within the range of the smaller wall-post buildings. At each end of the pit was a substantial posthole, these posts are generally thought to have supported a tent-like roof structure. Considerable debate has surrounded the function of the pit in *Grubenhäuser*, and whether the floor of the pit represented the floor level within the building (a truly sunken floor, the traditional interpretation) or whether the pit should be seen as an under-floor storage place or 'cellar' beneath a wooden floor at ground level (an interpretation that has become increasingly popular in recent years). At Catholme, the excavators favoured the traditional interpretation, noting that in all but five cases lines of stakeholes or postholes were found around the edges of the pit bottoms, indicating revetting of the sides of the pits with hurdles or planking. The entrances to the *Grubenhäuser* seem to have been at one corner, suggested by a bulge in the corner of the pit; entrance from the ends would have been obstructed by the posts supporting the roof.

Whatever the correct interpretation of the architecture of *Grubenhäuser*, they are usually viewed as ancillary buildings of some sort, associated with storage or craft activities, rather than dwellings. A common find from *Grubenhäuser* are clay loomweights, suggesting that often if not exclusively these buildings were used as weaving sheds (the damp atmosphere would have been good for the storage of wool or vegetable fibre). This is supported at Catholme, where loomweights, generally fragmentary, were recovered from the bottom of five of the *Grubenhäuser* (Fig 8.7). Other than this, however, the excavation provided no evidence of the function of the various buildings, although it may be assumed that the dwellings were amongst the larger buildings and that the smaller buildings served ancillary functions.

In addition to the shallow boundary ditches of enclosures and the buildings, other significant features of the Anglo-Saxon settlement included fire-pits, green-stained pits and human burials. Six fire-pits were uncovered, a typical example being a shallow sub-rectangular pit, *c* 2m long by 1m wide, containing a layer of fire-cracked stones on top of an ashy soil with charcoal. The hot stones were presumably used for slow drying or cooking, perhaps roasting meat for a feast. The fire-pits were generally located adjacent to boundaries and away from buildings, presumably because of the fire risk. At least thirteen pits were characterised by a yellowish-green staining on their bottom and sides, and some of these had a pair of associated postholes, one either side of the pit, indicating a superstructure of some sort. The function of these pits is not known; suitably lined they could have been used in such activities as tanning, dying or brewing. Alternatively they might have been cesspits. Most of the green-stained pits were sited in peripheral locations like the fire-pits but three were located inside buildings and appeared to be contemporary with them. Finally, two inhumation burials and a third possible example were uncovered. The bone was very poorly

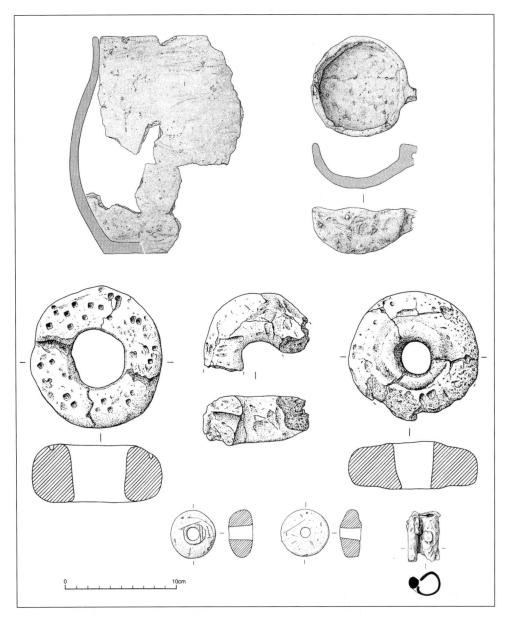

Figure 8.7 Finds from the Anglo-Saxon settlement at Catholme. Top left: globular jar; top right: cup; middle row: clay loomweights; bottom: fired clay spindle whorls; bottom right: iron barrel padlock

preserved, in one case (accompanied by an iron knife) surviving just as dark staining. The location of the two definite human burials is interesting. Both were located at the entrances to enclosures, which is likely to have had symbolic significance. How these burials relate to the (presumably) more formal cemetery associated with the settlement is not known.

The finds from the Catholme excavation were meagre and unprepossessing (Fig 8.7). Most were recovered from the pits of *Grubenhäuser* but much of this material was probably debris that accumulated after the buildings had fallen into disuse. Evidence of weaving was provided by the loomweights mentioned above, together with four clay spindle-whorls. Iron working on site was attested by slag, although not in large quantities. Both iron-smelting slag (a by-product of the primary production of iron from ore) and smithing slag (a by-product of the secondary working of iron to make artefacts) were present, much of it in three distinct clusters, but unfortunately none was associated with a furnace, hearth or workshop structure (Brown 2002). Iron artefacts themselves were few and far between, and comprised such everyday items as knives (seventeen examples), shears, an awl, a hook, a pin and a buckle loop. Somewhat less commonplace is a fragment of a barrel padlock, perhaps from a casket or box in which precious items were kept (Fig 8.7).

The main category of find was coarse, undecorated handmade pottery, including globular jars, bowls, a platter and small cups (Vince 2002). Examination of the fabrics suggested that while most of the pottery contained inclusions (eg rock fragments) that could have been obtained locally, some may have come from further afield. This simple, undecorated pottery is not of much help for dating purposes.

Taking all this evidence together, a picture can be formed of the Anglo-Saxon settlement at Catholme. In a number of fundamental respects this picture is not very different from the picture we formed of the Iron Age farmsteads at Fisherwick or Whitemoor Haye – a seemingly low-status and largely self-sufficient farming community. We have no direct evidence of the crops grown and bone preservation was so poor that little can be said of the animals reared other than that they included cattle, sheep, pigs and horses (Harman 2002). None of the buildings was particularly large and, given their decidedly irregular construction, they cannot have been impressive. A principal difference to the Iron Age situation (apart from the style of the architecture, a point we will return to later) is that rather than individual farmsteads, each presumably occupied by a separate family, we now have an agglomeration of 'farmsteads', each again presumably occupied by a different family, forming a small village. Some at least of these 'farmsteads' were contained within their own enclosures within the settlement as a whole. No single building or enclosure was obviously distinguishable from the rest in a way that suggests the residence of a village headman or some other special function, although here we have to be cautious because evidently only part – perhaps only about half – of the settlement was excavated. The central enclosure within the excavated area (VII on Fig 8.4) does seem to stand out somewhat from the rest, and late in its life it was extended southwards and the distinctive L-shaped building mentioned earlier, one of the largest in the settlement, was built within it. However, the distinctiveness (if any) of this enclosure and building cluster is subtle and it is central only to the excavated area and not necessarily to the settlement itself.

Another difference from the Iron Age homesteads is that the Catholme settlement was evidently long-lived, surviving perhaps for three centuries, whereas the Iron Age homesteads, to judge from the apparent low density of occupation within them, may have been occupied only for a generation or two before being turned over to other uses. Given this, and to emphasise a point made earlier, the impression of a densely occupied settlement that one gains by glancing briefly at the overall plan of the Catholme settlement is misleading. Only a few of the buildings would have been in use at any one time, leaving plenty of space for animals and other purposes. (Sixty-five buildings have been identified. Allowing a generous estimate of a life of 50 years for each of these buildings, over a period of 300 years on average only about eleven would have been in use at any one time. If there were two ancillary buildings for each house, this would amount to just four households functioning at any one time, say eight if the settlement was in fact double the size of the excavated area.) Catholme was a small place.

In some contrast to the impression of a small community of subsistence-level farmers – peasants, basically – that we gain from the settlement at Catholme, is the impression we gain from the finds from the adjacent, and almost certainly associated, cemetery (confusingly given the different name of 'Wychnor'). Here we find, in the male graves, the spears and shields of warriors, and the gilded cruciform brooch from the grave of a woman (it may be safely assumed by analogy) is hardly peasant attire. This does not make the inhabitants of the Catholme settlement particularly important people on the wider stage (the fantastic riches of the Sutton Hoo ship burial, contemporary with Catholme, show what a really important person looks like) but locally they may have counted for something. The grave goods from the Wychnor cemetery are comparable with those from thousands of burials that have been found in rural locations across much of England, and although the associated settlement evidence is rarely found, small, unprepossessing villages or hamlets like Catholme can be reasonably assumed. However, unlike the jewellery of their womenfolk, the shields and spears of the menfolk were not just for show in these violent times. Who were these people and how did they fit in to society? This is a much-debated question.

Anglo-Saxons and Britons

The Anglo-Saxons conquered and settled a land that was already occupied by Britons. A basic narrative of events in Britain between AD 410 and around AD 600 (about the time of the establishment of the Anglo-Saxon settlement at Catholme) is provided by a handful of historical sources. These include a contemporary source, *The Ruin of Britain*, written in the 540s by a British monk called Gildas, and two later sources. These are the *Ecclesiastical History of the English People*, completed in 731 by 'The Venerable' Bede, a monk in the Northumbrian monastery of Jarrow, and *The Anglo-Saxon Chronicle*, a late (9th-century) Saxon compilation of annals. All were written with a different purpose and bias (Gildas's is an apoplectic rant against the evil behaviour of the British rulers of his day with dire warnings of the consequences) and none is considered to be entirely reliable.

Gildas tells us that the British, under the leadership of a 'proud tyrant' named Vortigern, brought in the first Saxons as mercenaries to defend the east coast against attacks by the Picts and Scots. Bede adds that the Saxons were led by the brothers Hengist and Horsa, and that their arrival dates to around AD 450.

Then, according to Gildas, the mercenaries rebelled and many years of fighting followed, culminating in a major British victory, perhaps around AD 500, at an unidentified location called *Mons Badonicus*. The ensuing period of peace lasted only to Gildas's day (the 540s) when he tells us that there were five British kingdoms ruled by wicked 'tyrants'. The *Chronicle* then tells us that the West Saxons were on the move, advancing northwards from Wessex to capture a large part of the south Midlands in 571 and winning a decisive battle at Dyrham (Gloucestershire) in 577, at which the 'kings' of Gloucester, Cirencester and Bath were present and their towns were subsequently taken.

There is no good reason to doubt the bare bones of this narrative, which is largely borne out by the archaeological evidence. A number of Iron Age hillforts in the West Country, most notably South Cadbury in Somerset, were reoccupied and refortified during this period. These must have been the strongholds of British warlords. That life of a sort continued in towns is shown both by archaeology and by the reference to 'kings' of Gloucester, Cirencester and Bath at the battle of Dyrham. Finally, archaeology also shows the steady spread of pagan Anglo-Saxon cemeteries inland: northwards from Wessex, up the Thames valley and westwards from East Anglia. While the fragmentary and biased historical sources simplify things down into a few major personalities and battles, the archaeological evidence hints at a much more complex pattern of events.

There are few historical clues as to what happened in the area we are interested in, the Tame valley and the Middle Trent, but the archaeological evidence needs to be assessed in the light of the historical outline provided above. Like the West Country, this was an area where Anglo-Saxon warriors and settlers arrived comparatively late, and it lies at the western limit of the distribution of pagan cemeteries. We therefore have a period, essentially most of the 5th century and into the 6th, when the area must have continued to be occupied by Britons before any significant Anglo-Saxon presence made itself felt. As at Gloucester, Cirencester and Bath, some continuation of occupation at the Staffordshire towns of Wall and Penkridge on Watling Street is likely. Significantly, whilst the vast majority of place names in Staffordshire are English in origin, the names Lichfield (close by Wall) and Penkridge preserve in modified form the Romano-British names of *Letocetum* and *Pennocrucium*. Archaeological evidence for continuity has also been claimed but this is best illustrated further down Watling Street at Wroxeter. Here, meticulous excavations in the baths basilica, directed by Philip Barker, have demonstrated a long period of post-Roman occupation in the former capital of the Cornovii (White and Barker 1998). The most dramatic aspect of this was the 'Great Rebuilding' of around AD 530–70, when a series of buildings of timber-framed construction, many of them substantial and dominated by a massive hall, were laid out within and around the shell of the former baths basilica (Fig 8.8). The rebuilding shows every sign of planning and the command of a skilled labour force on a major scale. Who ordered this building project? The most likely answer is an unknown local potentate or warlord, a descendant of one of the leading families of the Cornovii perhaps, similar to the 'kings' of Gloucester,

Cirencester and Bath of around the same period. Something similar is perfectly plausible for Wall also.

Although continuity of occupation well into the 5th and 6th centuries is demonstrable at a number of Roman towns, the nature of these places would have changed fundamentally. Coinage, a Roman-style market economy, industrial-scale production of pottery and other goods had all disappeared, so that it is probably better to characterise this continuity as 'life in towns' rather than 'town life' in the sense that a classical Roman would understand it. With the collapse of wider administrative structures, communities fragmented and turned in on themselves; their horizons shrank. But if 'towns' like Wroxeter and perhaps Wall survived as centres of some sort they cannot have done so in a vacuum, and their most intimate relationship would have been with their immediate rural hinterland. For Wall this would have included the Where Rivers Meet area but the difficulty is that rural occupation in this period – the 5th and 6th centuries up to the arrival of the Anglo-Saxons – is next to invisible, not just in the study area but much more widely.

Unfortunately, the Britons of the period appear not to have used pottery to any extent (vessels of wood and leather must be presumed), nor did they build their settlements or bury their dead in a manner that leaves a recognisable archaeological trace. Staffordshire as a whole is almost entirely a blank (Kinsley

Figure 8.8
Reconstruction drawing of the 'Great Rebuilding' at Wroxeter

2003). Reoccupation of hillforts, including the possible example at Borough Hill in the Where Rivers Meet area, in a similar fashion to South Cadbury and other hillforts in the West Country, is a possibility but as no significant excavation has taken place on Staffordshire hillforts (or at Borough Hill just over the border in Derbyshire), this must remain speculation.

For almost the whole of rural Staffordshire, the only tantalising glimpse of possible British activity provided by archaeology for this period comes from an excavation undertaken in 1990–91 at Tucklesholme Farm in the study area (Hughes 1991). The excavation was of what was presumed to be an early Bronze Age ring-ditch (the ploughed-out remains of a round barrow), described in Chapter 5 above. Just outside the ring-ditch a sub-rectangular pit was uncovered, 2m long by 1.25m wide and 0.55m deep, with evidence of burning at its base. Its fills included one with a lot of charcoal, tiny fragments of burnt bone and substantial elements of burnt timbers, perhaps from a box or basket. The pit would therefore seem to be associated with a cremation burial. The surprise came when radiocarbon dates were obtained for the burnt timbers. These turned out to fall in the 5th century AD and not the Bronze Age as expected. It is possible that the samples were contaminated but there is no good reason not to take the radiocarbon dating at face value. Whether this external burial was broadly contemporary with the ring-ditch or whether it was made around 2000 years later at the edge of an ancient barrow cannot be determined.

Archaeological visibility only returns with the pagan Anglo-Saxon burials (described above) at Catholme/Wychnor and at Tucklesholme itself, which form part of a wider grouping in the Middle Trent valley. In the past these would have been taken at face value as the graves of Germanic intruders, and the Germanic origins of the material culture (jewellery, weapons) is not in doubt. Given the marginal location of the area in the distribution of early Anglo-Saxon burials, it has more recently been suggested that the Wychnor cemetery 'is equally likely to represent the adoption of Germanic cultural styles by the native inhabitants' (Kinsley 2003). This is an extreme view; a slightly stronger argument can be made that the Catholme 'Anglo-Saxon' settlement was substantially or even wholly native (*ibid*). This finds some support in the contention that the settlement developed from an adjacent 3rd- to 4th-century Romano-British settlement indicated by pottery scatters recovered during fieldwalking (see above). However, this is hardly compelling, especially as the crucial period (the 5th century) is missing. The *Grubenhaus* is undoubtedly a Germanic type of structure, with its precedents on the continent, although there is nothing especially Germanic about the wall-post structures.

Until we learn how to recognise 5th-century British rural settlements and burials in the area and examples are excavated, the debate is perhaps fruitless. By the 6th century the Anglo-Saxons had been in Britain for several generations and no doubt much intermarriage and interbreeding between the two populations had taken place, so that to be ethnically Anglo-Saxon was different to being Anglo-Saxon 'by blood' (irrespective of how people saw themselves). This is different, however, from the idea that the natives adopted Anglo-Saxon material culture, burial traditions and architectural styles without there being a significant, and dominant, intrusive Anglo-Saxon population. There is little reason at present to abandon the more traditional view.

The survival of a native British population is not seriously in doubt, although it is likely that economic collapse, warfare, climatic deterioration and plague, all of which are documented, probably led to a substantial decline in population from the Roman period. Continuity of aspects of landscape organisation and use is not incompatible with 'elite dominance' of a native population by a (potentially quite small) intrusive group. Place-name evidence in Staffordshire provides a further indication of British survival, with some 30 names from the county indicating contact between the speakers of Old English and British (Kinsley 2003; Gelling 1992). These include Celtic river names such as Trent and Tame, and names deriving from *cumbre*, the Old English version of *Cymry* (the name the British gave to themselves), such as is found at Comberford to the south of the study area (Gelling 1978). A less-flattering reference to a British community might be found in place names with a 'Wal-' element, as in Walton-on-Trent in the study area. This derives from Old English *walh*, which had two meanings, not necessarily contradictory: 'Welshman' and 'serf' (*ibid*).

Whatever the nature of the early interaction between native and Anglo-Saxon, the Where Rivers Meet area rapidly became English and indeed lies in the heartland of one of the greatest of the Anglo-Saxon kingdoms, Mercia.

In the shadow of Offa

The radiocarbon dates from the Catholme settlement suggest that it had a long life, from at least the 7th century through to the 9th century. This means that the settlement was occupied at a time when the local region was at the heart of English history – the late 8th century, the time of Offa, greatest king of Mercia, the greatest kingdom in Britain at the time. His secular 'capital' was at Tamworth, just a short distance up the Tame, and the ecclesiastical centre at Lichfield, successor to Roman Wall (Letocetum), was even closer – both were just a day's journey away.

The origins of Mercia and the six other major kingdoms of England (Kent, Sussex, Wessex, East Anglia, Essex and Northumbria) lie in the 6th century, when they began to form out of the smaller 'kingdoms' that had preceded them (Fig 8.9). To the west and north lay British kingdoms, such as Dumnonia (Devon and Cornwall), and Dyfed, Powys and Gwynedd (Wales). Much of the history of the 7th and 8th centuries is the history of warfare and alliance between these kingdoms, with first one English kingdom and then another rising to dominance. The kings of these dominant states were referred to by Bede and other sources as *Bretwaldas*, meaning 'wide-rulers', although this is unlikely to be a formal office. Initially these kingdoms were pagan but from around 600 their kings converted to Christianity (at least nominally and with some backsliding); quite how this affected the majority of the population is a difficult question.

One of the earliest of the great kings of Mercia was Penda (died 655), and

Figure 8.9 The major
kingdoms of Britain
in the 6th to 8th
centuries and Offa's
Dyke

the historical sources provide some details of his struggles with Northumbria (top kingdom at the time). In his attempt to halt Northumbrian expansion the pagan Penda made common cause with Cadwallon, the Christian British king of Gwynedd, against the Christian English king (and *Bretwalda*) Oswald of Northumbria. Cadwallon, Oswald and eventually Penda all died in these wars, the fortunes of which went this way and that. If we were to judge by the settlement at Catholme, life went on as normal throughout all this warfare, which ranged widely across the land and required warriors to fight it. But a settlement in the heartland of Mercia cannot have been unaffected by such events, showing how the historical and archaeological records often tell different stories, both probably misleading in different ways. The challenge is to attempt to resolve the archaeological and historical records, not through seeking direct archaeological evidence of battle and destruction (which is rare and almost always ambiguous) but through trying to explore, tentatively, the way in which archaeological patterns might 'mesh' with the wider political and cultural scene. Unfortunately, this challenge can hardly be engaged given the current state of archaeological knowledge.

Figure 8.10 Silver penny of Offa

Although Penda was defeated and killed in battle in 655, Mercia's star was in the ascendant. Its greatest king Offa (died 796) flourished in the second half of the 8th century and ruled over all of the English with the exception of Northumbria. He is also of course credited with the building of Offa's Dyke to hold the Welsh at bay, a massive engineering work twice the length of Hadrian's Wall. By Offa's time Mercia had been Christian for a century (how is this reflected at Catholme and what are we to make of the two or three graves discovered within the settlement?), trade was once again flourishing and towns as centres of trade had re-emerged. Coinage in regular use had reappeared also, best symbolised by the beautiful pennies bearing Offa's name (Fig 8.10). These gained a wider circulation than any currency since Roman times and, interestingly, are found not only in hoards but frequently individually, indicating their use for everyday transactions. A silver coin of Offa, a metal-detector find, has been reported from the Where Rivers Meet area.

Just as Wall did in Roman times, Offa's 'capital' at Tamworth and cathedral at Lichfield (which he briefly raised to an archbishopric in competition with Canterbury) must have had an effect on their hinterlands. The word 'capital' is usually given in inverted commas when applied to Tamworth because Offa, like other kings of the period, had no capital as such but was peripatetic. His court moved about from place to place, receiving hospitality and collecting taxes and food. A formal tribute system is found in a document known as the *Tribal Hidage*, which would appear to be a Mercian tribute list and sets out the taxes required from different tribes or regions comprising Mercia and other kingdoms. From this we learn that the people in the Tame valley and environs were called the Tomsaetan and occupied the heartland of the Mercian empire, including the royal church at Repton, the bishopric at Lichfield, and Tamworth itself, if not a capital in the modern sense then at least the place where Offa and the other Mercian kings liked to spend Christmas in the royal hall. This again emphasises just how impoverished our archaeological impression of the Where Rivers Meet area must be and how much more work remains to be done.

Close encounters with Vikings

If the settlement at Catholme survived into the late 9th century, as the radiocarbon dating suggests (Garton and Kinsley 2002), then it would have passed through another major political and cultural transition: incorporation into the Danelaw. This was the area of England, north and east of Watling Street, which in a treaty of 886 with the Viking king Guthram, Alfred the Great of Wessex conceded to the Danes, and where Danish law rather than English law applied.

The events leading up to this treaty were momentous and violent, and cannot but have affected the inhabitants of Catholme. They began remotely enough with a series of Viking raids, mainly in the north of Britain and including the plundering of the monasteries of Lindisfarne, Jarrow and Iona, in the last years of Offa's reign. These were isolated incidents but from 835 the attacks became more regular and in 865 a Danish 'Great Army' landed in East Anglia, then turned northwards to capture York in 866. Within three years of the arrival of this army the once great kingdoms of Northumbria and East Anglia had fallen; Mercia and Wessex held out. In 871 a new Danish army landed and in the same year Alfred the Great succeeded to the throne of Wessex. His reign started badly and after a series of minor defeats he had to buy the Danes off. They left Wessex alone for five years and turned their attention instead to Mercia, which fell in 874.

According to the *Anglo-Saxon Chronicle*, in the winter of 873/74 the Great Danish Army made its camp at Repton, Derbyshire, in the territory of the Tomsaetan and just 18km (12 miles) from Catholme. The choice of campsite cannot have been coincidental, but was instead highly symbolic. The Danes were pagans and Repton, where a monastery had been founded, was a church of the Mercian royal family. Excavations by Martin Biddle (Biddle and Kjølbye-Biddle 1992) uncovered a large enclosure by the Trent that used the monastery church as a gatehouse. Outside the enclosure was a massive stone structure covered by an earth mound, which may have been constructed as a mausoleum for the Mercian royal family. However, the Vikings had evidently used it as a charnel house for some of their dead. The bones of some 250 people were buried there, 80% of them robust males in the age range 15–45 years, the skulls stacked on top of the long bones. This suggests that the bodies had first been buried elsewhere or exposed until defleshed before being deposited in the tomb. Others were buried in the church itself. One, a warrior who had been killed by a blow to the top of his leg, was accompanied by a sword, knife, key, boar's tusk and jackdaw bone, and was wearing a Thor's hammer silver amulet.

The presence of this hostile army so close to home must have had just as profound an effect as the arrival of the Roman army some eight centuries earlier. A decade later, the Where Rivers Meet area found itself at a boundary zone once again, just the 'wrong' side of the border of the Danelaw, which carved Mercia in two. English power had now passed to the kingdom of Wessex. The extent of Viking settlement within the Danelaw is uncertain, and we have similar problems of interpretation to those involving the Anglo-Saxons four centuries earlier.

As with the Anglo-Saxon settlement, one line of evidence is provided by place names. In the north and east of England a large number of place names (for example numerous names ending in –*by* and –*thorp*) are in the language spoken by the Vikings, Old Norse. However, the main concentration of such names does not extend into our area, and charters show that by the 10th century even the smallest features of the landscape had Old English names, indicating that whatever the situation had been earlier, English was by then the language of the mass of the population. Only a handful of names show Scandinavian influence, but significantly include examples ending in –*holme*, from the Old Norse *holmr*, island, such as Catholme, Fatholme, Tucklesholme and Borough Holme. These appear to be hybrid names combining an Old English element with an Old Norse suffix. Thus 'Catholme' may combine an Anglo-Saxon personal name, *Catta*, with *holmr* (Losco-Bradley and Kinsley 2002). These 'islands' would have been defined as the areas of dry land within the floodplains between the multiple channels of the rivers (see Chapter 3). There is no indication, however, of any changes in the archaeological record of the settlement at Catholme that can be associated with these events, unless of course the eventual abandonment of the settlement is to be associated with them.

The abandonment of the settlement at Catholme marks the end of the story we have been tracing, and the further development of the landscape in the medieval period and beyond lies outside the scope of this book.

Conclusion

We hope that we have succeeded in this book in conveying something of the richness of the ancient landscapes that have been revealed at the confluence of the Trent and the Tame, and some idea of the methods that have been used to explore them. Prior to the commencement of sand and gravel quarrying, which began on a large scale in the 1960s, almost nothing was known about these landscapes, and there was very little 'on the ground' to suggest their existence. Most of what we now know about these landscapes has come about, directly or indirectly, as a consequence of quarrying. This is the positive side of things. The negative side of things is that quarrying has now destroyed a very large portion of the archaeological remains that once survived, and all that we now have is the archaeological record that we have attempted to summarise and interpret in the preceding chapters. We have not shied away from pointing to the many gaps and biases in this record, and the difficulties of interpretation that arise from these.

However, we have good reason to end on a positive note. The work of the Where Rivers Meet project has provided a practical demonstration of how a range of new technologies can be deployed to help us to model and interpret ancient landscapes. These technologies also help us to predict in a much more rigorous manner than has previously been possible where in the landscape archaeological remains might survive and what type of preservation might be anticipated. Most of the archaeological investigations described in this book were carried out before the tools for such 'predictive landscape modelling' became available. Despite this, an enormous amount has been learned over the past 40 years, as we hope to have shown. It is exciting (if a little chastening) to imagine how much more could have been learned if the techniques and resources we have today had been available 40 years ago. It is even more exciting to imagine what will be achieved in future decades, when campaigns of archaeological excavation and investigation can benefit from the outset from the tools and approaches now available (and others yet unimagined). While the Where Rivers Meet project was underway, some of our colleagues at the University of Birmingham (and some members of the Where Rivers Meet team) were engaged on a project which has mapped, on a huge scale, the drowned landscapes of the southern North Sea using seismic data (Gaffney, Fitch and Smith 2009). This is the 'Doggerland' to which we referred in Chapter 4. We have little doubt that we are still just at the beginning of a revolution in landscape archaeology.

References

Acreman, M C, 1989 Extreme historical UK floods and maximum flood estimation, *J Institution of Water and Environmental Management*, **3**, 404–12

Atkinson, R J C, Piggott, C M, & Sandars, N, 1951 *Excavations at Dorchester, Oxon.* Oxford: Ashmolean

Bain, K, Hancox, E, & Hewson, M, 2004 Catholme landscape ground truthing project 2004: post-excavation assessment. Unpubl report, Birmingham Archaeology Report **1356**

Barber, M, 2007 The Blank Country? Neolithic enclosures and landscapes in the West Midlands, in Garwood (ed) 2007c, 79–96

Barclay, G, & Bayliss, A, 1999 Cursus monuments and the radiocarbon problem, in A Barclay & J Harding (eds), *Pathways and ceremonies: the cursus monuments of Britain and Ireland.* Oxford: Oxbow

Biddle, M, & Kjølbye-Biddle, B, 1992 Repton and the Vikings, *Antiquity*, **66**, 36–51

Brennand, M, & Taylor, M, 2003 The survey and excavation of a Bronze Age timber circle at Holme-next-the-Sea, Norfolk, 1998–99, *Proc Prehist Soc*, **69**, 1–84

Brown, A G, Cooper, L, Salisbury, C R, & Smith, D N, 2001 Late Holocene channel changes of the Middle Trent: channel response to a thousand year flood record, *Geomorphology*, **39**, 69–82

Brown, K, 2002 Metal slag, in Losco-Bradley & Kinsley (eds) 2002, 113–15

Bunch M A, & Riley, M S, 2004 *Where Rivers Meet project: a preliminary report on hydrogeological modelling.* Upubl report, School of Geography, Earth and Environmental Sciences, University of Birmingham

Buteux, S, Brooks, S, Candy, I, Coates, G, Coope, R, Currant, A, Field, M, Greig, J, Howard, A, Limbrey, S, Paddock, E, Schreve, D, Smith, D, & Toms, P, 2003 The Whitemoor Haye woolly rhino site, Whitemoor Haye Quarry, Staffordshire (SK 173127): assessment report on scientific investigations funded by the ALSF through a grant administered by English Nature. Unpubl report, Birmingham University Field Archaeology Unit

Campbell, J (ed), 1982 *The Anglo-Saxons.* Oxford: Phaidon

Challis, A J, & Harding, D W, 1975 *Later prehistory from the Trent to the Tyne.* BAR Brit Ser, **20**. Oxford: British Archaeological Reports

Chapman, H P, 2005 Rethinking the 'cursus problem': investigating the Neolithic landscape archaeology of Rudston, East Yorkshire, UK, using GIS, *Proc Prehist Soc*, **71**, 80–100

Chapman, H P, 2006 *Landscape archaeology and GIS.* Stroud: Tempus

Chapman, H P, & Cheetham, J L, 2002 Monitoring and modelling saturation as a proxy indicator for *in situ* preservation in wetlands: a GIS-based approach, *J Archaeol Sci*, **29**, 277–89

Chapman, H P, Hewson, M, & Wilkes, M S, forthcoming The Catholme Ceremonial Complex, Staffordshire, UK, *Proc Prehist Soc*

Childe, V G, 1936 *Man makes himself.* London: Watts and Co

Clarke, D L, 1970 *Beaker pottery of Great Britain and Ireland.* Cambridge: Cambridge University Press

Cleal, R M J, Walker, K E, & Montague, R, 1995 *Stonehenge in its landscape: twentieth-century excavations,* English Heritage Archaeol Rep, **10**. London: English Heritage

Coates, G, 2000 An archaeological evaluation of the site of the recycling unit, Alrewas Quarry, Staffordshire. Unpubl report, Birmingham University Field Archaeology Unit Report, **702**

Coates, G, 2002 *A prehistoric and Romano-British landscape: excavations at Whitemoor Haye Quarry, Staffordshire, 1997–1999,* BAR Brit Ser, **340**. Oxford: British Archaeological Reports

Coates, G, & Wooward, A, 2002 Discussion, in Coates 2002, 79–90

Coope, R, & Smith, D, 2003 The coleoptera, in Buteux *et al* 2003, 17–18

Cooper, T, 2008 *Laying the Foundations: a history and archaeology of the Trent Valley sand and gravel industry.* York: Council for British Archaeology

Currant, A, & Schreve, D, 2003 Assessment of vertebrate remains, in Buteux *et al* 2003, 1116

Davies, N S, & Sambrook Smith, G, 2004 Where Rivers Meet: geological, palaeofluvial and hydrogeological analysis of the study area. Unpubl report, School of Geography, Earth and Environmental Sciences, University of Birmingham

Davies, N S, & Sambrook Smith, G, 2006 Signatures of Quaternary fluvial response, Upper River Trent, Staffordshire, UK: A synthesis of outcrop, documentary and GPR data, *Zeitschrift für Geomorphology NF,* **50** (3). Berlin-Stuttgart: Gerbrüder Brontraeger, 347–74

Deegan, A, & Cox, C, 1995 Barton-under-Needwood, SK2018, Staffordshire: aerial photographic assessment. Unpubl report, Air Photo Services

Dixon, P, 2002 The reconstruction of the buildings, in Losco-Bradley & Kinsley 2002, 89–99

Esmonde Cleary, A S, 1999 Roman Britain: civil and rural society, in J Hunter & I Ralston (eds), *The Archaeology of Britain: an introduction from the Upper Palaeolithic to the Industrial Revolution.* London: Routledge, 157–75

Evans, TN, 2006 Ritual monuments and natural places: an assessment of the Neolithic and early Bronze Age landscape architecture at the confluence of the Rivers Trent, Tame and Mease, Staffordshire. Unpubl MA Dissertation, University of Birmingham

Evans, J, 2007 The Romano-British pottery, in Hewson 2007, 81–7

Field, M, 2003 Assessment of plant macrofossils, in Buteux *et al* 2003, 21–4

Gaffney, C F, & Gater, J A, 2003 *Revealing the buried past: geophysics for archaeologists.* Stroud: Tempus

Gaffney, V, Fitch, S, & Smith, D, 2009 *Europe's Lost World: the rediscovery of Doggerland.* York: Council for British Archaeology

Gaffney, V, Thomson, K, & Fitch, S, 2007 *Mapping Doggerland: the Mesolithic landscapes of the southern North Sea.* Oxford: Archaeopress

Garton, D, Elliott, L, & Salisbury, C R, 2001 Aston-upon-Trent, Argosy Washolme, *Derbyshire Archaeol J,* **121**, 196–200

Garton, D, Howard, A, & Pearce, M, 1996 Neolithic riverside ritual? Excavations at Langford Lowfields, Nottinghamshire, in R J A Wilson (ed), *From River Trent to Raqqa*, Nottingham Studies in Archaeol **1**. Nottingham: Department of Archaeology, University of Nottingham, 9–11

Garton, D, Howard, A, & Pearce, M, 1997 Archaeological investigations at Langford Quarry, Nottinghamshire, 1995–96, *Tarmac Papers*, **1**, 29–40

Garton, D, & Kinsley, G, 2002 Radiocarbon dates, in Losco-Bradley & Kinsley 2002, 120–3

Garwood, P, 2007a Late Neolithic and early Bronze Age funerary monuments and burial traditions in the west Midlands, in Garwood (ed) 2007c, 134–65

Garwood, P, 2007b Regions, cultural identity and social change, *c* 4500–1500 BC: the west Midlands in context, in Garwood (ed) 2007c, 194–215

Garwood, P, 2007c *The undiscovered country: the earlier prehistory of the west Midlands* (The Making of the West Midlands Vol. 1). Oxford: Oxbow

Gearey, B R, & Chapman, H P, 2006 Planning policy, *in situ* preservation and wetland archaeology in the United Kingdom – some present concerns. *Conservation and Management of Archaeological Sites*, **7**, 179–82

Gearey, B R, Chapman, D J, & Kent, M, 2000 Palaeoecological Evidence for the Prehistoric Settlement of Bodmin Moor, Cornwall, South-West England: Part II – Land-Use Changes from the Neolithic to the Present, *J Archaeol Sci*, **27**, 493–508

Gelling, M, 1978 *Signposts to the past: place-names and the history of England.* London: Dent

Gelling, M, 1984 *Place-names in the landscape: the geographical roots of Britain's place-names.* London: Phoenix Press

Gelling, M, 1992 *The West Midlands in the Early Middle Ages.* Leicester: Leicester University Press

Gibson, A, 1998 *Stonehenge and timber circles.* Stroud: Tempus

Gibson, A, & Loveday, R, 1989 Excavation at the cursus monument of Aston Upon Trent, Derbyshire, in A Gibson (ed), *Midlands prehistory: some recent and current researches into the prehistory of central England*, BAR Brit Ser, **204**. Oxford: British Archaeological Reports, 27–54

Greig, J R A, Osborne, P J, Smith, C A, & Williams, P, 1979 The landscape of the Fisherwick area during the Iron Age, in Smith (ed) 1979, 93–103

Greig, J R A, 2007 Priorities in Mesolithic, Neolithic and Bronze Age environmental archaeology in the west Midlands, in Garwood (ed) 2007c, 39–50

Guilbert, G, 1996 Findern is dead, long live Potlock: the story of a cursus on the Trent gravels, *PAST*, **24** (November), 10–12

Guilbert, G, 2004 Borough Hill, Walton-upon-Trent – if not a hill fort then what?, *Derbyshire Archaeol J*, **124**, 248–57

Guilbert, G, forthcoming Report on excavations at Fatholme

Hancocks, A, 2002 Romano-British pottery, in Coates 2002, 53–60

Harding, A F, 1981 Excavations in the prehistoric ritual complex near Milfield, Northumberland, *Proc Prehist Soc*, **47**, 87–135

Harman, M, 2002 Animal bones, in Losco-Bradley & Kinsley 2002, 115

Hedges, J D, & Buckley, D G, 1981 *Springfield cursus and the cursus problem.* Chelmsford: Essex County Council

Hewson, M, 2007 *Excavations at Whitemoor Haye Quarry, Stafforshire, 2002–2004: A prehistoric and Romano-British landscape*, Birmingham Archaeol Monogr Series 2, BAR Brit Ser, **428**. Oxford: Archaeopress

Hoare, R C, 1812 *The Ancient History of South Wiltshire*. Volume I. London: William Miller

Hodder, M, 1982 The prehistory of the Lichfield area, *Trans S Staffordshire Archaeol Hist Soc*, **12**, 13–23

Howard, A J, & Knight, D, 2004 The Pleistocene background, in Knight & Howard 2004, 9–29

Hughes, E G, 1991 The excavation of a ring-ditch at Tucklesholme Farm, Barton-under-Needwood, Staffordshire, 1990–1991: an interim report. Unpubl report, Birmingham University Field Archaeology Unit Report, **163**

Hughes, E G, & Hovey, J, 2002 National Memorial Arboretum site, Alrewas, in Coates 2002, 9–13

Jones, A E, 1992 Catholme, Staffordshire: an archaeological evaluation 1992. Unpubl report, Birmingham University Field Archaeology Unit Report, **209**

Jordan D, 2005 The geoarchaeology of deposits at Catholme. Unpubl report, Terra Nova Ltd

Kinsley, G, 2002 The Wychnor cemetery, in Losco-Bradley & Kinsley 2002, 23–7

Kinsley, G, 2003 Anglo-Saxon Staffordshire: an overview. Available: http://www.arch-ant.bham.ac.uk/research/fieldwork_research_themes/projects/wmrrfa/seminar4/Gavin%20Kinsley.doc Accessed: 18 September 2008

Knight, D, & Howard, A J, 2004 *Trent valley landscapes*. King's Lynn: Heritage

Leary, R, 2002 Romano-British pottery from excavations and fieldwalking, in Losco-Bradley & Kinsley 2002, 20–3

Lees, D, 1984 The Sanctuary: a Neolithic calendar?, *Institute of Mathematics and its Applications*, **20**, 109–14

Losco-Bradley, S, 1984 Fatholme, Barton-under-Needwood, Staffordshire, *Proc Prehist Soc*, **50**, 402

Losco-Bradley, S, & Kinsley, G, 2002 *Catholme: an Anglo-Saxon settlement on the Trent gravels in Staffordshire*, Nottingham Studies in Archaeol, **3**. Nottingham: Department of Archaeology, University of Nottingham

Losco-Bradley, S, & Wheeler, H, 1984 Anglo-Saxon settlement in the Trent Valley: some aspects, in M Faull (ed), *Studies in Late Anglo-Saxon settlement*. Oxford: Oxford University Department for External Studies, 101–14

Loveday, R, 2004 Contextualising monuments: the exceptional potential of the middle Trent valley, *Derbyshire Archaeol J*, **124**, 1–12

Loveday, R, 2006 *Inscribed across the landscape: the cursus enigma*. Stroud: Tempus

Loveday, R, & Petchey, M, 1982 Oblong ditches: a discussion and some new evidence, *Aerial Archaeol*, **8**, 17–24

Malone, C, 1994 *The Prehistoric Monuments of Avebury*. London: English Heritage

Martin, H, 2001 An archaeological watching brief and salvage recording at Whitemoor Haye. Unpubl report, Birmingham University Field Archaeology Unit Report, **794**

Martin, A, & Allen, C S M, 2001 Two prehistoric ring ditches and an associated Bronze Age cremation cemetery at Tucklesholme Farm, Barton-under-Needwood, Staffordshire, *Trans Staffordshire Archaeol Hist Soc*, **39**, 1–15

Meeson, R A, 1991 Willowbrook Farm, Alrewas, Staffordshire: the site of a barrow and possible Neolithic/Bronze Age building. Unpubl report, Department of Planning and Economic Development, Staffordshire County Council

Miles, H, 1969 Excavations at Fisherwick, Staffs, 1968 – A Romano-British farmstead and a Neolithic occupation site. *Trans Staffordshire Archaeol Hist Soc*, **10**, 1969, 1–23

Morris, E L, 2002 Briquetage, in Coates 2002, 52–3

Neilson, C, 2001 Archaeological excavations at Whitemoor Haye Quarry, Alrewas, Staffordshire, Areas D, E, G, & H: an interim report. Unpubl report, Birmingham University Field Archaeology Unit Report, **704**

Neilson, C, 2002 Archaeological excavations at Barton Business Park, Barton-under-Needwood, Staffordshire, 2001. Unpubl report, Birmingham University Field Archaeology Unit Report, **842**

O'Brien, C, 1974 Interim note on excavations near Alrewas. Unpublished report, Trent Valley Archaeological Research Committee

Oswald, A, Dyer, C, and Barber, M, 2001 *The creation of monuments: Neolithic causewayed enclosures in the British Isles*. London: English Heritage

Palmer, R, 1976, Interrupted ditch enclosures in Britain: the use of aerial photography for comparative studies, *Proc Prehist Soc*, **42**, 161–86

Piggott, S, 1958 Native economies and the Roman occupation of Northern Britain, in I A Richmond (ed), *Roman and Native in North Britain*. Edinburgh: Nelson

Piggott, S, 1965 *Ancient Europe*. Edinburgh: Edinburgh University Press

Plot, R, 1686 *The Natural History of Staffordshire*. Oxford: The Theatre

Pryor, F, 1992 Special section: current research at Flag Fen, Peterborough, *Antiquity*, **66**, 439–531

Pryor, F, 1998 *Etton: excavations at a Neolithic causewayed enclosure near Maxey, Cambridgeshire, 1982–1987*, English Heritage Archaeol Rep, **18**. London: English Heritage

Pryor, F M M, & French, C A I, 1985, Archaeology and environment in the Lower Welland Valley, *E Anglian Archaeol*, **27**, 1–337

Renfrew, C, 1987 *Archaeology and language*. London: Jonathan Cape.

Salisbury, H, 2002 Preface, in Losco-Bradley & Kinsley 2002, xi–xii

Samuels, J, 1979 Baked clay fragments and mudwalling, in Smith (ed) 1979, 59–60

Saracino, E P, 1990 Interim report: archaeological evaluations at Willowbrook Farm, Alrewas, Staffordshire (TR31032C-STALWF90). Unpubl report, Tempus Reparatum

Saracino, E P, 1991 An archaeological assessment of Willowbrook Farm, Alrewas, Staffordshire. Unpubl report, Tempus Reparatum

Schreve, DC, Howard, AJ, Currant, AP, Brooks, S, Buteux, STE, Coope, GR, Crocker, BT, Field, MH, Greenward, M, Silva, B, Smith, D, Tetlow, E and Toms, P, forthcoming A Middle Devensian woolly rhinoceros from Whitemoor Haye Quarry, Staffordshire (UK): palaeoenvironmental context and significance, *J Quaternary Sci*

Smith, C A, 1976 Second report on excavations at Fisherwick, Staffs, 1973 – ice-wedge casts and a middle Bronze Age settlement, *Trans S Staffordshire Archaeol Hist Soc*, **16**, 1–17

Smith, C A (ed), 1979 *Fisherwick: the reconstruction of an Iron Age landscape*, BAR Brit Ser, **61**. Oxford: British Archaeological Reports

Smith C A, 1980 The historical development of the landscape in the parishes of Alrewas, Fisherwick and Whittington: a retrogressive analysis, *Trans S Staffordshire Archaeol Hist Soc*, **20**, 1–14

Smith, D, 2002 Insect remains, in Coates 2002, 67–72

Spikins, P, 1999 *Mesolithic northern England: environment, population and settlement*, BAR Brit Ser, **283**. Oxford: Archaeopress

Taylor, J, 2006 The Roman period, in N J Cooper (ed), *The Archaeology of the East Midlands: an archaeological resource assessment and research agenda*, Leicester Archaeol Monogr, **13**. Leicester: School of Archaeology and Ancient History, University of Leicester, 137–59

Toms, P, 2003 Optical dating sampling and assessment of potential, in Buteux *et al* 2003, 29–31

Vince, A, 2002 Anglo-Saxon pottery, in Losco-Bradley & Kinsley 2002, 102–8

Vine, P M, 1982 *The Neolithic and Bronze Age cultures of the middle and upper Trent basin*, BAR Brit Ser, **105**. Oxford: British Archaeological Reports

Wainwright, G J, 1968 Durrington Walls: a ceremonial enclosure of the second millennium BC, *Antiquity*, **42**, 20–6

Wainwright, G J, & Longworth, I H, 1971 *Durrington Walls: Excavations 1966–1968*, Rep Res Comm Soc Antiq London, **29**. London: Society of Antiquaries

Wardle, C, 2003 Roman Staffordshire: the five towns and beyond. Available: http://www.arch-ant.bham.ac.uk/research/fieldwork_research_themes/projects/wmrrfa/seminar3/Chris%20Wardle.doc Accessed: 18 September 2008

Watters, M.S, 2003 *Where Rivers Meet project: geophysical survey at Catholme*. Upubl report, Visual and Spatial Technology Centre, University of Birmingham

Whimster, R, 1989 *The emerging past: air photography and the buried landscape*. Swindon: RCHME

White, R, & Barker, P, 1998 *Wroxeter: life and death of a Roman city*. Stroud: Tempus

Wilkes, S M, & Barratt, G, 2004 Where Rivers Meet project: digital landscape modelling and analysis. Unpubl report, Visual and Spatial Technology Centre, University of Birmingham

Windell, D, 1989 Late Neolithic 'ritual focus' at West Cotton, Northamptonshire, in A Gibson (ed), *Midlands prehistory: some recent and current researches in the prehistory of central England*, BAR Brit Ser, **204**. Oxford: British Archaeological Reports, 85–94

Winterbottom, S J, & Long, D, 2006 From abstract digital models to rich virtual environments: landscape contexts in Kilmartin Glen, Scotland, *J Archaeol Sci*, **33**, 1356–67

Woodward, A, 2002 The prehistoric pottery, in Coates 2002, 43–52

Woodward, A, 2007 Ceremonial landscapes and ritual deposits in the Neolithic and Bronze Age periods in the west Midlands, in Garwood (ed) 2007c, 182–93

Index

use of metal 94, 97, 98,
Bronze Age–Iron Age transition 93–5
burial practices 98, 100
    cremation, cremations 16, 66, 70, 81, 85, 86,
      90, 96, 98, 99, 147, 149, 161
    disposal in water 100
    excarnation, excarnated remains 61, 66, 100,
      165
    inhumation, inhumations 72, 73, 81, 86, 96,
      147, 149, 150, 155
burials 56, 81, 83, 86, 90, 97, 100, 102, 155,
    156, 160, 161, 165
    flat cemeteries 98–9, 100
    urnfields 96, 98

Catholme (Staffs) **17**, 18, 38, 52, 101, 102, 131,
    143, 166
Catholme Anglo-Saxon settlement 150, **151**,
    152–8, 161, 162, 164, 165, 166
    Grubenhäuser 18, 150–1, 153, 155, 156, 161
    phasing of 152
    wall-post buildings 151, 152, 153, 154, 157,
      161
Catholme Ceremonial Complex **4**, 7–8, 30, **31**,
    32, 55, 66, **67**, 76, 78, 79, 80, 84, 91–2, 106,
    107
    cursus 65, 66, **67**, 68, 76, 87, 89, 90, 107
    interpretation of 87, 89
    phasing of 88, 89, 90
    pit-alignments 76–7, 90–1, 105–6
    'sunburst' monument 66, 67, 68–72, 74, 76,
      79, 83, 89, 90
    'woodhenge' 2, 7–8, 66, 67, 73–6, 78–9,
      89–90, 93, 107
Catholme Farm 2, 7, 39, 40, 55, **74**, 87
cave art 50, 57
Celts, the 96–7, 122, 126
ceremonial practices 56, 59, 61, 63, 65, 79, 86,
    87, 90, 92, 126
climate
    historic 44, 45, 46, 48, 50, 59, 97
climate change 5, 37, **38**, 45, 50–1, 52, 97, 162
coinage 129, 145, 160, 164
communications 60 *also see* droveways; track-
    ways
    Roman roads 131–3, 134, 139, 144, 145, 159,
      165
    routeways 62, 107

cropmarks **11**, 15–16, 18, 64, 65, 68, 78, 79,
    101, 102, 117, 121, 135, 138, 139, 142–3
    factors influencing 8, 12–13, 16, 33, **34**, 84,
      142, 150
    plots of 7, **12**, 19, 28, 110, **111**, 113,

Danelaw, the 165
data sources
    British Geological Survey 6–7, 26
    Historic Environment Records 7, 19, 27, 145
    Ordnance Survey 6, 23, 24, 26, 27, 52
dating techniques 22, 152
    Optically Stimulated Luminescence (OSL)
      44, 49
    radiocarbon 22, 32, 44, 49, 71, 74, 83, 85, 98,
      100, 101, 102, 105, 152, 161, 162, 165
Derbyshire 1, 7, 19, 27, 50, 53, 134, 145, 161,
    165
Devensian, the 37–8, 101
Doggerland 37, 46, 53, 167
drainage 7, 21, 33, 36, 37, 51, 113, 120, 136
droveways 18, 113, 121, 126, 135, 143 *also see*
    communications
Durrington Walls, Wilts 14, 73

early humans 49–50
earthworks 90, 122
economy 56–7, 126, 131, 145, 147, 160, 162
Elford (Staffs) **4**, **17**, 21
enclosures 77–9, 101–2
English Heritage 1, 18
environment, the 27, 114
    historic 43–4, 46–7, 48
exchange 57, 62, 83, 94, 121, 145 *also see* trade

farming 14–15, 21, 52, 56–7, 58, 60, 114–15,
    121, 126, 157
    arable 14–15, 97, 102, 106, 114, 115, 121, 135
    expansion of across Europe 58–9
    pastoral 97, 102, 115, 139, 143 *also see* live-
      stock
Fatholme (Staffs) 51, 52, 79, 87, 131, 166
fauna 51, 52 *also see* Ice Age, the, animals;
    megafauna
faunal remains 100, 105, 110–11, 114, 157
    insects 44, 48–9, 110–11, 114, 128, 137
fieldwalking 18, 20, 53, 87, 134, 142, 143, 152,
    161